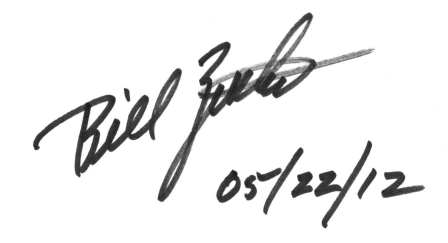

Bill Zettler
05/22/12

ILLINOIS PENSION SCAM:

HOW POLITICIANS AND UNIONS CONSPIRED TO BANKRUPT OUR CHILDREN'S FUTURE

BY

BILL ZETTLER
APRIL 1, 2012

ISBN-10: 0615627749
ISBN-13: 9780615627748

"In God we Trust all others bring data."

W. Edward Deming

TABLE OF CONTENTS

FOLLOW THE MONEY

HOW THE ILLINOIS EDUCATION ASSOCIATION BANKRUPTED ILLINOIS

Forward by Jack Roeser

The Situation

FOR 15 YEARS the Family Taxpayers Foundation and the ChampionNews.net have made available online the salaries and resulting pensions of all the teachers and administrators in Illinois. Since 2006 Bill Zettler has been presenting his very readable analysis of the unfolding financial lurch, stumble and fall of the K12 school system's 870 Districts.

I, Jack Roeser, was President of an Arlington Heights home owner organization over 40 years ago when District 59 went for a referendum to raise taxes. We opposed it and defeated that tax increase, but it opened the door to the massive mismanagement of the public schools. I continued the analysis of District 59 and others who were wasting our taxes and giving the kids a poor education. It's been a fascinating trip going to school board meetings and being a skunk at a picnic. The IEA (Illinois Education Association) emerged as the driving force of the ever increasing cost to the taxpayers. The kids are the excuse for the spending of all the ever increasing taxes, and the parents were there to pay the taxes. The teachers became victims by the mismanagement by the IEA, and AFT Unions. You will see in Zettler's articles the woeful mismanagement by the IEA in salaries, pensions, buildings, etc., everything they touch. The system runs at all because about 50% of the teachers have brought their personal integrity to the job, while all too many others surrendered to mismanagement and retired while still on the payroll. The tragic result of all this mismanagement was exposed long ago in 1993 in Forbes Magazine in a revelatory article named the National "Extortion" Association, Parent of IEA.

Graphs showed how student achievement went down as the Union presence and salaries went up. The trends continue to these days.

Zettler points out that the K12 system has run the cost of educating one student one year is $16,000. Imagine, an average class of 25 students costs $400,000 per year. The teacher is paid about $60,000. Overhead of $340,000 is inexcusable.

A clue to the Union management style is in the frank statement of the President of the AFT, "When school children pay union dues I'll represent the interests of the school children."

The Result

The State cannot pay the promised teacher pensions which are over $80 Billion in deficit and growing worse quickly. Zettler will show you salaries and pensions over $200,000 per year, some over $300,000.

Follow the Money

The teachers pay dues to the IEA and other Unions ranging from $500 to over $1,000 per year. This amounts to about $80 million a year in Illinois.

In 1986, the U. S. Supreme Court ruled in Chicago Teachers Local 1 v Hudson[112] that a union must explain to nonunion workers the purposes for any fees it collects from them. The Court considered it essential for unions to provide adequate information about the portion of financial cost charged for collective bargaining to employees who object to fee payments. School boards must therefore establish contractual agreements which minimize any possibility the objecting employee is subsidizing any union political or ideological activities.

The Hudson decision (and the Beck decision in 1988) proclaims that 80% of those dues are spent on Union politics, on the politicians in Springfield and locally as they please. The large majority goes to the Democrats and Michael Madigan, Speaker of the Illinois House got over a $1,000,000 in recent years, as did his daughter, the Illinois Attorney General.

All that money has corrupted the political process well beyond just the K12 schools. So what we have to face now is that Illinois is basically bankrupt, cannot pay its bills, and that includes the pensions promised the teachers. Many teachers are aware that the IEA Union is their enemy who has used their dues to ruin their pension and to bankrupt the State as well.

Illinois has the worst credit rating of any State. Democratic Speaker Mike Madigan passed $3.7 billion bond issue to pay those outrageous pensions one more year. That can't continue.

Madigan and the IEA say the Illinois Constitution says that the promised pension cannot be reduced. Well we think that shows how desperately incompetent the IEA and Madigan are.

They may claim that a state can't technically go bankrupt, but they can't stop the financial crash that has already arrived.

Illinois has the reputation for being the most corrupt State of all, and also the most bankrupt.

Madigan, the Democrats and the IEA have caused this financial mess, they have lied to us for years. The facts of their mess are revealed in Zettler articles in this book.

It is now apparent that the IEA and their Union have dominated the politics of Illinois by using that 80% of the dues that was used only for political purposes according to the Hudson decision of the U.S. Supreme Court.

The IEA Union has bankrupted Illinois and thereby become the enemy of the teachers who expected a pension that they now know can't be paid. ⟺

INTRODUCTION

"An error does not become truth by reason of multiplied propagation, nor does truth become error because nobody sees it." — Mahatma Gandhi

THE STATE OF the Illinois State Pensions is perhaps the most talked about subject in Illinois these days. Seemingly every news organization, media outlet, and hundreds of blogs, each with slightly different perspectives, bombard IL citizens with suspect arguments, disingenuous public relations sound-bites and much ignorance of the subject matter. The latter seems mostly to come from those who are members of the pension systems.

Since I have been studying and writing about the pension systems since 2001 Jack Roeser, founder of the Family Taxpayers Foundation and the Championnews.net, has asked me to write a short "book" outlining what I have learned over the last 10 years. Most of my writing, over 150 articles, has appeared on the Championnews.net website.

The material I have used for research over the last 10 years has almost entirely come from state government sources including Actuarial Reports, CAFR's (Comprehensive Annual Financial Reports), CGFA (Commission on Government Forecasting and Accountability) Reports and on occasion the state budget.

Some people collect stamps: I collect actuarial reports. For TRS (Teachers Retirement System) I have every one going back to 1969. I may be the only person in IL who has read every Actuarial Report, all 55 of them, issued by the five state pension funds since 2000. Believe me these will never be best sellers.

Although not an actuary I have spent the last 40 years developing software for scientific, statistical and financial applications ranging from war-games to sophisticated multi-company financial statements. In other words I have worked with and extensively analyzed many numbers based systems and Actuarial Science is all about numbers. I have tried to apply my numbers experience to my writing to explain, in as simple a manner as I can, the enormous complexity of pension math. That pension/actuarial math includes large doses of statistics, economics, accounting and demographics. By law each pension system must provide an Actuarial Report at the end of each year. To give you an idea of what is contained in an actuarial report the 2010 Teachers Retirement System Actuarial Report is 78 pages long and contains 61 pages of tables and charts. Most of the rest are formulas and explanations of assumptions being used in the 61 pages of tables. Obviously if you don't like numbers or are not used to using numbers, it can be overwhelming and/or sleep inducing. But in actuality the actuarial reports are the ultimate source of all correct explanations of what has and will happen to the pension systems. If they are not the source of what you are reading and hearing then what you are reading and hearing is probably wrong.

Other sources of information used in my research have come from the ISBE (Illinois State Board of Education) for teacher salaries and via FOIA (Freedom of Information Act) requests to the 5 state pension systems for current pensions and other retirement data. For teacher salaries we have records going back to 1999 and for pensions back to 2005.

All the information used in this book is public information and is available on the internet from various sources including, but not limited to, the Family Taxpayers Foundation, the Chicago Sun-times and openthebooks.com. What I have done with this book is analyze this public data in different ways, a technique called "data mining". I am able to do this because of the huge amount of data I have collected over the years.

Since much of my work has been concentrated on teacher pensions I have been accused of teacher bashing and even teacher hating which is understandable but not true. The reason so much of my attention is concentrated on teachers is the fact that K thru university (TRS and

SURS) represent about 80% of the pension costs and liabilities. They also have the highest salaries, the highest pensions (96 of Top 100 pensions are educators, see Appendix A), the shortest work years and by and large the shortest careers. In the case of K-12 the number of $100,000 salaries has increased more than four-fold in the last 10 years from 3,026 to 14,866. Since pensions are directly related to salaries a four-fold increase in $100,000 salaries means a more than four-fold increase in $100,000 pensions. See Appendix B item 29 for more details.

There is also much more data available for teachers especially K-12 and this lends itself to the kind of analysis I have done in this book. And if I may throw a compliment their way, the TRS (Teachers Retirement System) has by far the best Actuarial Reports in the state and in fact the best I have seen of the several states I have studied. Their reports should be the standard for all Actuarial Reports in IL.

This is not to say state workers aren't part of the problem too. Some state workers such as troopers can retire at age 50 on 80% of their last year's salary after only 27 years work. In fact over 150 retired state police have pensions over $100,000. In addition just about every state worker who works 40 years, and many who work as little as 35 years, has an initial retirement income (SERS pension plus Social Security) greater than their take home pay at retirement. Private sector workers have nothing comparable to this political largesse.

Are all of my conclusions correct? Of course not and there are certainly math errors in some of my analysis. Also there may be date errors since the material presented covers a span of several years. With certainty there are grammatical errors, lack of proper antecedents, typos, etc. which scores of English teachers will quickly and accurately point out. My purpose is to provide an alternative world-view of Illinois state pensions in opposition to the view of those who directly benefit from the current official viewpoint.

As for the title of the book I define "scam" as a lack of honesty and transparency when it comes to describing the problem. At best IL politicians and unions are disingenuous at worst deceitful. Here are 3 major points that are being ignored by the powers that be:

1. The huge numbers being discussed ($85 billion unfunded etc.) are a "Rosy", best case scenario. We need to know what the numbers will be in a "worst" case scenario or at least a "worse case" scenario.

2. Under this "Rosy" scenario we are going to pay $200 billion in pension taxes between now and 2032. What would this number be in a 'worse" case?

3. Under this "Rosy" scenario, after paying in $200 billion, we will leave our children with an unfunded pension debt almost twice what it is now ($160 billion vs. $85 billion). What would this number be in a "worse case?

Does ignoring every possible outcome except the "Rosy" scenario sound like a reasonable, responsible approach or a political kick-the-can-down-the-road-approach i.e. a scam?

And remember the people waiting down the road to catch that kicked can are our children and grandchildren.

Although the book is broken up into 5 broad categories it should be treated more like a reference manual than a book you read from page 1 to the end.

Chapter 1: How Did We Get Here? Excessive pension benefits lead the way.
Chapter 2: How bad is the problem?
Chapter 3: Pension Mythology.
Chapter 4: You Cannot Control Pensions Unless You Control Salaries.
Chapter 5: What we need to do to solve the problem.

An overview of all the state pensions systems is the first item in Appendix A. It shows the various numbers associated with each system as of June 30, 2011 the latest Actuarial Data available. I call this chart the "Pension Numbers Matrix."

If you would like to see a brief summary look at Appendix B for charts and tables that relate to the pensions systems. Each of them refers back to the chapter in the book that relate to that chart.

To give readers a head start I have chosen 10 sub-chapters that I think are most important and recommend you read those first then any others that might interest you.

1. **Taxpayers have contributed more, not less, than the 1995 Fifty year pension funding law required.**

   Most people are familiar with the 1995 pension funding law that set up a schedule of payments that would result in 90% pension funding by 2045 for all the state pension systems. The schedule of state payments given to us in 1995 has been exceeded. So why are we being told we have to pay more when we have already overpaid?

   See Chapter 3.1 "Pension Crisis: Politicians and Unions Lied To Us in 1995 and Have Been Lying to Us Ever Since."

2. **Since 2001 taxpayers have contributed 230% more than teachers to the Teachers Retirement System.**

   The most vociferous group in demanding more from taxpayers are teacher unions and their members. Hardly a day passes without a strident claim by a teacher or union honcho or one of their many political lackeys that the taxpayer (AKA the state) has not made their contribution while the dutiful teachers always make theirs. Good job by the unions convincing their membership but unfortunately for them it is patently not true. See Chapter 2.2 "Taxpayers Have Contributed 230% more than Teachers Since 2001".

3. **Less than 1% of state retirees worked 40 years.**

   If you work in the private sector from age 22 to 62 and retire on early Social Security at a maximum of $22,000 you will have worked 40 years. It is extremely rare for state workers to work that long in spite of the large pensions. In fact the Top 100 Pensions average only 31 years work in IL for their average $227,000 pension. And educators are not the only employees with a good deal. Most state employees (SERS) who work at least 40 years will have retirement income greater than their final salary take-home-pay (pension plus Social Security). See Chapter 2.8 "Average State Pensions Are Far Above Average".

4. **The supposedly "modest" average state pensions are worth 4 times Social Security.**

   The word "modest" is used by media, union members and politicians to describe IL state pensions in order to minimize the huge cost to taxpayers. But when you look closer you find that the average state employee works less than 25 years and in more than half the cases only 9 months a year (educators). So why are pensions worth 4 times Social Security for 9-month employees working partial (25-years) careers considered "modest"? The highest pensions are 8 to 10 times Social Security. See Chapter 2.8 "Average State Pensions Are Far Above Average.".

5. **State retirees have used more than 132,000 years of sick-leave credit to receive extra pension without actually having to work for it.**

   Employees in the state pensions can accrue sick leave at the rate of 10 to 15 days per year and use them as "work years" when they retire. In TRS a "work year" is only 170 days (34 weeks) so in about 20 years or so a teacher will have the maximum two years already accrued well before they retire. In some school districts sick days are given away or can be purchased outright at the time of retirement for $20/day. I show an example of a teacher who paid $6,800 at her time of retirement for 340 days (2 years) sick leave credit that boosted her pension by $4,800/year. See Chapter 1.4 "Retired Teachers Getting Pensions for 157,700 years They Never Worked".

6. **Over 44,000 retirees have annual pensions greater than their total contributions over their entire career.**

   This is an indication that employee contributions are much too low. As a comparison, the maximum Social Security at age 62 is $22,000 after about $130,000 in employee contributions over the recipient's career. So even if you lived to age 125 with cost-of-living-adjustments your annual Social Security would never exceed your contributions. See Chapter 1.8 "Should Public Employees Have pensions Greater Than Their Career pension Contributions?"

7. **The reason TRS pension liability is so high is because teachers are vastly overpaid compared to adjoining states.**

   The way IL pensions are calculated a doubling of salary results in a doubling of pension payments. The top teacher salary in IL for 2011, $203,000 for a suburban Phys-ed teacher, is $108,000 more than the top teacher in Kentucky. It is also $95,000 higher than WI, $92,000 higher than IA and $83,000 higher than MO highest teacher salaries. See Chapter 4.12 "Why Is Illinois's Top Teacher salary $108,000 more Than Kentucky's?"

8. **If IL teachers had the same salary and pension schedule as Wisconsin we would save more than $4 billion/yr. enough to make the annual pension payment.**

   WI teachers (and administrators) have much lower salaries than their IL peers and their maximum pension is not reached until age 65. If the same rules applied to IL we would save $4 billion/yr. even including the Social Security cost associated with WI. See Chapter 4.5 "Wisconsin: Top Teacher Salary $89K Less Than IL Top Teacher Salary" and See Chapter 4.6 "IL School Administrators Make 67% More than Wisconsin's".

9. **If the pension rules in effect in 1970 when the "Pension Guarantee" was added to the state constitution were still in effect there would be no unfunded pension liability.**
   In December 1970 the phrase "shall not be diminished or impaired" was added to the IL state constitution guaranteeing pensions for state employees. One month later in January 1971 new laws were passed increasing pension benefits by 11% to 53%. Boy, that didn't take long. Pension benefits were increased by another 17-30% in 1998. See Chapter 1.1 "IL Pensions: More than 130 benefit increases since 1970 are the major cause of unfunded liability."

10. **Teachers' unions have given IL politicians of both parties more than $50 million in contributions since 1995.**
    Unions give politicians $10's of millions and get $10's of billions back in increased pension benefits. Rod Blagojevich gets $1.8 million from teacher unions then pushes $10 billion pension bond thru the legislature. See Chapter 2.6 "Teacher Unions Give Politicians $10's of millions in Contributions, Politicians Give Teacher Union Members $10's of Billions in Benefits."

So strap on your seatbelt and get ready for a rough ride through "The Matrix" the Pension Numbers Matrix.

Bill Zettler
April 1, 2012

CHAPTER 1:

HOW DID WE GET HERE?
EXCESSIVE PENSION BENEFITS LEAD THE WAY.

"I know that two and two make four although I must say if by any sort of process I could convert 2+2 into five it would give me much greater pleasure."

— Lord Byron

1.1) IL Pensions: More than 130 benefit increases since 1970 are the major cause of unfunded liability.

I̤T IS INTERESTING to note that with all of the clamor and posturing by various union and political types about the "sacredness" of the Constitutional Pension guarantee no one has taken the time to see what pension rules were in place at the Constitutional Convention of 1970.

That is up until now. If pension rules were the same now as when we guaranteed pensions during the 1970 Constitutional Convention there would currently be a pension surplus not a pension deficit.

That means the current $44 billion TRS (Teachers Retirement System) unfunded and the future $73 billion future projected unfunded by 2032 is entirely due to pension benefit enhancements passed by Springfield politicians over the ensuing years. As politicians grubbily grabbed all the teacher union dollars they could get, the retirees inexorably became pension millionaires via evermore goodies added to the so-called "guarantee".

Pension rules on 12/15/1970 when Constitutional pension guarantee was approved.

Pension accrual rate: 1.5% per year worked.

Maximum pension:
Age 60 = 60% max.
Age 61 = 61 and 2/3 % max.
Age 62 = 63 and 1/3% max.
Age 63 = 65% max.
Age 64 = 66 and 2/3% max.
Age 65 = 68 and 1/3% max.
Age 66 = 70% max.

½ year sick-leave credit allowed
COLA = 1.5% Not compounded
Years worked for maximum payout = 45
Early Retirement Option (ERO) - No

Current pension rules:

Pension accrual rate: 2.2% per year
Maximum Pension: age 54.5 = 75%
2 years sick-leave credit.
COLA 3% Compounded.
Years worked for maximum payout = 33
Here's a comparison of all the changes since 1970. You can see for yourself the unfunded pension liabilities, at least for teachers, has been driven by benefit increases not covered by employee contribution increases.

Comparison 1970 Pension Rules vs. 2011 Pension Rules

	1970	2011	Increase
Age for max pension	66	54.5	11.5 years
Years worked for max.	45	33	33%
Annual accrual rate	1.50%	2.20%	46%
Maximum rate	70%	75%	7%
Cost-of-living-adj.	1.5% not compounded	3% Compounded	600%
Sick-leave credit yrs.	0.5	2	400%
Total pension Payout 100,000 Salary and max retirement.	$1.54 million	$3.29 million	113%
Teacher contribution rate	6%	8%	33%

Here is a better way to look at the effect benefit increases have had on the cost of pensions versus the amount teachers contribute to their ever growing pensions:

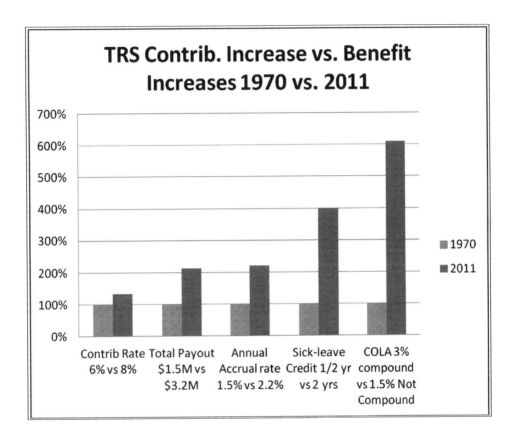

The COLA (Cost-of-living adjustment) differential is so great because life expectancy at age 54 (2011) is 30 years vs. 20 years for a 66 year old (1970).

If the rules in effect in 1970 when the pension guarantee was approved were still in effect we would have a surplus in the TRS fund not a deficit.

Benefit increases were handed out every year for the last 41 years except 1976 and 1992.
The pension-pillaging of the taxpayer accelerated after the Constitution was approved on Dec. 15, 1970.

In some years there were multiple legislative dates where benefits were handed out. For example in 1991 new benefit provisions went into effect on Jan 1, Feb 1, July 1 and Nov 19.

Before 1970 there were few substantive changes to the pension rights granted to retirees. Afterwards the teacher unions worked their legislative magic and got increased benefit after increased benefit passed starting immediately in 1971. It was like Custer at the Little Big Horn – except the taxpayers didn't know about the slaughter until 40 years later.

Here is a **partial list** of the 130 TRS pension enhancements passed by a compliant legislature at the expense of every Illinois taxpayer:

1971 – Pension maximum rose to 75% from 60%.
     Annual COLA rose to 2% from 1.5%
     No pension reduction if younger than 60 with 35 years service.
1972 – 85 sick days (1/2 year service) allowed for early retirement.
1973 – Survivor benefits paid at age 50 instead of 55.
1978 – Annual COLA rose to 3% from 2% (not compounded)
1979 – ERO (Early Retirement Option) allowed.
1980 – Retiree health insurance program established.
1982 – Employer pick-up of employee contributions allowed.
1983 – Unmarried children over 18 eligible for health insurance coverage.
1984 – Sick leave credit upped to 170 days from 85 days.
1990 – 3% COLA compounded.
1990 – Survivors get COLA.
1990 – Disability and pensions added for part-time and substitute teachers.
1991 – Retiree health care premiums 75% subsidy.
1998 – Waive Early Retirement cost – 34 work-years becomes 35 years for pension.
1999 – ERO extended to 2005.
2000 – All teachers allowed 20% salary increases increasing pension payments.
2002 - ERI (Early Retirement Incentive) enacted.
2003 – "Pipeline" and "Modified" ERO programs enacted.
2006 – Disability recipients allowed to teach and still receive disability payments.

Every one of those items added to taxpayer cost, $100's of billions over the decades. Just the COLA going from 1.5% not compounded to 3% compounded increases the pension payout by 30% over a 30 year retirement life expectancy.

Based upon this 130 item, 40 year rap-sheet teachers should be paying at least 15%.
Just the pension alone demands 13% and the benefit enhancements are not limited to just pensions. In 1991 alone there were enhancements for optional service credit, survivors' annuities, disability retirement, backdating benefits by 90 days, and annual increases for revisionary annuities. Each one of these benefits adds to the cost of TRS and in none of these cases were the teachers asked to contribute more. Every single cost was born by the taxpayer. Multiply this by over 100 other benefit increases since 1970 and taxpayers liability has increased enormously.

Although union leaders complain that 8% is high enough many 401K contributors in the private sector, making $100,000 salary can contribute 21% including their 6.2% for Social Security. And of course 401K's are not guaranteed like state pensions are.

Constitutional provisions cannot be reversed but legislative ones can be.
The problem with constitutional amendments is that they can only be revoked (maybe) by another constitutional amendment. However, legislative public acts are reversed or revoked all the time.

If the legislature passed legislation that increased benefits over and above what was approved in 1970 why can't they pass new legislation revoking all those increases?

What should be done.
Initiate legislation reversing most or all of the above with the goal of returning to the pension rules that were in effect when the constitutional pension clause was approved on Dec. 15, 1970. The 95% of Illinois workers paying for, but not benefitting from, the State Pension System demand it.

Contracts are abrogated all the time. Hundreds of state vendors have not been paid for months, some more than a year. Why should a pension contract be any different? ═

1.2) ERO (Early Retirement Option):
How Benefit Enhancements Drive Up Pension Costs.

I N THE LAST chapter I documented how more than 130 benefit increases for the TRS (Teachers Retirement System) have been passed by the legislature since the "Pension Guarantee" amendment to the constitution was passed in 1970. The overwhelming majority of these benefits have been paid for by the taxpayer not the employees. This is just one of the more egregious examples of how benefit enhancements affect the overall cost of providing long-term pension benefits to public employees.

ERO – Early Retirement Option (2004).

The normal full- retirement age for TRS is 60 or you must have 35 years "service credit" (not actual years worked). If you are a teacher and want to retire before age 60 you must pay a penalty of 6%/yr. off of your pension for very year less than 60 or every year short of 35 years "service credit."

Therefore ERO was devised to allow retiring teachers to avoid the early retirement penalty. Like virtually every benefit enhancement since 1970 the cost burden of this benefit is predominately passed on to the taxpayer.

ERO Example:
Assumptions:
Teacher retires at age 55 with 30 years of creditable service.
Teacher's average pensionable salary is $100,000.
Teacher's highest salary is $120,000.

Full pension = $66,000/yr. (30 years times 2.2% per year).
Discounted pension (because she does not have 35 years and is not age 60) = $46,000.

So under rules in place prior to passing the ERO legislation in 2004, this teacher could either wait until she is 60 to collect $66,000 or she could start taking $46,000 at age 55. With ERO she can receive the full $66,000 at age 55. That means she will receive $330,000 between ages 55 and 60 with ERO that she would not have received otherwise. But over her expected lifetime at age 55 she will receive $700,000 more in pension payments under ERO than under the previous plan.

What does she pay for this? A measly .4% of salary (only since 2004) or about $400/yr. (why bother?) plus 11.5% of her highest salary for each year under age 60 or $69,000. And at most suburban schools the $69,000 is picked up by the school district so she pays virtually nothing for a $700,000 pension benefit.

In addition to the employees portion the local school district i.e. the taxpayers, must also contribute to ERO in the amount of 23.5% and these amounts can be substantial. As of Nov. 2011 about 988 retirees have had the local district pay out more than $100,000 to allow them to retire early without the discount normally applied to early retirees.

Below is a list of those retirees who received more than $200,000 in ERO payments by their employer, the local school districts:

ERO (Early Retirement Option) Payments Over $200,000				
Made by Local Taxpayers for Benefit of Retiring Employees				
NAME	SCHOOL	ERO Payment by School	Annual Pension	Years Work In IL
Codell, Neil C	Niles TWP CHSD 219	361,097	163,344	20
Herrmann, Mary B	Winnetka SD 36	287,875	131,560	14
Petersen, Jerry D	Community HSD 218	285,686	140,080	16
Steyskal, James L	Reavis TWP HSD 220	253,383	139,471	30
Vogler-Corboy, Dale A	Niles TWP CHSD 219	251,630	96,991	19
Wardzala, Edward J	Lake Park CHSD 108	251,338	129,917	31
Gonzalez, Janet E	Adlai Stevenson HSD 125	226,579	122,748	23
Peterson, David W	SEJA 804 NSSED	223,631	141,598	31
Surber, Rebecca L	Woodridge SD 68	217,165	119,299	31
McGee, Glenn W	Wilmette SD 39	209,903	184,119	32
Brown, Timothy F	Consolidated HSD 230	209,652	131,020	21
Sostak, Susan P	Norridge SD 80	207,423	85,431	22
Heuerman, Steven L	Niles TWP CHSD 219	206,672	115,108	31
Sorensen, Larry W	Park Ridge CCSD 64	205,472	97,150	26
Broughton, Cynthia A	ISBE - Assistant Supt	205,114	126,455	32
Stramaglia, Michael F	Schiller Park SD 81	203,275	107,228	22
Nielsen-Hall, Denise M	Deerfield School District 109	201,541	110,895	32

SOURCE: *Teachers Retirement System.*

Notice how few years have actually been worked. The average of the group is 25 years. That's because "service credit" years are used for pension calculation not actual on-the-ground years and those include non-work items such as sick-leave and Optional Service credits. Yes, you can become an Illinois pension millionaire without working too long in Illinois.

Fortunately (maybe) for beleaguered IL taxpayers, the ERO law terminates June 30, 2013 and will disappear unless renewed by the state legislature. Let's hope they have more sense now than they did when they first passed this law in 2004. ═

1.3) ERO (Early Retirement Option): How The IEA + Politicians Plunder Taxpayers for $1 Billion.

Teachers already retire early – why do they need an option to retire even earlier? Well if you are a public union (IEA – Illinois Education Association) and you give politicians over $50 million in political contributions since 1995 you can ask for and receive just about anything you want.

The ERO is one of the most pernicious giveaways because it confounds the taxpayer by taking money from all over the place. And when you add it all up it comes to $620 million from local taxpayers and at least $505 million from state taxpayers and that's only thru 2010: it's scheduled to continue thru 2013.

Under current law unless you have 35 years Service Credit (NOTE: for more than 90% of TRS retirees Service Credit is more than actual years worked) you cannot receive your full 2.2% of salary for each year of Service Credit. It is discounted by 6%/yr. for each year under age 60. So if you wanted to retire at age 58 (TRS average) with 25 years Service Credit (TRS Average) and did not have ERO your pension would be reduced by 12% (2 years under age 60 times 6%/yr.).

So with the ERO law passed in 2004 teachers can retire as early as age 54 with less than 35 years Service Credit and not be penalized by the 6%/yr. discount.

Table 1: ERO School Payment vs. Career Employee Contributions.
Here is an example of how the taxpayer is being ripped off for absolutely no reason.

Note that in every case but one the ERO payment by the local taxpayer (school district) to allow the employee to retire without a discount exceeds the total amount paid in to the pension system by the employee during his entire career!

Note: "-" Indicates Records without available data

Table 2: Total School District Cost Final Year of Employment.
A $772,000 cost for one employee for one year? How is that possible?

It's possible because of the complete lack of transparency by local school boards. Shouldn't this kind of expenditure have an open meeting with public input before it is approved? If you had a $772,000 contract for a roof repair you'd have all kinds of meetings and debate before the money was spent. But when it comes to the 80% plus of the budget representing employee compensation everything is done behind closed doors without public comment.

The following two tables show the amounts involved using the Top 20 ERO abusers. These abusers are not alone – more than 12,000 retired TRS members have received ERO payments and more than 900 of those have been greater than $100,000.

Employee Contributions versus ERO School Contributions				
Name	Current Pension	School District	Employee Contrib.	School Dist. ERO Contrib.
Codell, Neil C	163,344	Niles TWP CHSD 219	234,371	361,097
Herrmann, Mary B	131,560	Winnetka SD 36	201,755	287,875
Petersen, Jerry D	140,080	Community HSD 218	–	285,686
Steyskal, James L	139,471	Reavis TWP HSD 220	199,755	253,383
Vogler-Corboy, Dale A	96,991	Niles TWP CHSD 219	151,247	251,630
Wardzala, Edward J	129,917	Lake Park CHSD 108	188,596	251,338
Gonzalez, Janet E	122,748	Adlai Stevenson HSD 125	162,397	226,579
Peterson, David W	141,598	SEJA 804 NSSED	189,567	223,631
McGee, Glenn W	184,119	Wilmette SD 39	260,525	209,903
Brown, Timothy F	131,020	Consolidated HSD 230	–	209,652
Heuerman, Steven L	115,108	Niles TWP CHSD 219	170,001	206,672
Sorensen, Larry W	97,150	Park Ridge CCSD 64	169,737	205,472
Broughton, Cynthia A	126,455	ISBE - Assistant Supt	163,408	205,114
Stramaglia, Michael F	107,228	Schiller Park SD 81	–	203,275
Nielsen-Hall, Denise M	110,895	Deerfield School District 109	174,362	201,541
Markavitch, Vickie L	91,613	Niles TWP CHSD 219	–	196,061
Schau, Pamela S	92,993	Maine TWP HSD 207	162,715	195,858

Mitz, William M	113,622	Adlai Stevenson HSD 125	182,810	195,781
Breunlin, Richard J	112,099	Palatine TWP HSD 211	179,938	191,502
Young, Jennifer	101,075	Adlai Stevenson HSD 125	125,457	187,999
Soc Security Age 62	*22,000*	*Social Security age 62*	*130,000*	-

TABLE 2: Total School District Cost Final Year of Employment							
Name	Annual Pension	School District	School Dist. ERO Contrib.	+	Last Annual Salary	=	Total School Cost Final Year
Codell, Neil C	163,344	Niles TWP CHSD 219	361,097	+	411,511	=	772,608
Herrmann, Mary B	131,560	Winnetka SD 36	287,875	+	245,000	=	532,875
Petersen, Jerry D	140,080	Community HSD 218	285,686	+	236,071	=	521,757
Steyskal, James L	139,471	Reavis TWP HSD 220	253,383	+	223,466	=	476,849
Vogler-Corboy, Dale A	96,991	Niles TWP CHSD 219	251,630	+	242,914	=	494,544
Wardzala, Edward J	129,917	Lake Park CHSD 108	251,338	+	225,169	=	476,507
Gonzalez, Janet E	122,748	Adlai Stevenson HSD 125	226,579	+	222,056	=	448,635
Peterson, David W	141,598	SEJA 804 NSSED	223,631	+	240,341	=	463,972
McGee, Glenn W	184,119	Wilmette SD 39	209,903	+	273,235	=	483,138
Brown, Timothy F	131,020	Consolidated HSD 230	209,652	+	216,986	=	426,638
Heuerman, Steven L	115,108	Niles TWP CHSD 219	206,672	+	187,278	=	393,949
Sorensen, Larry W	97,150	Park Ridge CCSD 64	205,472	+	174,870	=	380,342
Broughton, Cynthia A	126,455	ISBE - Assistant Supt	205,114	+	161,213	=	366,327
Stramaglia, Michael F	107,228	Schiller Park SD 81	203,275	+	223,709	=	426,984
Nielsen-Hall, Denise M	110,895	Deerfield School District 109	201,541	+	163,070	=	364,611
Markavitch, Vickie L	91,613	Niles TWP CHSD 219	196,061	+	163,384	=	359,445
Schau, Pamela S	92,993	Maine TWP HSD 207	195,858	+	178,137	=	373,995
Mitz, William M	113,622	Adlai Stevenson HSD 125	195,781	+	191,124	=	386,905
Breunlin, Richard J	112,099	Palatine TWP HSD 211	191,502	+	162,981	=	354,483
Young, Jennifer	101,075	Adlai Stevenson HSD 125	187,999	+	159,999	=	347,998

How much do teachers' pay for the ERO millions?

Turns out, not much.

The top man on our list, Neil Codell retired in 2009 and at the employee ERO cost of .4% of salary would have paid in about $56,000 on his $1.4 million in salary from 2005 thru Jan1, 2009 when he retired. I say would have because his employment contract actually called for the school district to pay his entire pension contribution so he paid zero.

So assuming he paid $56,000 what would he have received in return?

First, of course, is the $367,091 TRS contribution for his ERO paid for by the generous taxpayers of Niles District 219. So there's s 7 to 1 return on investment right off of the bat.

Secondly, because he was only 56 years old when he retired the ERO calculation erased the 24% discount he would have had to take if retired four years before full retirement age of 60. This increased his pension by $39,000 per year plus the 3%/yr. COLA for cash annuity cost of about $975,000.

So for no reason and beyond all logic and fairness we, the taxpayers, gave a man making $411,000/yr. a taxpayer funded bonus for early retirement worth more than $1.2 million.

And teachers claim these payments are guaranteed by the constitution.

If that's not an example of economic insanity I don't know what is.

End ERO now; do not wait until 2013. ⇐

1.4) Retired teachers getting pensions for 157,700 years they never worked. Should this be guaranteed by the Constitution?

I OFTEN READ letters-to-the-editor or get an email from a teacher that says something like: "I worked 30 years as a teacher and …". But when I check the official state records that teacher has worked 28 or 29 not the 30 mentioned.

Why is that? Well teachers get pensions paid on "Service Credit" not actually on the years worked in Illinois. "Service Credit" is a concept that boosts pensionable years worked in IL with giveaways that have been added over the years to increase teachers' pensions for no reason other than they are teachers.

I know of no private sector system where the workers receive pensions based upon more years than they have actually worked.

Service Credit scam 1: pensions paid on 75,000 years of sick leave never worked.
The major way to get Service Credit is via sick days. Every teacher's contract contains an allowance for "sick days" averaging about 12 days per year. If the teacher doesn't take the days off as sick leave (most of the suburban schools have 2-3 personal days on top of sick days so they can use those for real sick days) they can accrue them for up to 2 years Service Credit when they retire. In the other economic dimension teachers work in a year is 34 weeks or 170 days. Therefore a 54 year-old teacher who only worked 33 years can use 2 years sick leave to get the full 35-year pension. By the way our famous 54 years old, $189,000/yr. Music teacher did exactly that. Worked 33 years, took 2 years sick-leave credit and presto he retired on 75% or $130,000/yr.

Of course almost no one is sick twelve days a year, year after year after year, for decades. But in IL this is a public employee benefit called, euphemistically, "sick leave" to make it sound better. It is not "sick leave"; it is a political gift.

Some contracts give teachers extra sick leave so they can retire early. In District 214, a day's sick leave can be purchased for $20 at retirement meaning a teacher with a $100,000 pension can use all of her sick days then, just prior to retirement, purchase 340 days or two years Service Credit for $6,800 thereby increasing her pension by $4,400 per year, plus 3% COLA, for the rest of her life. That $4,400 extra pension payment that cost the teacher $6,800 will payout about $200,000 over a 30 year life expectancy. The $193,200 difference is paid for by you know whom: the taxpayer.

So should that $193,200 additional pension cost be guaranteed by the constitution?

Service Credit scam 2: "Optional Service Purchase": Pay $63,000 get $1.2 million.
Teachers may also "purchase" Service Credit, at an extreme discount, for teaching previously in other states.

Retirees have paid nominal amounts for 82,700 years of out-of-state work that by definition is not Illinois work. If it's not Illinois work why do Illinois taxpayers have to pay pensions for it?

On average teachers paid $3,100 for each "Optional Service" year and received $2,400/yr. pension increase for it. That $2,400 plus the 3% COLA for 25 years has a cash annuity value of $60,000 so teachers get a 20 to 1 return for every year of "Optional Service" purchased. The difference between what they pay and what they ultimately receive is paid for by the taxpayers of IL.

In one case a retiring superintendent paid $63,000 to "Purchase" 10 years service credit, which increased her pension by over $50,000. Since she was only 55 years old when she retired that extra $50,000/yr. had a cash annuity value of about $1.2 million. In other words taxpayers handed a school employee over $1 million pension bonus for absolutely no reason. This superintendent also received a $287,000 ERO payment from the school district to the TRS.

John Conyers paid even less: $27,909 for 10 years out-of-state service. Add in 2 years for sick leave and here's a man who only worked 18 years in IL but has a $230,000 pension thanks to the generous taxpayers of Illinois.

Were these million dollar giveaways guaranteed by the state constitution? If you ask the teachers the answer is "absolutely." If you ask me it is a total corruption of the purpose of pensions. Legal perhaps but totally corrupt.

Why do Illinois taxpayers have to pay pensions for work not done at all or done in another state?

As you can see in every single case the "Service Credit Years" used to calculate these very large pensions are considerably more than the years actually worked in Illinois.

Also note how young these people are: all of them 54 to 57 years of age.

TABLE : Service Credit Years versus Actual Years Worked					
Name	Age At Retire	Total Years Pension With Service Credit	Years Worked in IL	Current Pension	School District
Codell, Neil C	56	26	20	163,344	Niles TWP CHSD 219
Herrmann, Mary B	55	26	14	131,560	Winnetka SD 36
Petersen, Jerry D	55	26	16	140,080	Community HSD 218
Steyskal, James L	55	32	30	139,471	Reavis TWP HSD 220
Conyers, John A	57	30	18	230,724	Palatine CCSD 15
Wardzala, Edward J	55	34	31	129,917	Lake Park CHSD 108
Gonzalez, Janet E	55	28	23	122,748	Adlai Stevenson HSD 125
Peterson, David W	55	33	31	141,598	SEJA 804 NSSED
McGee, Glenn W	56	34	32	184,119	Wilmette SD 39
Brown, Timothy F	55	27	21	131,020	Consolidated HSD 230
Heuerman, Steven L	55	33	31	115,108	Niles TWP CHSD 219
Sorensen, Larry W	55	28	26	97,150	Park Ridge CCSD 64
Broughton, Cynthia A	55	34	32	126,455	ISBE - Assistant Supt
Stramaglia, Michael F	55	23	22	107,228	Schiller Park SD 81
Nielsen-Hall, Denise M	55	33	32	110,895	Deerfield School District 109
Markavitch, Vickie L	55	21	12	91,613	Niles TWP CHSD 219

Schau, Pamela S	55	24	16	92,993	Maine TWP HSD 207
Mitz, William M	55	34	31	113,622	Adlai Stevenson HSD 125
Breunlin, Richard J	54	35	33	112,099	Palatine TWP HSD 211
Young, Jennifer	54	34	29	101,075	Adlai Stevenson HSD 125

SOURCE: Teachers Retirement System

The purpose of government is not government employees.

The purpose of government is to provide for the common good at a level and for a cost agreed to by the voters and taxpayers. What possible common good (as opposed to personal good) is provided by a government that gives away billions of dollars to young retiring public employees?

And the moral question is similar: why are we giving billions away making public employees multi-millionaires while at the same time cutting public services to the truly needy? I thought progressive policies were designed to help poor people not millionaires?

So the teacher-political industrial complex has come down to these three corrupt concepts:
1. The complex is allowed to create a public service that is bereft of competition, cost control or measurement.
2. The complex is given license, by those they elect, to make laws and regulations (pension laws for example) that benefit themselves at the expense of the public.
3. The complex is provided benefit assurance by enforcement power over the taxpayers – if you don't pay your taxes we will seize your property to pay for those superior benefits.

At some point in time the 95% of IL citizens not enjoying the expensive benefits of public pension system must have control over the costs associated with the 5% who do have those benefits.

We cannot continue to elect politicians who ignore the will of the 95%.

SOURCE: Teacher Retirement System ⇐

1.5) Why Illinois Pensions Are in Trouble: $27,909 Gets You $3.5 Million in Pension Payments.

Retiree Gets $230,000 Pension For 18 Years Worked.

YOU DON'T HAVE to work long in the Illinois public schools to get multi-million dollar pensions. For example there is John Conyers who worked in Illinois at Palatine Elementary District 15 for 18 years and now has a pension of $230,000 per year after retiring in 2003.

Conyers actually retired with 30 years Illinois "Service Credit" although he only actually worked 18 years in Illinois. He did this mainly through a state pension process called "Purchased Optional Credit". Under this plan you can use your work years and salaries in another state, pay a discounted contribution and use those years, up to 10, in calculating your pension.

Of course, any discount to a public employee is an additional tax on Illinois taxpayers. And this one is a very big tax.

He also used about 2 years of sick leave credit. You cannot earn 2 years sick leave credit (340 days) in 18 years even if you never missed a day so the local district must have given him free sick days (say 170) as part of his contract. This results in more freebies to the employee from the taxpayer without the taxpayer's knowledge or approval.

So work 18 years, take 2 years sick leave credit and 10 years Optional Credit and you get a $230,000 pension.

Let's examine how much this costs Illinois taxpayers over the retiree's expected lifetime.

First his outrageous salary schedule – 58% increase over 3 years:
2000 - $223,000
2001 - $250,000
2002 - $300,000
2003 - $353,000

So he has 30 years service credit (only 18 work years) at 2.2% per year or 66% of the average of his last four years ($281,000) or about $185,000 pension to start with, increased by 3% per year leaves him with $230,000 pension today.

If he had received his pension only on the 18 years he actually worked his starting pension would have been about $110,000, bad enough but a lot better than $185,000.

So how much did Mr. Conyers have to pay to increase his pension by $75,000/yr.? Exactly $27,909, less than one-half of the first years increase. What a good deal for Mr. Conyers! What a terrible deal for Illinois taxpayers.

The total pension payout over a 30-year life expectancy including the automatic COLA of 3% for a starting pension of $185,000 is $8.7 million and for a starting pension of $110,000 is $5.2 million, a difference of $3.5 million for an investment of $29,238.37.

I don't want you to think I am picking on Mr. Conyers. Mary Van Der Bogart worked only 13 years for Winnetka SD 36 and now has a pension of $169,000 after getting two years credit for sick leave and buying 7 years credit for $34,000. Those credits are worth about $3 million in extra pension payments over a 30-year life expectancy.

In all, 109 K-12 retirees worked less than 30 years for $100,000+ pensions.

What public good is served by paying out $3 million pensions for less than $30,000?
There is certainly a personal good but where is the public good? What exactly is the justification for making people multi-millionaires with public tax dollars? Are there not better public purposes for the $3 million (on top of $5 million, remember) than adding to the wealth of an already vastly over-compensated public employee?

Homeless shelters are bursting at the seams, food pantries are empty and services for poor seniors are cut by $48 million but we can find $3 million to add to a $5 million pension for someone from Colorado who worked in Illinois for 18 years?

What the next governor should do.
The next governor needs to stand up and say that paying excessive salaries and pensions to public employees is immoral. That is not the proper or fair use of taxation nor does it do what taxation should do: provide for the common good.

The old, the sick and the hungry deserve the benefit of those taxes for that is truly providing for the common good. Using those taxes to enhance the multi-million dollar pensions of public employees who only spend a fraction of their careers in Illinois is in fact an immoral use of those tax dollars.

And he needs to emphasize the lack of transparency. Why are transactions like this not pubic knowledge? Why do we have to tweeze these facts out of decadal old bureaucratic archives to bring them to the public's attention? Could it be that politicians and bureaucrats don't want us to know? Of course they don't.

This is evidence of nonfeasance at best, malfeasance at worst. The next governor needs to end using taxes to provide for the individual good and instead insist on their use for their intended purpose, the common good.

Stand up and be counted, governor. Lead from the front like all good soldiers do.

SOURCE: Teacher Retirement System, Illinois State Board of Education. ⟵

1.6) Pension Insanity: $75,000 Salary Turns Into $155,000 Pension for One Kindergarten Teacher.

E VERY TIME I think I cannot possibly be any more cynical about public pensions and salaries than I already am, I find some new data to prove me wrong yet again. Yes it's true; I am still not cynical enough.

How is it possible in this time of want, where the Illinois Department of Human Services is cutting $90 million from services for poor children and the needy elderly, we still feel obligated to take taxpayer dollars and fund public pensions at 200% of a public employee's salary?

As you look at the following table of TRS members with pensions greater than their ending salaries ask yourself this question: what public good is being served by this use of tax dollars? And furthermore, why isn't this considered to be immoral?

Retired TRS Members with Pensions Greater Than Ending Salaries					
Name	School	Begin Annual pension	Ending Avg. Salary	Pension Greater By	
Smith, Annette T	Peoria SD 150	155,353	75,861	79,492	Elementary Teacher
Zender, Frances T	Community HSD 155	146,430	98,905	47,525	High School English
Watson, Arcelia R	Paxton-Buckley-Loda 10	100,498	63,570	36,928	Middle School Teacher
Emmons, Joyce R	Bradley School District	100,602	66,640	33,962	Special Ed
Ellman, Jean	SEJA 804 NSSED	115,987	92,846	23,141	Social Worker
Wassell, Fred J	New Berlin CUSD 16	76,308	53,648	22,660	Biology Teacher
Roth, Ruth C	Morton CUSD 709	91,056	77,674	13,382	High School English
Burtzos, Ioanna	Downers Grove GSD 58	87,352	78,526	8,827	Social Science Teacher
Ford, Gordon H	Springfield SD 186	75,575	67,755	7,820	Psychologist
Gordon, Melva E	Peoria SD 150	79,020	71,772	7,248	Elementary Teacher

Vondrak, Edward	Thornton TWP HSD 205	108,730	101,514	7,216	Phys ED
Ferguson, Ronald	Winnebago CUSD 323	74,912	68,724	6,188	Administrator
Lovett, Marna D	Rockford School District	85,495	79,422	6,073	Elementary Teacher
Hauptman, Gail C	Olympia CUSD 16	74,043	68,197	5,847	Special Ed
Full, James C	Freeport School District	75,487	71,113	4,374	Drivers Ed
Parker, John E	Granite City CUSD 9	76,997	73,051	3,945	Administrator
Hwastecki, Ralph	Northbrook-Glenview	85,473	83,067	2,406	Elementary Teacher
Giannamore,	Mundelein CHSD 120	128,830	127,352	1,478	Guidance Counselor
Kinnan, Anna P	Oak Park ESD 97	106,995	106,427	567	Elementary Teacher

These pension amounts are allowed by both the TRS and SURS using a series of calculations, which, if they exceed the normal pensions at 75% of salary, are given to the employees via a lifetime annuity.

This is another example of legal corruption.
We have this false idea that all corruption involves illegal actions. As we know the public pension system in Illinois was constructed in a legal framework of unlikely premises and assumptions that basically had no chance of long-term success. Instead, career politicians used it to reward long-term campaign contributors. See "Illinois Pensions and Intergenerational Theft" further on in this book.

In effect the pension system is a form of money laundering, whereby those who give money to politicians get their investment back many times over in salaries and benefits. That is how $50 million in political contributions by Illinois teachers K-University resulted in a $50 billion TRS pension deficit, 1,000 times the contributions received. See where the teacher contributions went under the chapter "Golden Handcuffs".

State employees who work a normal 45-year career will retire on more income than when they worked.
State employees are a group we haven't talked much about but on the whole they have the best pension deal in the state. A state employee who works from age 21 to age 66 (like most of us do in the private sector) will retire on take-home pay 20% or greater than when he worked.

That's because he gets 75% of his pay plus Social Security. So if he was making $80,000 and retired after 45 years he would get $60, 000 state pension and about $24,000 in Social Security or $84,000/yr. Additionally upon retirement he does not pay Social Security (7.65%) or pension contribution (4%) or state income tax (5%). Therefore his take-home pay goes from $68,000 to $84,000. Yes his retirement take-home exceeds his working salary.

Notice that by paying only 4% into the state pension he gets $5,000/mo. retirement income while paying 6.2% into Social Security he gets $2,000/mo. He pays less and gets more thanks to the generosity of the Illinois taxpayer.

How many private sector employees do you know who will be retiring on more than they made when they worked? Not many I would bet.

What the next governor should do.
The next governor should campaign on the theme "Hit the reset button on pensions."

 Let's take all public retirement benefits back to where they were in 1970 when the pensions were guaranteed. Get rid of early retirements, get rid of free health care and let's start over from that point.

How could the public employees complain? That is what was guaranteed, so that's what you will get. All the upgrades and increases folded into the plans in exchange for political contributions since then will be reversed.

In February this year there were two non-binding referendums on funding public pensions. Here is the exact question asked: "Shall the Illinois General Assembly and the Governor take immediate steps to implement meaningful pension reform which will relieve the unsustainable burden on local taxpayers?"

By overwhelming margins of 87% and 91% voters approved implementing "meaningful pension reform." In November at least 12 more communities will vote on this exact issue. I predict that the outcome will be result, once again, in overwhelming approval of "meaningful pension reform."

That should prove beyond a doubt that comprehensive pension reform is supported by a large majority of Illinois taxpayers and any successful politician is going to be out front in implementing this most important of reforms.

SOURCE: Teachers Retirement System. ⇐

1.7) Teacher's 41% Salary Increase Costs Taxpayers $1.3 Million in Extra Pension Payments.

Would you pay $15,000 over four years to get $1.3 million over the next 29?

IN MY LAST chapter "Pension Insanity" I documented how some teachers can get pensions more than twice their salaries. Unfortunately for us taxpayers, that's not the end of the insanity.

At many school districts, the last four years of a teacher's career is a goldmine of money. Most get 26% increases over the last four years (6%/yr. compounded). Since pensions are calculated on the four highest salaries these final four-year increases add mightily to the teachers pensions and as a byproduct millions and millions of dollars to the taxpayers pension cost.

Why do teachers get 6% increases each of their last four years?

Because under Illinois statute Public Act 94-0004 they can. Believe it or not, that law was put into effect to prevent schools from handing out 20% increases per year.

It has nothing to do with skill or work ethic or quality. You could be the best teacher in the school or the worst. Either way you get your 6% per year. It only has to do with the fact they are public employees with special political deals made with politicians who received over $50 million in political contributions from the Teachers Union. To see which politicians get the most from teachers see "Golden Handcuffs".

Our headline teacher is not the only one to get this kind of pension increase.

The headline teacher is our 56 year-old $189,000 music teacher from Hinsdale High School who retired last year on a beginning pension of $130,000/yr. As I wrote earlier he actually paid less into his pension system than a self-employed person with the same salary would pay into Social Security. The difference is the teacher gets $130,000 at age 54; the self-employed person gets $21,000 at age 62. To see the comparison of Social Security to teacher's pension see "Teacher Contributes Less for His $130K Pension Than You Do for Your $21K Social Security".

In the last four years of his career his salary went from $134,526 to $189,433. That 41% raise cost him only an additional $15,000 in pension contributions compared to what he would have paid if his salary had stayed at $134,526 but cost taxpayers $1.3 million in increased pension payments over his 30-year life expectancy. His 41% salary increase resulted in his first year pension going from $100,000 to $130,000. The resulting $30,000 annual increase is twice the $15,000 extra he paid in pension contributions. How's that compare to your 401K?

Using the same formula for two other teachers we looked at recently results in similar numbers. For our $191,000/yr. Phys Ed teacher described in *"$1 Million Payout to Two Teachers Proves Schools Should Pay for Pensions, Not the State"* the amounts would be $16,000 increase in pension contributions for $1.2 million in increased pension payments. Then for our *"$138 per hour 2nd Grade Teachers Will Bankrupt the State"* the contribution increase was $9,000 for $700,000 worth of increased pension payments.

Over their last four years these three teachers' annual raises averaged 7.5%, 12% and 8% respectively.

Working taxpayers are getting 1.5% raises, Social Security retirees zero, why are teachers getting 6-12% raises?
Avoca District 37 in Wilmette just signed a new teacher's contract guaranteeing a minimum of 6% increase each year for the next five years. Many teachers will get more than 6%. And since this is an elementary school district we know the contract calls for 6 hr. work-days for 37.5 weeks/yr.

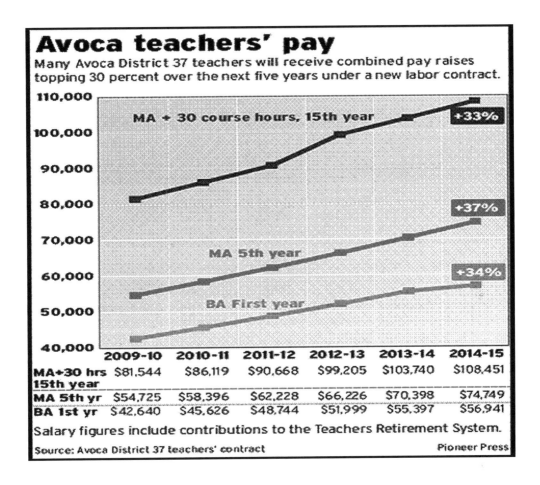

Avoca teachers' pay

Many Avoca District 37 teachers will receive combined pay raises topping 30 percent over the next five years under a new labor contract.

	2009-10	2010-11	2011-12	2012-13	2013-14	2014-15
MA+30 hrs 15th year	$81,544	$86,119	$90,668	$99,205	$103,740	$108,451
MA 5th yr	$54,725	$58,396	$62,228	$66,226	$70,398	$74,749
BA 1st yr	$42,640	$45,626	$48,744	$51,999	$55,397	$56,941

Salary figures include contributions to the Teachers Retirement System.

Source: Avoca District 37 teachers' contract   Pioneer Press

Thanks to Pioneer Press for above graph.

According to the Economic Policy Institute average worker's salary increases for 2010 will be 1.5%. I am certain the teachers would agree with this number because the president of the American Federation of Teachers, as well as the presidents of the AFL/CIO, SEIU and UAW unions, is on the board of directors of the Economic Policy Institute.

Federal employees will receive a 1.4% increase and according to Peter Orzag, President Obama's recent head of Economic Policy:
"…frankly, I think to a lot of Americans that sounds pretty good."

Part time employees with part time careers should not be getting multi-million dollar pensions.

By law teachers are supposed to work 35 years to receive the maximum 75% pension as opposed to 45 years for those of us in Social Security. As it turns out though, only 12% of the retirees since 2009 have actually worked 35 years although 38% have retired with 35 years or more credit.

How is that possible? It's possible because politicians have riddled the pension laws with numerous goodies to allow teachers to retire early from what is already early retirement. Sick leave, which runs from 10 to 15 days per year, can be accrued up to 340 days or two years teaching credit even though the teacher never stepped into a classroom for those two years. Some school districts give teachers a year of sick leave free as part of their contract. Why do they care, they don't have to pay the pensions. Our famous $189,000/yr. Music teacher actually only worked 33 years but took 2 years sick-leave credit to get his mind-boggling $130,000 pension at age 54.

Then there is ERO (Early Retirement Option) that allows schools to pay into TRS to allow teachers to retire with full pension even though they have not worked the requisite 35 years. These payments often run into the hundreds of thousands of dollars with the largest being $361,096 for Neil Codell former superintendent at Niles District 219.

So we have tens of thousands of teachers working part-time jobs at 9 months/yr. vs. 12 months/yr. for the rest of us and working careers that are typically less than 35 nine-month years vs. 45 or more 12-month years for private sector workers. In the case of our $189,000 music teacher he actually worked in the classroom less than 25 years (9 months times 33 years) for his $130,000 pension.

What the next governor should do:

The next governor should "hit the reset button" on pensions on three fronts.

First, revert the pensions to the rules that were in effect in 1970 when the pensions were supposedly "guaranteed" by the Constitution. That would make a full pension of 70% available at age 66 and an early 60% pension at age 60. Although still a much better deal than almost all Illinois taxpayers receive, it would be acceptable to most people.

Secondly "Share the cost" between the employees and the employers. Whatever plan is approved part of the solution must be equal sharing of risk between the employees and the employers. The current plan where the taxpayers assume all the investment risk is unsustainable and unacceptable.

Thirdly, move the cost of pensions to the local school districts. If Hinsdale wants to provide a 56 year-old music teacher with a $1.3 million pension boost over the last four years of his career then why should taxpayers in Peoria pay for it? Hinsdale should pay for it because they caused it to happen. To offset the increase in property taxes, lower the income tax rate by 50%.

The taxpayers of Illinois want complete, comprehensive pension reform and they want it now. It's not complicated – voters want public employees to have the same retirement and health care benefits as the private sector, no better and no worse.

SOURCES: Teachers Retirement System and Illinois State Board of Education. =

1.8) Should Public Employees Have Annual Pensions Greater Than Their Career Pension Contributions?

MY ANSWER WOULD be absolutely not but unfortunately for us taxpayers 20,603 state retirees do have pensions greater than the total amount they contributed to their pensions when they worked.

How does that compare with the Social Security (SS) pension system? A Social Security recipient who worked from college graduation to age 62 (40 years) and was at the maximum Social Security salary contribution limit ($106,400) would have paid in about $130,000 for his share of SS. His max SS pension at that time would be about $22,000 or about 16% of his contribution. If he lived 24 more years (his life expectancy at age 62) he would end up with about $37,000/yr. assuming a 2% CPI increase each year. That $37,000 at age 86 would represent about 26% of his contribution.

It turns out that 99.7% of state pension system retirees from age 50 to age 86 have pensions that exceed the 26% of contributions the maximum Social Security recipient receives at age 86. There is no comparison between Social Security and state pensions payouts since state pensions range from 4 times SS for the average pension (see "Average State Pensions Are Far Above Average") to 8 times SS for a $130,000/yr. music teacher pension (see "Teacher Contributes Less for His $130K Pension Than You Do for Your $21K Social Security").

Ignore the constant whining coming from public employees about how much they contribute – look at their actual amounts paid in.
Egged on by union bosses, teachers and other public employees are being quoted in the media and writing letters to the editor complaining that the amount they pay into their pensions easily justifies the payments out, which as we have constantly shown is patently not true. Teachers are constantly quoted as paying 9.4% or even 10% (rounding up I guess) when we know the pension contribution now is 8% and anyone retiring in the next few years has averaged only about 7.2% slightly higher than SS 6.2%.

So ignore the strident claims and look at the actual dollar amounts paid in over their career. What you will see in every case is a pension payout far in excess of what is justified based upon the amounts contributed by the employees themselves. By comparing those employee contribution and payout amounts with Social Security contributions and payout amounts you get a true picture of the distortions in the current state systems.

So what I have done to illustrate the huge differential between what we peons pay into and get out of Social Security compared to state retirees is compare our prototypical 86 year old Social Security maximum recipient with 10 of the most egregious under-payers in each of the 5 state systems.

GARS - General Assembly Retirement System.
Well, it should come as no surprise to anyone who has lived in IL for more than 24 hrs. that the most outrageous and costly examples of excessive pensions involve the politicians pension system. After all, thievery begins at home.

Note how the 86 year old Social Security recipient with the meager $37,000 pension has contributed vastly more than every pol in this table yet they are the ones pulling down 6 figure pensions.

Top 10 GARS (Politicians) with Annual Pensions Greater than career contributions				
Name	Annual Pension	Total Contrib.	Pension in Excess of Contrib.	Pension as Pct. Of Contrib.
Social Sec. Age 86	37,000	130,000	-93,000	26%
BERMAN, ARTHUR	203,428	109,293	94,135	186%
FRIEDLAND, JOHN	140,649	66,716	73,933	211%
THOMPSON, JAMES	127,215	84,996	42,219	150%
NETSCH, DAWN	121,720	87,778	33,943	139%
HOMER, THOMAS	120,021	78,093	41,927	154%
BOWMAN, H	115,447	73,377	42,071	157%
KARPIEL, DORIS	114,234	95,999	18,234	119%

DEGNAN, TIMOTHY	112,152	85,291	26,861	131%
MOLARO, ROBERT	112,074	109,860	2,214	102%
MCGREW, SAMUEL	110,407	76,963	33,444	143%

SERS – State Employee Retirement System.

About 95% of SERS employees only pay 4% into their retirement system. This is obvious by looking at the huge pensions with very small contributions. Once again our 86 year old max. SS guy pays much more in and gets much less out.

Oh, and by the way, those 95% of SERS retirees also get Social Security so add $25,000 to these numbers.

Top 10 SERS (State) with Annual Pensions Greater than career contributions					
Name	Final Employer	Annual Pension	Total Con-trib.	Pension in Excess of Contrib.	Pension as Pct. Of Contrib.
Social Sec. Age 86		37,000	130,000	-93,000	26%
PARWATIKAR, SADA	HUMAN SERVICES	179,097	121,041	58,056	148%
MODIR, KAMAL	HUMAN SERVICES	161,876	101,605	60,271	159%
BAIG, MIRZA	HUMAN SERVICES	135,465	124,340	11,126	109%
COOPER, KEITH	CORRECTIONS	119,089	94,287	24,802	126%
BAKER, MICHAEL	CORRECTIONS	116,050	77,520	38,530	150%
AHITOW, RODNEY	CORRECTIONS	113,754	101,847	11,906	112%
CASTRO, JOHN	CORRECTIONS	113,754	87,583	26,171	130%
OLEARY, MICHAEL	CORRECTIONS	113,754	108,897	4,857	104%
HARDY, STEPHEN	HUMAN SERVICES	113,650	86,948	26,702	131%
DOBUCKI, KENNETH	CORRECTIONS	112,830	90,804	22,025	124%

TRS – Teachers Retirement System.

Compared to the politicians TRS members look reasonable. But not really. Who wouldn't pay in $200,000 to their retirement system if they could get a $200,000 pension in their mid-fifties?

AN ILLINOIS PENSION SCAM

Top 10 TRS (Teachers) with Annual Pensions Greater than career contributions					
Last	Employer	Annual Pension	Total Contrib.	Pension in Excess of Contrib.	Pension as Pct. of Contrib.
Social Sec. Age 86		37,000	130,000	-93,000	26%
Conyers, John G	Palatine CCSD 15	230,726	217,805	12,921	106%
Baskin, Lawrence	Glen Ellyn CCSD 89	217,344	216,134	1,209	101%
Patton, Ronald C	Bloom TWP HSD 206	212,316	203,340	8,977	104%
Howard, Robert T	Community CSD 59	195,503	168,445	27,058	116%
Pekoe, Lawrence C	Deerfield School Dist109	189,853	139,232	50,621	136%
Schildt, Nicholas N	Quincy SD 172	188,994	163,010	25,983	116%
Geppert, Edward J	IL Federation Of Teachers	185,851	170,210	15,641	109%
McKanna, Robert A	Palatine CCSD 15	180,396	147,826	32,570	122%
Van Winkle, David	Valley View CUSD 365	179,929	170,188	9,741	106%
Anderson, John C	Lake County Special Ed	178,987	140,192	38,795	128%

SURS – State University Retirement System.

These are the big boys of the five state pension systems having all of the $300,000 plus pensions and most of the $200,000 plus. They have, in general, contributed more than the other retirees but their pensions are by far the most outrageous.

Top 10 SURS (University) with Annual Pensions Greater than career contributions						
Last	First	Employer	Annual Pension	Total Contrib.	Pension in Excess of Contrib.	Pension as Pct. Of Contrib.
		Social Security Age 86	37,000	130,000	-93,000	26%
Riad	Barmada	University of Illinois - Chicago	386,334	361,950	24,384	107%
Dan	Pavel	University of Illinois - Chicago	235,638	215,327	20,311	109%
Frederick	Neumann	University of Illinois - Urbana	231,767	227,101	4,666	102%
John	Swalec	Waubonsee Community College	223,891	146,673	77,218	153%
George	Jorndt	Triton College	215,161	180,700	34,461	119%
Sidney	Levitsky	University of Illinois - Chicago	213,252	184,505	28,748	116%

Philippe	Tondeur	University of Illinois - Urbana	205,243	198,691	6,552	103%
Peter	Beak	University of Illinois - Urbana	201,831	155,810	46,021	130%
Charles	Linke	University of Illinois - Urbana	201,162	190,775	10,387	105%
Louis	Hencken	Eastern Illinois University	198,420	182,195	16,225	109%

JRS – Judges Retirement System.

Judges tend to be in the system fewer years than other members but still pull down substantial pensions. These top10 averaged about 25 years to get their large 6-figure pensions and one of them actually contributed less than our SS recipient.

Column1	Column2	Column3	Column4	Column5
Top 10 JRS (Judges) with Annual Pensions Greater than career contributions				
Name	Annual Pension	Total Contrib.	Pension in Excess of Contrib.	Pension as Pct. Of Contrib.
Social Sec. Age 86	37,000	130,000	-93,000	26%
BARRY, TOBIAS	181,325	171,583	9,742	106%
MILLER, BENJAMIN	174,836	172,652	2,183	101%
LUCAS, RICHARD	171,181	154,218	16,963	111%
GREIMAN, ALAN	166,624	124,138	42,485	134%
MCNULTY, JILL	166,624	163,800	2,824	102%
COHEN, JUDITH	166,313	132,310	34,003	126%
COUSINS JR, WILLIAM	166,313	159,250	7,064	104%
TULLY, JOHN	166,300	148,775	17,525	112%
BARTH, FRANCIS	165,031	153,775	11,256	107%
INGLIS, LAWRENCE	164,551	157,394	7,157	105%

Employee contributions are too low and need to be increased substantially.

This is an example of number 3 in my "Four Rules of Too."

1. Salaries are too high.
2. Pensions are too high.
3. CONTRIBUTIONS ARE TOO LOW.
4. Retirement is too early.

The entire system is out of control and unsustainable. Massive reform is needed and soon.

We cannot afford to have public employees contributing less than Social Security recipients while at the same time receiving multiple times SS payments.

If Social Security is in big trouble with its modest payment schedule beginning at age 62, what kind of trouble are the IL pension systems in with its excessive 6-figure payouts beginning at age 50 (State Troopers)? ═

1.9) Should Part-time Public Employees with Partial Careers get Six-figure Pensions?

As Illinois stares into the pension payment abyss, we have to question the morality of unlimited pensions for part-time employees. Just last week the state announced $1.2 million in cuts to the meals on wheels program for poor seniors. However, the checks continue to be cut for the 5,400 state pensions with pensions in excess of $100,000.

The worst example would be school teachers (not administrators) with a 170-day work year contracts (182 day contract less 12 days sick leave) who have pensions in excess of $100,000.

Since we already know that most teachers do not work full careers (average 25 year careers with pensions equal to 400% of Social Security) and in fact fewer than 10% work even 35 years. Assuming an age of 22 at college graduation, 35 years would get you to age 57. Since those in the private sector can't take Social Security until age 62, we really should consider 40 years to be a minimal career for a full pension. Assuming 40 years is the definition of full-time career less than 1% of teachers work full careers before they retire. That means 99% do not work full careers.

Below I just list the ones with less than 35 years work in IL. And assuming they were 170-day-a-year teachers most of their careers they also worked 1/3 less than the average private sector worker (235 days vs. 170 days per year). So by definition they are part-time employees with partial careers receiving 6 figure pensions.

Notice the prevalence of non-academic teachers lead by 12 Phys Ed, 9 Guidance Counselors and 4 Music teachers not to mention teachers in Drama, cabinet making and Radio-TV whatever that is.

In closing do you know any private sector employee with less than 35 years worked who has a pension over $100,000? How about any private sector employee period?

If not why do public employees have such a good deal?

Because they control the politicians with $50 million of political contributions, that's why.

Teachers Who Work Less Than 35 Years Get $100,000 Pension			
Name	Yrs. Work	Yearly Pension	Job Description
Cleland, Janell A	30	158,266	English (Grades 9-12 Only)
Mackey, Robert J	30	102,837	Guidance Counselor
Hopkins, Donald	30	100,004	Physical Education
Chierico, David P	31	110,790	Physical Education
Mitz, William M	31	113,612	Physical Education
Giambeluca, Paul J	31	102,663	Learning Behavior Specialist I
Van Pelt, Jerry L	31	101,078	Director
Wensch, Thomas P	32	122,978	Director
Mohan, James J	32	114,687	Director
Darnell, Robert S	32	113,790	Director
Kalisiak, Roger A	32	108,747	Physical Education
Sincora, Craig D	32	108,330	Health Education
Moss, John H	32	104,099	Director
Capron, Victor T	32	101,826	Guidance Counselor
Kopecky, Brian G	32	106,815	Physical Education
Dale, Michael R	33	109,458	Geography (Grades 9-12 Only)
Samper, Laura J	33	102,296	Speech (Grades 9-12 Only)
Luebbe, Patricia A	33	100,775	Librarian/Media Specialist
Dryanski, Fred J	33	108,010	Physical Education
Pointer, Betty H	33	158,725	Director
Martin, John D	33	146,386	Director
Drollinger, Jack E	33	119,424	Director
Luehr, Gayle J	33	117,503	Physical Education
Curby, David G	33	113,506	Physical Education
Roeing, Roger D	33	112,209	Guidance Counselor
Breunlin, Richard J	33	112,099	Trigonometry (Grades 9-12 Only)
Bloch, James G	33	111,611	Director

Knuth, Martin J	33	110,007	Cross Categorical
Richmond, Lynn W	33	107,712	Director
Kolze, Michael R	33	107,371	World History (Grades 9-12 Only)
Brennan, John F	33	106,886	Spanish
Bluminberg, Deborah J	33	106,611	Guidance Counselor
Gross, Steven G	33	104,554	Cabinet Maker/Millworker
Rothchild, Susan J	33	103,680	Drama/Theatre Arts
Papich, Mary J	33	102,835	Director
Werneske, Donald A	33	102,612	Director
Kubowicz, Michael J	33	102,563	Physical Education
Hastings, Kendall R	33	102,166	Instrumental Music
Martin, Charles E	33	102,099	Instrumental Music
Gratkins, Nanette A	33	101,451	Physical Education
Trzyna, Christine A	33	101,010	Physical Education
Pass, Stephen K	33	100,920	Guidance Counselor
Schmitz, Alice J	33	100,862	Librarian/Media Specialist
Goad, Robert B	33	100,793	Vocal Music
Hoffmann, Susan L	33	100,725	Cross Categorical
Brunssen, Kim C	33	100,682	Instrumental Music
Ciancio, Robert L	33	100,606	World History (Grades 9-12 Only)
Oliver, Scott D	33	100,324	Computer Programming
Petrowsky, Dennis J	33	100,048	Psychologist
Zech, Deborah K	33	109,330	Director
Kray, Deborah L	34	102,555	French
Kasper, Keith G	34	103,638	Learning Behavior Specialist I
Finke, Kenneth E	34	103,247	Graphic Design/Commercial Art
Canning, Judy A	34	105,742	Algebra
Merilos, Martha K	34	101,397	U.S. History (Grades 9-12 Only)
Liesz, James A	34	114,420	English (Grades 9-12 Only)
Gilbert, Sandra D	34	111,835	Guidance Counselor
Maciejewski, Lee T	34	108,368	Physical Education
Botthof, Peter E	34	106,046	Algebra
Wilson, Gary F	34	103,765	Algebra

Harsy, Leonard G	34	102,472	Guidance Counselor
Kleckner, William J	34	102,468	Driver Education
Ogilvie, Peter H	34	101,929	Physics (Grades 9-12 Only)
Dineen, Thomas P	34	100,094	Health Education
Pinelli, Vincent C	34	102,655	Radio & TV Broadcasting
Hamilton, Sandra K	34	101,636	Guidance Counselor

1.10) Teacher Contributes Less for His $130K Pension Than You Do for Your $21K Social Security

Let's ask public employees to pay their fair share.

ACCORDING TO THE latest SBA (Small Business Administration) statistics there are over 1.1 million small businesses in Illinois. Their size ranges from one employee to 500 employees and in most cases, with very few exceptions, the owner pays 12.4% of his wages into the pension plan called Social Security.

On the other hand the 300,000 public employees in the state pension system pay an average of 7.9% into their far superior plans and for many fewer years – from 25 years for State Troopers to 34 for K-12 teachers. That compares to many Social Security recipients who have paid in for 40, 50 or even more years.

The result of this distorted, politically directed contribution scheme is multi-million dollar pensions for public employees paid for largely by private sector workers whose main pension plan, Social Security, is severely limited in scope and payout.

How does Social Security compare to state pensions?

The examples of public pension excess are almost too numerous to mention. In 2009 we have 13 state troopers retiring at age 50 with pensions in excess of $100,000. Six-figure pensions for middle-aged teachers and universities employees proliferate like flies on rotten meat. There is no upper limit for state pensions. We already have a $426,000 pension; can a $1 million pension be far behind?

Social Security, on the other hand, has limits. This year it is about $22,000 maximum at age 62.

Social Security recipients, on average, pay into the system longer and in the case of the self-employed and small businessmen pay a higher percentage of their income, 12.4%, than do, for example, teachers who pay 8%. Thus the total dollar contribution for Social Security contributors ends up much higher than those receiving the 6-figure state pensions. And the state pensions tend to start at an earlier age, 50 in case of troopers and as early as 54.5 in the case of teachers.

You don't have to be a math whiz to see that the state pensions, with lower payments in, higher payments out and years earlier retirement are unsustainable as currently legislated. After all, as we constantly hear in the media, Social Security is in big financial trouble. If $22,000 Social Security payouts at age 62 are financially unsustainable, what do you think $100,000 pensions at age 50 are going to do to future Illinois taxpayers?

Here's an example of the problem.
This chart shows the pension contributions in and pension payments out for two professional music teachers each making the same salary during their careers. The first is a music teacher working 9 months a year for 34 years and the second is a self-employed music teacher working 12 months a year for 40 years. As you can see the self-employed person pays much more in than the teacher but ends up getting only 1/7th as much out.

Pension Comparison		
Public Sector Employee vs. Private Sector Employee		
	Music Teacher Public Employee	**Music Teacher Self-Employee**
Years Worked	33	40
Ending Salary	189,000	189,000
Current Contribution Rate	8%	12.40%
Total Contributions	194,000	268,000
Pension At Age 54	130,000	zero
Pension At Age 62	150,000	22,000
Total Lifetime Pension Paid Out	5,800,000	800,000

Notice the self-employed worker contributes 38% more (268,000 vs. 194,000) than the teacher even though the teacher receives seven times as much in pension payments $5.8 million vs. $800,000.

What the next governor should do.
Require public employees to increase their contributions to at least match the level of a private sector self-employed person making the same salary.

In addition he should begin the process of increasing the retirement age back to 60 and the paid-out rate to 60% of salary, the retirement age and payout rate in effect when the constitutional guarantee was approved in 1970. ⇐

1.11) Work for the State 5 Years, Pay in Zero, Get $130,000 Pension. Work for Yourself 45 Years, Pay In $314,000 Get $28,000 Social Security.

Anybody see a problem here?

THIS IS WHAT happens when you live in a state with no accountability, no transparency and massive political malfeasance. You and I are in effect tax slaves whose purpose in life is to work and pay exorbitant taxes so the elitist politically connected public employees can live in luxury when they retire – on our dime of course.

The person from the first line of the title is Dr. Renee Hartz, a thoracic surgeon hired by the University of Illinois to teach surgery. I am only guessing about what she actually did because records of her activity are very limited. In a Freedom of Information Act request I asked for her contract or offer letter outlining her job responsibilities plus pay and benefits included in her job offer. Despite pay of $567,479.10 per annum from 1991 to 1995 there were no records related to her hiring. So who knows what she did or was supposed to do? However we do know she was paid a lot of money to do it.

Since those wages were as of 1991 in current terms in would be about $750,000. According to the American Medical Association, Cardio-thoracic surgeon's median income is $533,000 as of 2009. So her salary at U of I was about 30% above the median.

Although I was unable to get employment contract info I was able to get payroll records showing how her costs were distributed to various university departments including the "employer" (that's you and me and every other IL taxpayer) pension contributions and that is what I am basing this analysis on. Those records show the state picked up the employee contributions ($157,000) which is why I say she paid in zero for her pension. Even if she had paid the $157,000 her $130,000 pension is outrageous.

How many $1 million/yr. public "servants" can IL afford?

As we know, total compensation is what we taxpayers pay for, not just salary. In the case of Dr. Hartz that additional pay includes a pension worth more than $2 million cash or $400,000 per year worked. Then there were healthcare benefits, vacations, malpractice insurance, etc. all of which she would have had to pay for herself if she were a self-employed surgeon. So even in 1991 dollars she cost us well over $1 million a year. In current dollars that cost would be about $1.5 million/yr.

We were so generous in fact that we donated $49,124.18 tax-dollars to her pension account in 2009, fourteen years after she left state employment.

Our self-employed person, on the other hand, worked much longer and contributed much more to his pension plan called Social Security. He could even have been a thoracic surgeon. Not only did he contribute $314,000 for his meager $28,000/yr. pension he paid for all of his other fringe benefits too such as health insurance, vacations (if he took any) and if he was a doctor, malpractice insurance premiums. Compared to our "servant" he had a pretty raw deal. Of course he didn't have access to the unlimited, guaranteed funding provided by taxes.

I thought servants were supposed to work 7 days a week until they croaked?

Not our servants apparently. The days worked are fewer, the months worked are fewer and the years worked are fewer and, in some cases, as outlined below, much, much fewer.

If we consider someone in the private sector who graduated from college at the typical age of 22 he would work 40 years until the age of 62 to get the minimum Social Security (max. $22,000/yr.) and in a full career, 44 years to age 66 to get full benefits (max. $28,000/yr.).

If we look at the total number of retirees in the five state pension systems we come up with about 182,000. Of those 182,000 state retirees only 279 worked at least 44 years (less than ¼ of 1 %), only 1,311 worked at least 40 years (less than 1%) and only 18,108 (10%) worked even 35 years. That means 90% of the people pulling down state pensions did not work even to the equivalent of age 57 (age 22 plus 35 years work). Did 90% of the people you know in the private sector retire before age 57?

That also means you can ignore the pensions public relations gambit (paid for by the taxpayers of course) that the 5,400 state pensions over $100,000 represent only 2.3% of retirees. What they fail to mention is that less than 1% of state pension retirees work what the rest of us call full careers. We're paying 6-figure pensions for part-time employees.

The State University Retirement System (SURS) is the most amazing with zero, none, nada employees ever working more than 40 years before retiring. And of those who have retired since 2001 only 3 have worked more than 36 years. And keep in mind SURS employees pay zero for their excellent health insurance while working and while retired if they worked 20 years.

Keep these numbers in mind when you here politicians and union leaders talking about "modest" pensions. They are only modest because the vast majority are part-time employees with short careers. Private sector workers with similar careers to average TRS retirees (25 years worked, $46,000 pension) would be getting $12,000 or less if they retired on Social Security at age 62. So even at the low-end state pensions are at least 4 times better than Social Security when taking into account the younger retirement age of state workers. At the $100,000 level state retirees receive up to 10 times the value of Social Security. See previous chapter.

Instead of raising taxes by 75% let's raise employee pension contributions by 75%.
On average public employees in the IL retirement systems pay less than 7% for these Golden parachutes we call pensions. Raising them by 75% would raise the contribution to about 12% a deal any private sector employees would take in a heartbeat. Even then we taxpayers would be paying more than 150% of the employee's contribution.

The following list of $100,000 pensions with 20 or fewer years worked (top 50 of 133 total) is just one indicator of the out-of-control output of the public-employee/politician industrial complex. Public employees give the politicians millions in political contributions and the politicians give the public employees billions in pension contributions in return. Dr. Hartz and her $130,000 pension barely make the list at number 49.

Where will it end? Either massive reform or bankruptcy – the status quo is doomed to failure.

IL Pensions More Than $100,000 Work 20 Years or Less in IL			
Top 50 of 133 Total			
NAME	**Mo. Pension**	**Year Pension**	**Work Years**
1	Abcarian	$26,607	$319,286	20
2	Ausman	$24,342	$292,105	17
3	Moss	$19,724	$236,688	24
4	Pavel	$19,065	$228,774	20
5	Sandlow	$14,931	$179,173	20
6	Pappas	$14,886	$178,634	17
7	Ross	$14,707	$176,479	17
8	NICKELS, JOHN	$13,536	$162,428	20
9	Ripps	$13,532	$162,380	15
10	Brody	$13,015	$156,185	20
11	Ehrlich	$12,907	$154,886	20
12	Van Der Bogert, Mary R	$12,704	$152,453	20
13	Frohman	$12,601	$151,213	13
14	Goldberg	$12,516	$150,192	20
15	Bailie	$12,361	$148,328	18
16	DOUGLAS, LORETTA	$12,323	$147,882	20
17	JAFFE, AARON	$12,288	$147,451	20
18	MADDEN, JOHN	$12,288	$147,451	20
19	GILL, TIMOTHY	$12,249	$146,990	20
20	DOZIER, RONALD	$12,216	$146,590	20
21	HEISER, LARRY	$12,216	$146,590	20
22	Anderson	$12,181	$146,173	17
23	THOMPSON, PERRY	$12,130	$145,562	19
24	MILLER, GEORGE	$12,088	$145,050	20
25	Hughes	$12,030	$144,365	18
26	WILLIAMSON DARRELL G	$11,957	$143,479	20
27	ANDREWS, H	$11,857	$142,278	20
28	Moriarty	$11,840	$142,079	20
29	BRODHAY, STEPHEN	$11,739	$140,869	20

30	RIZZI, DOM	$11,724	$140,689	19
31	KENNEDY, JAMES	$11,681	$140,168	19
32	KUHAR, LUDWIG	$11,605	$139,260	20
33	Valli	$11,548	$138,581	20
34	KLITZ, CARSON	$11,461	$137,531	20
35	GAUSSELIN, EDWIN	$11,451	$137,408	20
36	TESCHNER, JOHN	$11,372	$136,461	20
37	MANNING JR, ROBERT	$11,361	$136,327	20
38	ROBINSON, RONALD	$11,357	$136,283	20
39	HETT, THOMAS	$11,275	$135,303	19
40	Erdoes	$11,266	$135,193	13
41	Wollstadt	$11,245	$134,943	17
42	DONNERSBERGER, DAVID	$11,111	$133,337	17
43	BERMAN, EDWIN	$11,093	$133,116	20
44	Cook	$11,061	$132,731	20
45	Gross	$11,059	$132,713	12
46	SEYMOUR, STEVEN	$10,904	$130,853	19
47	HOLT, LEO	$10,902	$130,826	18
48	SCHERMERHORN, THOMAS	$10,895	$130,737	18
49	Hartz	$10,870	$130,439	5
50	MC COOEY, BRENDAN	$10,833	$129,998	19
SOURCES:	Teachers Retirement System (TRS)			
	State University Retirement System (SURS)			
	State Employee Retirement System (SERS)			

1.12) $10 Million Pensions Are Here – Top 100 State Pensions Will Payout over $700 Million. Here's How to Save $2 Billion.

Springfield fiddles while taxpayers get burned.

WHERE IS THE pension reform we have been promised by various and sundry politicians? Tom Cross's SB 512 bill has been waved furtively in front of the Civic federation and some media outlets but there is apparently no action forthcoming in the near future.

In the meantime $400,000/yr. pension checks keep going out every month unabated. No one in Springfield seems to care that multi-millionaires on the public-pension dole are being paid while cuts are being made to meals-on-wheels for poor seniors and home health care for the seriously disabled. This seems curious to me since the progressives always seem to rail about doing more for the poor and needy. Certainly the people on this Top 100 list are neither poor nor needy so where is the outcry from the left? The only people complaining are the tea-partiers and conservatives.

Obama wants to tax the millionaires – let's start here in IL with the pension millionaires.
As it stands right at this moment IL pensions are not taxable at the state level. If we just taxed these Top 100 pension millionaires we could raise $1.1 million/yr. and reinstate the meals-on-wheels for poor seniors.

If we taxed all state pensions where family income exceeds $50,000 we would get about $200 million/yr.

Keep in mind a $40,000 pension at age 55 with a 3% COLA will pay out over $1.8 million assuming an average life expectancy.

Come on progressives let's tax those millionaires and help the poor. Shouldn't they pay a little more, their fair share?

Why do state retirees get 3% Cost-of-living-adjustments when Soc. Sec. Gets zero?
Another give away to the politically connected is the automatic 3% COLA. It cost taxpayers $200 million a year and it's compounded year after year. The COLA doubles all pensions in 24 years for absolutely no reason other than political favoritism.

If pensioneers' family income is greater than $50,000 then you don't get any COLA. That would save over $100 million/yr. and allow us to reinstate the $40 million in cuts to the Department of Aging and have some money left to pay down the $6 billion in past due bills.

Why do state retirees get free health care?
Under current law, if you work 20 years for the state or state universities you get free health care when you retire in addition to free health care when you were working. If all state employees and retirees paid 40% of their health care insurance we would save $1 billion per year.

Why do public employees get retirement pay for sick-leave?
Right now teachers can receive up to 2 years sick-leave credit towards their retirement meaning their pension is increased by 4.4% for the rest of their lives. They average about 1.5 years per retiree so over time that would amount to about 3.3% of retirement cost or about $200 million per year.

No one on the private sector gets sick-leave credit so therefore no one in the public sector should get it.

Eliminate all salary spiking to rein in top end pensions.
As it stands the worst teacher in each school district gets an automatic 26% salary increase (6% per year compounded) over his last 4 years for no reason. I say worst teacher because all full-retirement teachers are eligible (there is no "judging" in our school system – heavens forbid) therefore if follows logically that the worst teacher and the best teacher and all teachers in between would get the 26% salary increases. This raises already absurd pensions by more than a quarter for the benefit of no one except the politically connected.

Teachers are not alone in this ripping off of the taxpayer of course. Politicians are famous for appointing retiring/ lost-the-last-election politicians to high paying state jobs and then transferring a short work period to the politician's pension plan which pays 85% after 20 years.

And state employees such as state troopers jack up maximum overtime in their final year and then grab 80% of that final year as their pensions beginning as early as age 50. So far 28 troopers have retired at age 50 with pensions in excess of $100,000. A $100,000 pension at age 50 will payout an average of $5.7 million.

"Spiking" cost is hard to determine because it is hidden from view and very hard to track but if it is only 7% of pension costs that would be about $500 million/yr.

We could save $2 billion/yr. with these 5 simple non-pension-reform reforms.

$200 million/yr. – Tax the pension millionaires.
$100 million/yr. – "Adjust" the Cost of living adjustment.
$1 billion/yr. – Health care: public employees pay same as private sector employees.
$200 million/yr. – Eliminate sick leave pension payments.
$500 million/yr. – Put a spike thru the heart of payroll spiking by eliminating it.

TOTAL = $2 billion

There are no public employees or jobs worth $5 million pensions let alone $10 million.
What follow is just the Top 10 estimated pension payouts. The Top 100 totals $702 million.

Several items to note:

1. Compared to early retirement on Social Security none of these millionaires worked a full career.
2. The state pension payout ratio "Payout to Contrib. Ratio" runs to over 40 times compared to Soc. Sec. max. 6 times. By limiting pension payouts to 20 times contributions we would save 50% on these public pensions. Who except the politically entitled would think 20 times is unfair?
3. Every one of these Top 10 Payouts is a K-12 employee.
4. Assumes 30 year life expectancy.

Name	Employer	Current pension	In-state Years Service	Estimated Total Pension Payout	Employee Pension Contrib.	Pay-out to Contrib. Ratio
Social Security Max	Retire age 62	22,000	40	780,000	130,000	6
Curley, Mary M	Hinsdale CCSD 181	226,645	31	10,765,641	248,707	43
Catalani, Gary T	Community SD 200	237,195	35	10,721,225	289,150	37
Gmitro, Henry A	Community CSD 93	234,803	34	10,613,087	282,749	38
Murray, Laura L	HomewoodFloss-moor	238,882	36	10,248,021	298,590	34
Bangser, Henry S	New Trier HSD 203	261,681	32	9,889,792	275,365	36
Burns, Kevin G	Community HSD 218	206,495	34	9,808,492	223,196	44
Hintz, James S	Adlai Stevenson125	234,810	29	9,568,607	235,017	41
Many, Thomas W	Kildeer Country-side	201,405	33	9,566,755	288,263	33
Hager, Maureen L	North Shore SD 112	231,703	33	9,430,296	277,773	34
Johnson, Michael	IL AssocSchool-Boards	193,273	33	9,180,483	229,060	40

There is plenty politicians can do now without pension reform.

So what's the hold-up? It's the same old problem in IL – the politically entitled have more than enough political power to keep the entitlements coming regardless of what the taxpayer/voter thinks.

Perhaps only bankruptcy will solve the problem. If so the sooner the better. ⇐

1.13) Four State Retirees Received Cost-Of-Living-Adjustments of More Than $10,000 In 2011.

Quinn Cuts funding for handicapped but hands out $10,000 pension increases.

IF YOUR STATE pension exceeds $333,333 per year do you really need another $10,000 to make it thru the economic downturn at the expense of the 99.9% of Illinois citizens who do not have such pensions?

Apparently in Illinois it doesn't matter how much you are getting from the taxpayers, there is always more where that came from. Total COLA's (cost-of-living-adjustments) for the 205,000 state retirees will total more than $200 million this year compared to .00, zero, none, nada for the 270,000 Illinois Social Security recipients COLA's.

In fact you could argue that the median full time wage employee in Illinois, making about $35,000 per year, received a negative COLA of $700/yr. because his state income tax went up by 2%. And how much more state tax did the four $10,000 amigos pay? None – state pensions are not taxed.

So Joe Sixpack gets his taxes raised by $700 so that multi-millionaire state retiree Tapas Das Gupta can get a $12,053 tax-free raise in 2011. By the way, Mr. Das Gupta has received more than $2.5 million in pension payments so far.

Column1	Column2	Column3	Column4	Column5	Column6	Column7
First Name	Last Name	Retirement Employer	2011 Pension	2010 Pension	Pension Increase	Pension Paid To Date
Tapas	Das Gupta	University of Illinois - Chicago	414,471	402,418	12,053	2,548,333
Edward	Abraham	University of Illinois - Chicago	402,630	390,903	11,727	1,539,106
Riad	Barmada	University of Illinois - Chicago	386,334	375,086	11,248	4,205,585
Mahmood	Mafee	University of Illinois - Chicago	359,360	348,893	10,467	1,557,010

In case you are wondering more than 400 state retirees received COLA increases of more than $5,000 in 2011.

Here's how to save $2.26 billion for the pension system next year.

There are many ways to save money if there is enough political will. Here are four quick and easy ones:

1. If we tax pensions we could add $350 million in revenue.
2. Eliminate the 3% COLA and save $210 million.
3. Freeze salaries and save $850 million.
4. Increase employee contributions by 5% and save another $850 million.

But even if we saved $2.26 billion and used it all for pensions State Auditor General William Holland says we taxpayers would still have to pay $4.14 billion for pensions (including pension bond payments) or about 12% of the state budget. In other words we still have a big problem. And it gets worse – in 2015 Holland says the tab will be $7.9 billion.

As it stands right now we employer taxpayers are paying 4 times more than the employees and yet all we see and hear are how we are shortchanging the employees. The following chart should put that false argument to rest: ≡

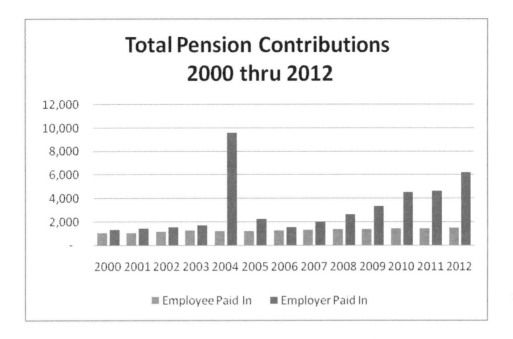

The large employer payment in 2004 was from the $10 billion pension bond established by Gov. Blagojevich. In total for the years 2000 thru 2012 taxpayers have paid in $43 billion (including bond interest) to the employees meager $17 billion. Why aren't the employees paying half of everything including the pension bond interest? That's what private sector employees do. If your 401K loses value does your employer make up the entire difference? No, of course not nor would you expect him to.

Why are public employees special?

Instead of a hiring freeze Quinn hires 19,000 new state workers and puts them in the old expensive pension plan.

Apparently Quinn doesn't see any budget problems because between April 14, 2010 when he signed the new Pension Reform Law and Dec 31, 2010 the state hired 19,000 new employees, not counting teachers according to the State Journal Register newspaper. Every one of the 19,000 is automatically grandfathered into the old expensive (for taxpayers that is) pension plan. That means another potential 19,000 pension millionaires over the coming decades.

And, no, they are not replacing retired personnel. Only 3,197 state employees retired in 2010.

Can you imagine if IBM was losing billions of dollars every year, going to their stockholders and saying "Yes, we are losing billions every year but things aren't that bad, we're going to hire 19,000 new employees, give them the best pension plan in the country and, by the way, continue handing out average 5% salary increases." The CEO would be fired but unfortunately we cannot fire Illinois CEO until 2014.

We need more businessmen and accountants and far fewer lawyers in Springfield if we are ever going to solve our budget and pension problems. Otherwise 1000's of moving vans with former Illinois residents' assets will be heading to Wisconsin, Indiana and Missouri and they won't be coming back either. Why would they? ⇐

1.14) State University Top 25 Pensions Average $277,000 for 29 years work.

Top 100 SURS retirees (all years) average $217,000 for only 28 years work.

ONE OF THE state pension systems we don't talk about much is SURS (State University Retirement System). SURS is the system with the dubious distinction of having the Top 10 pensions in the state's history.

Top 10 Pensions in History are all SURS			
First	**Last**	**Mo. Pension**	**Annual pension**
Tapas	Das Gupta	34,539	414,471
Edward	Abraham	33,553	402,630
Riad	Barmada	32,194	386,334
Mahmood	Mafee	29,947	359,360
Herand	Abcarian	27,405	328,865
Ronald	Albrecht	27,302	327,623
James	Ausman	25,072	300,868
Jacob	Wilensky	23,371	280,450
Phillip	Forman	22,782	273,389
Joel	Sugar	22,176	266,113

Under SURS employees pay only 7% of their salary (slightly more than Social Security's 6.2%) and can retire with 80% pensions with 36 years "Service Credit".

Now "Service Credit" does not mean years actually worked because it includes sick leave "credits" and "Purchased Credits" that can be used in lieu of actually working. In fact of the 2,400 academic retirees in the last two years exactly one has worked the full 36 years. All the others have worked less than the maximum required years and of the Top 100 pensions for 2009-2010 (averaging $150,000/yr.) the average years worked is 28.

Teacher years are like dog years – 28 years is really 21 years.

If you are a college academic and teach 36 weeks a year (two 18-week semesters) then your 28 nine-month work years are the equivalent of 21 twelve-month work years the rest of us work. So looking at the Top 100 SURS pensions for 2009-2010 that way we have $150,000 pensions for what the rest of us would call an average of 21 years of work.

Twenty-one years is exactly ½ of the 42 years most of us work before we can draw on Social Security.

SURS Top 100 retirees for 2009-2010, on average, paid less into the pension system for their $150,000 than self-employed making the same salary do into Social Security for $22,000.

If you work from age 21 to age 62, and make the same salary as the Top 100, you can retire on about $22,000/yr. in Social Security. However the key point is you would have paid more into Social Security for your $22,000 over your 41 years of self-employment than the $150,000 SURS retiree would have paid into his pension plan over his 28 work years. In other words the SURS public employee gets 5 times as much retirement pay for less money invested and he gets it at an earlier age. What's not to like if you're a public employee?

SURS employees get free health care too.

If you are a state or university employee you get free health care while you work and after you retire if you have worked at least 20 years. The total health care cost for the state is in excess of $2 million a year. If we asked state employees to pick up ½ of their very generous health care cost the state would save over $1 billion.

So here we are with another case where state employees retire in their 50's with 6-figure pensions and free health care after paying into the retirement system what is a pittance compared to the costs. Taxpayers, of course, are stuck with picking up the difference in costs.

What the next governor should do.

The next governor needs to be a teacher. He needs to explain to the citizens of Illinois where all the tax dollars go. And when he does people will see that public employees' total compensation including salaries, pensions, health care, holidays, sick leave, vacation etc. is far beyond what their peers in the private sector earn.

Then he needs to compare public compensation to other groups such as Wisconsin K-12 teachers whose compensation including pension costs is 45% less than Illinois. See WI comparison to IL in chapter 4.5. Furthermore he needs to have a public sector commission look at compensation costs job by job from custodian to administrator with the goal of bringing the public compensation back down to parity with the private sector.

For example how many hours a week does a college faculty member actually teach? Since they get 3 months a year off while still pulling down a full salary is it too much to ask that they put in more time during the limited 9-month work year? How about we ask them to teach one more hour per day in exchange for the 9-month work year?

The governor should lead the way by decreasing the governor's salary significantly from $180,000 to $120,000 and should forego all pension accruals during his term in office.

His $120,000 salary will allow him to argue for a maximum $10,000/mo. salary limitation for all public employees until the budget is balanced. This would save $1.5 billion a year including pension costs.

After all who has a more important job the governor or the 18,000 state employees, including K-Univ., currently making more than $10,000/mo.?

And finally, how many taxpayers think a $10,000/mo. public salary is a hardship? ═

1.15) $1 Million Payout to Two Teachers Proves Schools Should Pay for Pensions, Not the State.

Why does Quinn want to raise taxes to make teachers millionaires?

I F WE NEEDED any more evidence that the Illinois public school system is of the teachers, by the teachers and for the teachers these financial transactions should provide the final proof.

The school district in question is Stevenson District 125 in Lincolnshire. In 2010 they provided ERO (Early Retirement Option) and "Excess Salary Cost" payments to the state to allow two teachers to retire early.

What are ERO and "Excess Salary Cost"?

ERO was passed by the legislature in 1979 and since then has been enhanced several times. Basically ERO allows teachers who are too young or have too few years work to qualify for undiscounted pensions. The local school district pays the ERO out of local property taxes and sends it to the state in the year the teacher retires. These payments can exceed $300,000 as in the case of Dist. 125's Robert Lyons, a History teacher.

Keep in mind teachers can already retire on full pension at age 54 so ERO is earlier than early.

"Excess Salary Cost" is a charge to the local schools by the TRS for handing out huge pay raises (anything in excess of 6%) in the last 4 years of a teacher's employment. There is no reason to hand out huge salary increases except to raise the level of the pension earned by the teacher. In the case of William Mitz, Physical Education teacher, this "Excess Salary Cost" paid for by the local property taxpayers added up to more than $102,000 for the $68,000 or 55% worth of salary increases he earned in the last 3 years of his employment.

Mitz Salaries 2007-2010:

2010	191,124
2009	176,504
2008	147,087
2007	123,194

How does that 55% increase compare to your salary increase since 2007?

How much does this add up to for two teachers?

So when you add the extra retirement payments to the outrageous 9-month salaries from the generous taxpayers of District 125 you get the following:

Name	Retirement Date	School's ERO and Excess Salary Pension Cost	Last Year's Salary	Total School Cost for One Employee for 1 Year	Subject Taught
Mitz, William M	6/4/2010	297,970.60	191,124	489,094.60	Phys Ed
Lyons, Robert E	6/4/2010	303,050.48	151,961	455,011.48	History

So that's $944,000. But as they say on the TV ads "That's not all folks!" They also receive family health insurance worth $19,000 each and as we know 30% of the salary ($102,000) is paid into the state pension system for each teacher. Add in 15 sick days and 3 personal days per year and you have well over $1 million in total compensation for two teachers.

It's not just District 125. Here are some more examples:

ERO (Early Retirement Option) Payouts Over $200,000				
Name	School District	Annual Pension	Final Average Salary	School Dist. ERO Payout
Codell, Neil C	Niles TWP CHSD 219	163,344	321,862	394,910
Mitz, William M	Adlai Stevenson HSD 125	113,616	159,477	297,971
Mellen, Nanette L	Danville CCSD 118	139,644	186,199	287,085

Petersen, Jerry D	Community HSD 218	135,996	190,380	285,686
Vogler-Corboy, Dale A	Niles TWP CHSD 219	96,996	209,937	262,234
Wardzala, Edward J	Lake Park CHSD 108	129,912	176,513	251,338
Schau, Pamela S	Maine TWP HSD 207	92,988	175,182	244,263
Peterson, David W	SEJA 804 NSSED	141,600	195,038	223,631
Lyons, Robert E	Adlai Stevenson HSD 125	71,892	134,536	222,034
Emde, Barbara L	Kildeer Countryside CCSD 96	57,288	102,770	210,217
McGee, Glenn W	Wilmette SD 39	184,116	247,341	209,903
Brown, Timothy F	Consolidated HSD 230	127,200	173,941	209,652
Broughton, Cynthia A	ISBE - Assistant Supt	126,456	170,740	207,611
Nielsen-Hall, Denise M	Deerfield School District 109	110,892	153,590	206,071
Stramaglia, Michael F	Schiller Park SD 81	104,100	131,214	203,275
Mical, Alice L	Wilmette SD 39	81,840	161,745	201,463

Let's cut the income tax rate in half and move the pensions to the local school districts.
As we mentioned before it is obvious these districts can pay their own pension cost. After all those allowing these outrageous salaries should pay the pensions incurred by those salaries. Why should people who don't live in the district and who do not have a say in the salary schedule have to pay the six-figure pensions that result from these excessive salaries?

Cutting the income tax to 1.5% from 3% would save the taxpayers about $4.2 billion just about the exact amount of the pension payment for 2011. The schools would then be liable for the salaries and the pensions and rightfully so. Maybe if they have to pay the pensions they will pay more attention to the salaries and early retirement payments they grant to their employees.

In addition cancel the 3% pension COLA and initiate the state income tax on pensions over $20,000 (currently pensions are not taxed). This would raise about $250 million, which could be used as tax credits for low-income homeowners.

What the next governor should do.
The next governor needs to begin the process of placing pension cost on those who control the salaries. It makes no sense to have those who pay the pension cost i.e. the state, have no control over the salaries that determine those pension costs. As we have seen before you cannot control pensions unless you control salaries.

Although K-12 is the most obvious example, state departments, especially universities, should also be charged with expensing pension costs. Their annual budgets would include pension costs and if they exceed it cuts would have to be made. They cannot raise salaries willy-nilly and expect others to fund the pension costs. The salaries and the pensions must be the responsibility of the same party.

Teachers who make $191,000/yr. and retire with a pension of $113,000 after working 31 nine-month years, needs to become a thing of the past. While Illinois taxpayers struggle to make ends meet, teachers' work in a privileged environment of high-paying guaranteed jobs, 3 months a year off, early retirement on top of early retirement, all at an extremely high cost to the hardworking taxpayers of Illinois. Schoolteachers and all public employees need to live and work in the same employment environment as the taxpayer does. No guarantees, no short work years, and retirement at 65 just like the rest of us. The days of special deals for teachers must end

CHAPTER 2:

<u>HOW BAD IS THE PROBLEM?</u>

"If 50 people say you're drunk you probably outta lie down."

— Jim Rockford, Rockford Files

2.1) QUESTION: How Much Do Taxpayers Owe For Unfunded State Pensions?
ANSWER: No One Knows But It Is Certainly More Than The Oft-quoted $85 Billion.

How computer models can be used for political purposes.

S O WHAT DO Global Warming and Al Gore have in common with Illinois' unfunded pension liability?

They both use "computer models" to come up with the wrong answer.

Most people have heard of global warming models (GCM – General Circulation Models) the unbelievably complex computer programs that attempt to project climate forward 100 years. These GCM projects are the most complex scientific and mathematical problem solving effort ever attempted by humans making the Manhattan Project and putting a man on the moon comparable to a four year-old's finger painting versus a Rembrandt.

Likewise Actuarial Reports like those provided to the various Illinois pension systems are also computer models though few people call them by that name. They too are very complex though nothing close to the scale of climate models.

Computer models do not "predict" they offer possible scenarios.

As the UN explicitly states in its latest climate change report regarding model output: "Scenarios are images of the future, or alternative futures. They are neither predictions nor forecasts."

So following the UN's description of models, Actuarial Reports are not predictions. But on the contrary if you read newspapers or listen to politicians and union members the output of the Actuarial Reports are indeed factual, not one possibility out of an infinite number of possibilities. This leads to false expectations and mass confusion.

Computer models can be programmed to generate whatever results you want.

Eons ago I worked on computerized models called "war games" a designation that should really be called "war models". In this particular model we used some of the most powerful computers in the world at the time to simulate "pretend" Soviet bombers coming over the North Pole and attacking the US. The programs generated "pretend" radar signals so military personnel could practice shooting the bombers down with "pretend" Nike missiles (like the ones that used to be in Vernon Hills) and "pretend" F-104 fighter jets. These models provided a very important training tool that allowed defense personnel to see the many, many different possibilities ("Scenarios" in UN parlance) of Soviet bomber attack missions.

Well to make a long story short(er) one Saturday, late in the day, three of us programmers were given 2 hours of computer time to fine tune some of the software. Computer time in those days was like water in the Gobi desert – when you got it you used every drop. Being young (and therefore by definition stupid) we decided to use the time instead to see what would happen if we gave the Soviet bombers only half a tank of fuel. To great peals of laughter we watched as 500 Soviet bombers dropped off of the radar screens like rocks somewhere in the Canadian tundra north of the Arctic Circle. By changing just one model assumption out of 100's to a nonsensical value we were able to generate the exact, though extremely unlikely, outcome we wanted to see. It was that simple.

Similarly climate models use an assumption for CO_2 that makes no sense. Since CO_2 measurement was standardized in 1958 at Mona Loa volcano in Hawaii, atmospheric CO_2 accumulation has increased consistently at about .5 to .6% per year. However the model uses 1% per year almost double what is happening in the real world.

Why is this important? Because the rate of CO_2 accumulation, like the pension investment return rate, is compounded over a long period of time, 100 years for CO_2 and 35 years for pensions. So CO_2 in the real world looks like it will double in 120 years while the model insists it will be only 70 years. Obviously assuming a 50-year difference in CO_2 doubling makes as much sense as loading a bomber with half a tank of fuel or guessing that investments will return 8.5%/yr. for 35 years. All three assumptions give you nonsensical results not facts.

So what does all this have to do with pensions?
Glad you asked.

Now that we have seen what unlikely assumptions can do to results in "war models" and "climate models" we can turn our attention to what they do in "pension models", AKA Annual Actuarial Reports.

In pension models assumptions are made for assets, life expectancy, annual salary increases, total liability, ROI (Return On Investment), as well as a few minor things we won't go into.

Assets – when $50 is $75:
This should be straightforward. If you have $100 you have $100. Well, in an Actuarial model not necessarily. If things go bad in the pension investment world you can call upon a legal method called "smoothing" to make things look better now at the cost of looking worse later. For example if you had $100 last year but only $50 this year you can average them and say Actuarial Assets are $75 instead of $50. Kicking the can down the road is what it should be called because the losses you do not recognize today must be recognized in the future. No matter how you try to rationalize smoothing it is deception.

So in Illinois when you lose $25 billion you suddenly discover "smoothing" and it looks like you only lost $6 billion. That's what they did last year but to the credit of the actuaries they called Illinois out on it. Here's the quote from the TRS (Teachers Retirement System) report from 2009:

"With the introduction of five-year smoothed asset value in 2009 schedules cannot serve as a realistic projection because they do not reflect deferred losses."

So actuaries said don't do it but TRS trustees, 6 of whom by law must be teachers or retired teachers, said, "Yes we can!"

Liabilities and ROI – just a wild guess:
In "pension models" the liability of the pension is calculated by "guessing" how much money we need in the bank today to pay for pensions up to 35 years in the future a financial term called Present Value. In order to do that you need to know the current salary, estimated salary increases, mortality rates, pension payout rates, etc. But the biggest single determinate of future liability is the assumed Interest Rate (IR). The higher the interest rate guess the lower the amount of money we need in the bank today to pay for the future pensions. So guessing 4%

would make the pension liability twice as much as guessing 8% ($270 billion vs. $135 billion) so GUESS which one politicians, union bosses and pension trustees prefer? Right, 8%.

Using an average of 8% IR in our "pension model" gives us today's quoted liability of $135 billion and since we have about $50 billion in the bank our Unfunded Liability is $85 billion ($135B - $50B). But the 8% assumption is also used for ROI and is just a guess; no one knows for sure what the return on assets will be for the next year let alone for the next 35 years. The fact that this 8% (8.5% in case of the TRS) is just a guess is nowhere to be found in the conversations we hear from politicians, unions and the media. It is presented to us as a fact, a fait accompli when in reality it is a guess and retrospectively a very bad guess.

But since these are "models" we really could use any interest rate to calculate our liabilities and ROI. The 8% currently being used is just one of an infinite number of interest rates we could use to "guess" what our liability is. We could theoretically use 10.3% (used by the City of Evanston at one time for its pensions) or 2.5% or even –1.0%. In a "model" those are all legitimate choices. If we use lower IR in our "model" our Unfunded Liability goes up and our ROI goes down.

So how did the powers that be do in the 10-year period 2000-2009? About 2.7% ROI per year, a number that if continued into the future would bankrupt the state in a few years. Oops.

"Pension models" are about to become more realistic.
In the next 2 years two new calculations (model assumptions) will be required by public pension funds using lower Interest Rates than current ones. The first is from GASB (Government Accounting Standards Board) that will require public pensions to use a blended rate, a higher one for assets actually held and a much lower one for the unfunded balances. This will require pension funds to use a lower IR for both its liability calculation and its Return On Investment assumption. According to Boston College's Center for Retirement Research Illinois' new interest rate will be 4.7% meaning IL unfunded pension liability is $185 billion not $85 billion. GASB' model says we owe another $100 billion. How do we pay for that?

Ditto for "The Public Pension Transparency Act" introduced Feb. 9, 2011 in the US Congress. This law, if passed, will require all public pensions to use what is called the "Risk Free Rate" or the rate on US treasury bonds currently about 4%. The theory is since pension payouts are guaranteed the assets used to fund them should be guaranteed also and the nearest thing to a financial guarantee is the US Treasury Bonds. Any other asset is too risky, as we have seen in the last 2 years.

How much will Illinois owe under these two new "model" assumptions?
The people managing the current pension Ponzi scheme are about to be called out. Here is the estimated Unfunded Liability using the three different Interest Rate Assumptions:

Current Guess: 8% $85 Billion
GASB Guess: 4.7% $185 Billion
Risk Free Guess: 4% $220 Billion

In addition to the pension liability taxpayers also have liability for $15 billion in pension bonds and $24 billion in unfunded retiree health care. All state employees get free health care when they work and when they retire if they have worked at least 20 years.

So under the "Risk Free" model we owe about $260 billion for public employee retirements. That's more than $50,000 per Illinois household. And unlike your mortgage this amount will go up every year because the annual costs cannot be paid ($10 billion in interest charges alone) and thus gets added to the debt. And unlike your mortgage you cannot walk away from your share of the pension debt unless you leave the state, which is exactly what many people will do. In 2034 this would be at least $100,000 per household and growing, a wonderful legacy to leave our children.

As bad as these numbers seem they do not include what we owe for local employees enrolled in the IMRF (Illinois Municipal Retirement Fund) or the 640 local Police and Fire pension funds. That's at least another $40 billion so we're up to about $300 billion.

Employees pay zero towards that $300 billion unfunded liability.
Every penny of the bad "guesses" in ROI is paid for by the taxpayers. And that is in addition to the "Normal Costs" that have to be paid every year as our share of the pension cost.

Here's a chart that makes the difference between taxpayer payments and employee payments more clear:

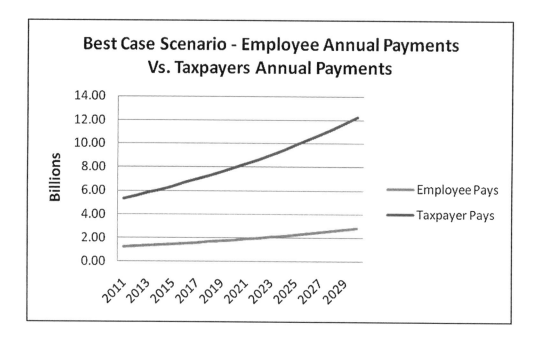

Since this is the "Best Case" any other outcome would send the upper taxpayer line into the stratosphere. Even using a Best Case outcome shows how unsustainable and unfair the pension system is. How can politicians and public employees ask taxpayers to pay 400% more than the employees all the way out to 2030? Whatever happened to 50-50?

When does disinformation become fraud?
Now that we know the facts presented to us as the "real" pension liability are indeed not facts but one "model" guess out of many should we insist on other guesses too? Yes we must insist they give us at least three scenarios (thank you UN) – current, 4.7% and 4%. After all they are going to have to do this anyway if the new rules and regulations come to pass. That way we would at least have an idea how wobbly this whole house of cards is.

There would be almost no additional cost to do so since the actuarial software would generate the frightening numbers with little additional effort. And once Illinois taxpayers (and hopefully politicians) see these enormous numbers the game will be over – real pension reform will be mandated instead of the current meager efforts analogous to anxious minnows nibbling on a whale's carcass.

SOURCES: CGFA March 2010 Five State Systems Combined.
             Teachers Retirement System Actuarial Report June 30, 2010
             State University Retirement System Actuarial Report June 30, 2010
             State Employees Retirement System Actuarial Report June 30, 2010

2.2) Taxpayers Have Contributed 230% More Than Teachers Since 2001.

A N UNENDING CASCADE of misinformation continues to come out of Springfield, union headquarters and the media so let me say it loud and clear:

We Taxpayers Have OVERPAID Into Pensions Not UNDERPAID.

Let's keep it simple:

Is $20 billion greater than $8.7 billion?

If the answer is "Yes" then we taxpayers have paid more for teacher pensions from 2001-2011 than teachers have. $11.3 billion more. That's 230% MORE.

The way I look at it the taxpayers are due a refund with interest.

Teachers vs. Taxpayers			
State Pension Contributions to TRS 2001 - 2011			
In millions of dollars			
YEAR	Taxpayer Contrib. (Employer)	Teacher Contrib. (Employee)	Taxpayer to Teacher %
2001	821	643	128%
2002	907	681	133%
2003	1,021	732	139%
2004	5,489	769	714%
2005	1,055	762	138%
2006	658	799	82%

2007	854	826	103%
2008	1,172	865	135%
2009	1,604	876	183%
2010	2,200	899	245%
2011	2,300	910	253%
TOTAL>>	18,081	8,762	206%
Pension Bond Interest	2,072	-	
Total Paid In	20,153	8,762	230%
SOURCE: Teachers' Retirement System of the State of Illinois			
June 30, 2010 - 2011			
Actuarial Valuation of Pension Benefits.			

SOURCE: Teacher Retirement System Actuarial Reports – June 30, 2001 & June 30, 2011

If the Teachers Retirement System loses $12 billion why do taxpayers have to pay for it?
The other dirty little secret we never talk about is how the taxpayer is responsible for every salary increase, every early retirement, every benefit increase and every dollar of investment loss. Which is exactly why we taxpayers (not the "state") are contributing 400% more than employees this year.

Seven members of the 13 Member TRS Board of Trustees are current or former employees of the public school system. So "teachers" are making the investment decisions for the TRS but the "taxpayer" (formerly known as the "state") is required to make up all loses via higher contributions i.e. higher taxes. Taxpayers are also required to pay 100% of the interest on all Pension Obligation Bonds, an amount now approaching $1 billion/yr. Since they are in charge why aren't teachers paying instead of taxpayers?

For more than a decade taxpayers have paid more than any reasonable system should require – 230% more in the case of TRS. Please note every single year taxpayers paid more than employees except in 2006.

Why are state pensions so expensive – the "Four Rules of Too".

1. Retirement is "Too Early":
State Police can retire at 50, teachers 54 and others at 55. Compare this with Social Security full retirement at 66. A person retiring at 50 will, on average, spend more time retired that he did working. That is very expensive proposition.

2. Pensions are "Too High":
From a maximum of 75% of salary for teachers to 80% for State Police and University employees to 85% for legislators to 75% plus Social Security for state employees plus 3%/yr. COLA, pensions are very expensive to finance. When combined with early retirement, costs are off the charts.

3. Salaries are "Too High":
Since pensions are percentages of salaries and are without any upper limit, high salaries lead to high pensions. State police earning $175,000, Phys Ed teachers $203,000 and school superintendents $368,000 have led to 5,400 state pensions in excess of $100,000/yr. growing at 25%/yr. This projects to 25,000 pensions over $100K by 2020.

4. Contributions are "Too low":
About 99% of state employees pay less into their retirement system than we do into SS and 401K and they pay for fewer years since they retire earlier than we do. Since they retire up to 16 years earlier on much higher pensions they should be contributing much more than the private sector not less. Because they are not paying their fair share the extra cost must be picked up by the taxpayers of IL.

See "Four Rules of Too" (Chapter 4.3).

Illinois pension and retiree health care costs are creating an economic dead-end.
The Census Bureau just reported that Chicago now has its lowest population in the last 100 years. Mayor Daley says the new pension requirements for Chicago pensions will raise property taxes by 60% (Bloomberg Dec 21, 2010). Do you think raising property taxes by 60% will lead to more people moving to Chicago or moving from Chicago? Moving *from* Chicago of course.

Use the same logic for the state. Will potential new employers look at Illinois and see $1 trillion in pension and health care benefits owed to retired public employees over the next 35 years as a reason to relocate here or as a reason to relocate to Indiana, Wisconsin or Ohio? Anybody with common sense would choose someplace other than Illinois to relocate.

Do you think these numbers oriented businessmen will notice that this years $6.8 billion tax increase exactly matches this year's pension cost ($6.2 billion) and retiree health care cost ($600 million)? Yes, I think they will notice.

Will the pension supporters' whining that pensions are "owed" or "promised" have any effect on these decisions? Yes, it will have a negative effect.

If Illinois wants to avoid becoming a Michigan and Chicago a Detroit then comprehensive, meaningful pension reform needs to be completed soon. Decisions to come to Illinois or leave Illinois are being made every day.

Every day we avoid making tough pension cost decisions more taxpayers leave Illinois. Who is going to pay the pensions when all the taxpayers have left? ⇐

2.3) Taxpayer Pension Contribution for Gov. Quinn in 2011: $140,000

Legislators will get $55,000 pension – no wonder they are against pension reform.

THE TITLE OF this article tells you everything you need to know about Illinois pensions: they cannot be paid, they will not be paid and they should not be paid.

It is not just Quinn of course but everyone in GARS (General Assembly Retirement System) is receiving 82% of their salary as a pension contribution. That means each state rep and senator will be receiving over $55,000 in pension contributions from the generous Illinois taxpayers on their $67,836 salary. So these part time jobs called state representative and state senator are paying over $120,000/yr. Not bad for government work.

And that puts Quinn at over $300,000/yr. – talk about overpaid.

So what would they be getting if they were paid like the average private sector taxpayer? About 11% (6.2% Social Security + 5% 401K matching contribution) meaning Quinn's employer contribution would be about $14,000 (Social Security stops at $106,800 and Quinn's salary is $170,000) and legislators about $7,500. So Quinn's current $140,000 taxpayer pension contribution is about 10 times more than what they would have to pay if he was under Social Security and a 401K-retirement system like most taxpayers.

Why the pensions cannot be paid #1: even the best-case scenario cannot be paid.

Unbelievably the 82% of salary pension contribution is a best-case scenario and is almost certainly too low. I predict right now that without massive pension cuts including to current retirees and current employees, taxpayer contributions for the Governor and other legislators will exceed 100% of their salary by 2015.

All of the pension systems have overestimated revenues and underestimated costs since at least 1996. All six factors used in calculating the $80 billion unfunded since 2001 have been negative i.e. increased the unfunded and thus taxpayer liability. These include salary increases, benefit increases, investment losses and lower mortality rates among others.

Since taxpayers are stuck with paying every pension penny that results from these items their required actuarial payments have sky rocketed to the benefit of no one but the employees

This is evidenced by the fact that the Employer Contributions (better known as taxpayer contributions) have been 250% more than employee contributions since 2000 even as the unfunded pension has increased by 500% from $15 billion to $80 billion.

This proves that the problem is not that taxpayers are not contributing enough it is because the pensions cost too much and the employees contribute too little. The costs must come down; the taxpayers are paying more than their fair share.

Here is a chart of pension contributions since 2000. Note that in every year taxpayers have contributed more than employees including 300% more in 2010.

Taxpayer Vs. Employee Pension Contributions 2000-2010
In Billions of Dollars Includes Interest on Pension Bonds

	Taxpayer Payments	Employee Payments	Dollar Diff.	Pct. More
2000	1.313	1.031	0.282	127%
2001	1.434	1.060	0.374	135%
2002	1.549	1.130	0.419	137%
2003	1.702	1.263	0.439	135%
2004	9.592	1.213	8.379	791%
2005	2.263	1.223	1.040	185%
2006	1.544	1.266	0.278	122%
2007	1.969	1.313	0.656	150%
2008	2.599	1.379	1.220	188%
2009	3.326	1.391	1.935	239%
2010	4.490	1.420	3.070	316%
TOTAL	31.781	13.689	18.092	232%

Why the pensions cannot be paid #2: more conservative regulations are coming in 2012.
As most people know now, every public institution from the smallest school to the US government has underestimated pension costs to the tune of trillions of dollars in total. A public non-profit organization called GASB (Government Accounting Standards Board) is assigned the responsibility to determine what accounting rules should be followed to assure full funding of public pensions and reasonable costs for taxpayers.

GASB has determined that the biggest flaw has been the assumed interest rate being used by public institutions to determine their pension liability. Basically the higher the interest rate assumption, the lower the supposed/imaginary unfunded liability will be. As you might guess IL has used the highest rate allowed under current rules, 8.5%. This has lead IL to the largest per capita pension liability in the country.

The reason politicians and unions like high interest rate assumptions is that it makes the contribution requirements by both employee and employer look more reasonable i.e. lower. Who doesn't want lower contribution rates? Taxpayers like them, politicians like them and employees like them. The problem is these estimated contribution rates are "pretend" numbers that deteriorate rapidly when investment returns do not return 8.5%/yr., year after year after year.

And guess who gets stuck with the tab, every single penny, if the "estimators" are wrong? Taxpayers of course which is why we are paying 82% of legislators salaries into their pension accounts and more than 40% into judges retirement accounts and more than 30% into everyone else's retirement accounts. And remember those percentages are best-case scenarios.

To make a long story short, by 2012 GASB has said it will come up with new rules on interest assumptions and 8.5% will never be seen again. The rate IL will have to use will be somewhere around 4.7% meaning the unfunded liability will jump from $85 billion to $185 billion in an instant.

Since we cannot pay $85 billion how are we going to pay $185 billion?

GASB is the 800 lb. Gorilla in the room that everyone is ignoring. But come 2012, that gorilla is going to tear the bejebbers out of the room and then everyone will realize what I am saying now: the pensions cannot be paid.

Why the pensions cannot be paid #3: it's a cash-flow problem.

Think of the $85 billion unfunded pension liability as the taxpayers 30 year "pension mortgage." That means our monthly payment for interest only is $680 million or $8.1 billion/yr. or about the same as the total sales taxes collected by IL. Note that only taxpayers have to pay for the unfunded pension mortgage, while public employees, representing just 5% of the workers in IL, pay zero.

And like you and your mortgage we still have daily pension expenses to pay in addition to our $8.1 billion annual "pension mortgage" payment. Those pension expenses other than the "mortgage" include pension payouts to retirees, salaries and expenses of pension staff and facilities, and broker/investment costs. In 2010 those expenses totaled $7.2 billion and are growing at more than 8%/yr. So our total expenses in 2010 were $15.3 billion. The unfunded liability is amortized over 30 years and the annual interest charges are basically just added to the unfunded balance. This is the reason the unfunded liability grows from $85 billion in 2010 to $160 billion in 2032 even though we make all of our scheduled payments in full and the funds return their unlikely 8.5% per year.

So consider the Rube Goldberg nature of this so-called plan. We pay $176 billion in pension taxes between 2011 and 2032 and at that point hand over to our children and grandchildren and great-grandchildren an unfunded debt of $165 billion almost twice what it is now. And that is a best-case scenario.

On the income side we have employee contributions of $1.4 billion, taxpayer contribution of $3.9 billion and an excellent 14% investment return yielding $6.7 billion for a total of $12 billion. Note that in spite of the constant tsk-tsking by the press and union officials of payment "shortages" by the state, taxpayers are paying 300% more than employees paid in 2010. Also note that employee contributions are less than 10% of our cash flow out.

Including an unsustainable 14% ROI we still have a $2.5 billion negative pension cash flow for 2010. This negative cash flow is projected to grow every year and will be, best-case scenario, at least $5 billion in 2020 despite an $8.9 billion payment by IL taxpayers scheduled for 2020.

So under "best-case" scenario we are scheduled to have more than a $35 billion total negative pension cash flow over the next 10 years. This is not a solution it is a recipe for financial disaster.

And, no, the so-called pension reforms enacted by the legislature will have virtually no effect over the next 10 years.

Why the pensions WILL NOT be paid: taxpayers have spoken.
In the last 10 months 17 non-binding referendums on the need to reform pensions have been presented to Illinois voters in various communities around the state. By an overwhelming margin of 83 % these referendums have been approved.

Taxpayers want significant reforms not the nibbling at the edges the governor and legislature have given us. Enforce the pension rules in effect when the pension guarantee was made and there would be no pension deficit. All the bennies and increases handed out like candy to the politically connected over the last 40 years need to be reversed.

Those politicians who ignore this issue will be replaced beginning in 2012. This does not bode well for Democrats beholden to public sector unions and their political contributions.

Why the pensions SHOULD NOT be paid: the issue of fairness overwhelms all others.
News outlets report almost daily on the disproportionate compensation advantage public employees have over their peers in the private sector. Pensions are so out of whack that it is not unusual for public retirees to have pension payouts five to eight times that of their peers in the private sector.

Quinn's idea to increase taxes on the $40,000 worker to pay for the $400,000 pensions of the non-worker is not going to fly. Instead let's have zero $100,000 pensions starting immediately with the politicians.

To reiterate: The 95% of Illinois workers who do not have state pensions are angry and they are not going to take it anymore. Taxpayer pension payments more than double employee payments are more than enough. Any employer in the private sector that contributed 230% of his employee's pension contribution would be bankrupt which is exactly what IL is for the very same reason. And most certainly that employer would not have to listen to his employees complain and whine that 230% more was not enough.

Dystopian Future Awaits State Retirees Unless Big Changes Are Made Soon.

Pensions that cannot be paid are going to be cut one way or the other. It would be much better for current retirees and workers to work on compromise than to wait for the inevitable de facto pension bankruptcy. Recently Pritchard, Alabama filed for bankruptcy unable to pay the required pensions and unable to get pensioners to take pension reductions. Now Pritchard retirees have nothing.

To speed up compromise the state should withhold pension payments (a la Chris Christy in NJ) until a viable solution is reached and use that money to make payments to other entities that have contracts with the state namely the vendors currently owed about $7 billion. Why are contracts with public employees the only ones deemed sacrosanct?

Based upon current payout ratios the IL state pensions have about 7 years of assets left before they run out of money if the state withholds payments.

The days of the taxpayer paying for decades of back-room political deals and every instance of political malfeasance and nonfeasance are over. We have reached our limit and big changes must be made and soon. Otherwise we will put people in office that will make the needed changes.

SOURCES: General Assembly Actuarial Report June 30, 2010
              IL Commission on Government Forecasting and Accountability ⇐

2.4) Illinois Pensions: Rob the Poor and Give It to The Rich.

Help the needy or help the greedy?

ILLINOIS DEPT. OF Human Services (DHS) recently announced some planned cuts:

- DHS to cut $150 million, expected to affect 178,000 children and adults
- Dept. on Aging to cut $40.8 million

That's $190 million in cuts to the most needy among us. Where could we possibly find $190 million to replace those cuts?

Easy. Just eliminate the pension COLA (Cost Of Living Adjustment) and you have $210 million. As every Social Security recipient knows there was no COLA this year anyway.

And here is another way to get $350 million. Just require Illinois pensions to be taxed. Right now Illinois pensions, including the 5,400 pensions in excess of $100,000 are not taxed at the state level. Do you think these multi-multi-millionaires can afford to pay taxes like you and I do? I think so.

What do public employees think about their pensions?

The highest pension in Illinois currently is Dr. Alon Winnie, at $460,000 +. He gets a pension from SURS and Cook County. He has collected more than $3 million since retiring but doesn't think that's excessive: "If you were with a good company, you'd have a helluva lot better benefits." That was a quote from the Sun-Times.

Excuse me, better benefits than $460,000/yr. pension? Exactly where could you get a better deal than that? That is a typical comment from a public employee; he has sacrificed for us and now, in his dotage, must eat dog food three days a week to make ends meet on his paltry $460,000. Mother Teresa without the vow of poverty I guess.

Three examples of robbing the poor and giving it to the rich.
Thirty-seven public school employees received raises of more than $35,000 last year. Why did I choose $35,000 as a comparison? Because $35,000 is the median full-time wage in Illinois. In other words, 37 school employees received raises greater than the annual wages of half of Illinois full-time workers. These poor working stiffs are paying property taxes for outrageous salaries and $1,000 year in income tax to fund $400,000 pensions for people who pay no income tax.

Rob the poor and give it to the rich.

Last year the average annual Social Security pension payment was $12,800. Our $460,000 Illinois pensioner received a tax-free $13,800 annual increase.

Rob the poor and give it to the rich.

An unemployed construction worker pulling in $400 a week in unemployment compensation will earn about $20,000 on which he will pay about $1,000 in state income tax. Our other $400,000 pensioner, Tapas Gupta, will pay zero, nothing, nada on his $414,000 pension. So the unemployed guy making $20,000 pays income tax to fund the $414,000 pensioner's pension but the pensioner pays zero income tax.

Rob the poor and give it to the rich.

What the next governor should do:
Institute an immediate cancellation of COLA and apply that to the $190 million in DHS cuts. Also apply the income tax to state pensions and use it to give a $20,000 deduction per tax return thus removing our unemployed construction worker and pensioners with total income less than $20,000 from the tax rolls.

These would be two very popular options with the 95% of Illinois workers (and voters) that are not part of the lucrative state pension system. Not so popular with the 5%. ⧫

2.5) "We are the $99K"; Art Teacher Equates her $99,000 Pension to Social Security.

A RETIRED ART TEACHER from Palatine District 211, recently wrote a letter to the editor of the Daily Herald defending her and other public employees' pensions by equating them to Social Security. In fact she wrote the following: "My pension = your Social Security".

There are so many errors, myths, delusions, misinformation and bad math in her letter it is difficult to know where to start. I guess we should give a-retired-art-teacher some slack since she was an art teacher not a math teacher. Of course that raises the first question: why does an Art Teacher, who retired at age 57 after working 36 nine-month years, have a pension of $99,000 to begin with?

Since this is a rather lengthy article, and you may be short of time, I will give you the summary results first, comparing the Art teacher with her peer in the private sector making the same salary but paying into Social Security. A more detailed explanation follows the letter that follows the summary.

Art Teacher's pension compared to peer's Social Security pension:
1. Teacher paid in $139,000 and receives $99,000 at age 63.
2. Teacher's peer paid in $135,000 and receives $23,000 at age 63.
3. At age 63 teacher had already received $564,000 in pension payments.
4. At age 63 peer had received zero in Social Security payments.
5. Teacher worked 36, 9-month years and retired at age 57.
6. Peer worked 42, 12-month years and retired at age 63.
7. At age 74 teacher's annual pension will exceed 100% of teacher's total contributions.
8. At age 74 peer's Social Security will be less than 25% of her total contributions.
9. Since 2001 teachers have contributed less than half as much to TRS as taxpayers have.

Art Teacher's letter to the editor:
"If your boss balanced his budget by not paying your Social Security pension benefits, your boss would be fined, shut down or in jail. (1) When the Illinois legislature did not pay my pension benefits they called it a "pension holiday" and got re-elected and praised for balancing the budget.

"Illinois teachers do not receive Social Security. They pay into their pension fund instead. Currently, the TRS rate is more than 10 percent. (2) The only reason some teachers earn more in their pensions than Social Security recipients do is because they paid at a higher rate. (3)

"If a retired teacher's spouse should die, the teacher does not even collect his or her late spouse's Social Security (4). If teachers earn Social Security credits doing other jobs, they are only entitled to about 25 percent of the benefits they earned. (5) It is unbelievable. (6)

"The organizations lobbying to convince legislators that public employees don't deserve their pensions work for Wall Street corporations that have already stolen your private pensions in 401(k) s. (7) They are multimillionaires who claim they Stand For Children when in fact they stand for greed. (8)

"Past pension holidays mean that the vast majority of money in the Illinois Teachers Retirement System is money that teachers earned and contributed. (9)

"My pension = your Social Security. We must protect them both. (10)"

Retired Art teacher
Palatine

1. If your boss balanced his budget by not paying your Social Security pension benefits, your boss would be fined, shut down or in jail. (1)
First of all it is "pension contributions" not "pension benefits". Theoretically "contributions" are made first then later "benefits" are paid. If my employer had to pay 30% of my salary for my pension, as taxpayers have to do for teachers, he would be "shut down" for sure because he would be out of business. No business could possibly survive those kinds of retirement benefits. However, since taxpayers are forced to pay taxes, any amount can be exacted from them by the

political process for the benefit of only one small group – teachers. On the other hand employer Social Security contributions are 6.2% about one-fifth the taxpayer contribution to TRS.

2. Currently, the TRS rate is more than 10 percent.

No it is not 10% - the current teacher contribution for beginning pension is 7.5%. Another .5% is for the automatic 3% COLA (Cost-of-living-allowance). When a-retired-art-teacher started teaching in 1969 her contribution was 5.5% for pension and .5%. for COLA so over her 36 year career she averaged 7.2%. Other moneys contributed by teachers (1.4%) to the TRS have nothing to do with their current pension payment.

3. The only reason some teachers earn more in their pensions than Social Security recipients do is because they paid at a higher rate.

No again. The reason a-retired-art-teacher receives a $99,000 pension at age 63 instead of the maximum $23,000 at age 63 for Social Security is because the taxpayers of IL guarantee it. A-retired-art-teacher paid in (contributed) $139,104 to her pension. Someone on Social Security working until age 63, earning the same salary as a-retired-art-teacher, would have paid in about $135,000. So no a-retired-art-teacher your massive $99,000 pension vs. your peers Social Security pension of $23,000 has absolutely nothing to do with your greater contributions. It has only to do with legal political corruption.

4. If a retired teacher's spouse should die, the teacher does not even collect his or her late spouse's Social Security.

Neither does any other spouse whose pension (Social Security) exceeds their spouse's which at max. would be about $28,000. So why should a millionaire like a-retired-art-teacher, getting $99,000/yr. get her spouses Social Security too? A-retired-art-teacher will collect $3.5 million over her expected lifetime – isn't that more than enough?

5. If teachers earn Social Security credits doing other jobs, they are only entitled to about 25 percent of the benefits they earned.

That's because Social Security is designed to be "Progressive" in its benefits with wage earners at the low end receiving 90% of their average earnings while those at the top end (like a-retired-art-teacher who earned more than $450,000 over her last four years) earn at a rate as low as 15%.

6. **It is unbelievable.**

You are right a-retired-art-teacher, it is unbelievable that a public employee with a tax-payer funded pension of $99,000 who retired at age 57 believes she deserves even more from the taxpayer than the $3.5 million she is already scheduled to receive. Unbelievably unbelievable.

7. **The organizations lobbying to convince legislators that public employees don't deserve their pensions** work **for Wall Street corporations that have already stolen your private pensions in 401(k) s.**

Well I for one have never worked for a Wall Street Corp. nor do I know anyone else who has. What we are more concerned about is public sector unions conniving with politicians to steal our children and grandchildren's money by making multi-millionaires out of public employees who retire when they are 57. I think I speak for most taxpayers when I say no public employee who worked 36 nine-month years deserves a $99,000 pension. Twice Social Security would be generous but more than 4 times Social Security is unacceptable and unsustainable.

8. **They are multimillionaires who claim they Stand For Children when in fact they stand for greed.**

I would agree with you a-retired-art-teacher. Paying a 57 year-old Art teacher $3.5 million not to work certainly does nothing for schoolchildren. It's not really for the kids is it?

9. **Past pension holidays mean that the vast majority of money in the Illinois Teachers Retirement System is money that teachers earned and contributed.**

As the following chart shows, since 2001 taxpayers have contributed more than twice what teachers have contributed. It seems to me if anyone should be upping their contributions it should be the teachers. Why don't they match us dollar for dollar? That would seem fair and the $10 billion ($17.8 billion vs. $7.8 billion) the teachers have shorted the system would go a long way towards solving our $46 billion TRS unfunded pension liability. Taxpayers should start complaining about how little teachers contribute.

Teachers vs. Taxpayers

State Pension Contributions to TRS 2001 - 2010

In millions of dollars

YEAR	Taxpayer Contrib. (Employer)	Teacher Contrib. (Employee)	Taxpayer to Teacher %
2001	821	643	128%
2002	907	681	133%
2003	1,021	732	139%
2004	5,489	769	714%
2005	1,055	762	138%
2006	658	799	82%
2007	854	826	103%
2008	1,172	865	135%
2009	1,604	876	183%
2010	2,200	899	245%
TOTAL>>	15,781	7,852	201%
Pension Bond Interest	2,072	0	
Total Paid In	17,853	7,852	227%

SOURCE: Teachers' Retirement System of the State of Illinois

June 30, 2010

Actuarial Valuation of Pension Benefits.

10. My pension = your Social Security. We must protect them both.

No a-retired-art-teacher there is no comparison between your $99K pension and your peers' $23k on Social Security as per the following:

a. You paid in a total of $139,000 and receive $99,000 at age 63.

b. Your peer paid in a total of $135,000 and receives $23,000 at age 63.

c. At age 63 you had already received $564,000 in pension payments.

d. At age 63 your peer had received zero in Social Security payments.

e. You worked 36 9-month years and retired at age 57.

f. Your peer worked 42 12-month years and retired at age 63.

g. At age 74 your annual pension will exceed 100% of your total contributions.

h. At age 74 your peer's Social Security will be less than 25% of her total contributions.

i. Since 2001 teachers have contributed less than half as much as taxpayers have.

The IEA's endless public relations campaign brainwashes everyone.

The Illinois Education Association (IEA) brainwashes not only politicians, the media and the public but also their own members by making them believe they not only deserve their pensions but have also "paid" for them. Nothing could be further from the truth as we have shown here.

Teacher pensions are unearned, un-payable and unsustainable. The sooner everyone realizes this, the sooner a long-term solution will be reached.

Until then pension bankruptcy is only a few bad investment years away. ⸺

2.6) Teacher Unions Give Politicians $10's of Millions in Contributions, Politicians Give Teacher Union Members $10's of Billions in Benefits.

If A Golden Apple Award for Teachers, Why Not A Golden Handcuff Award for Politicians?
SINCE TEACHERS HAVE the Golden Apple Award I thought it only appropriate to have a similar award for politicians called the "Golden Handcuff Award." Whereas the Golden Apple recognizes the highest achievement in the classroom, the Golden Handcuff would recognize those politicians with the highest achievement in garnering political contributions from the teacher unions. To get the Golden Handcuff Award you must have received at least $100,000 in teacher union contributions.

I call it the Golden Handcuff because once you have received money from the unions you are no longer able to lift anything heavier than a 5-figure contribution check. The heavy lifting involved in curbing $170,000 Drivers Ed teacher salaries, $400,000 administrator salaries, ten-million dollar pensions, free health care, vouchers, endless property tax increases etc. cannot be done when you are encumbered with the Golden Handcuffs. No sir, all you can do after your Golden handcuffs are snapped closed is sign on to (or sponsor) bills providing more money and benefits to the teachers. Things are good if you are an Illinois politician and you avoid talking about any of these troublesome issues.

$51 Million Reasons Why Teacher Salaries, Pensions and Benefits Continue To Go Up.
Although the state does have a website to track political contributions **(http://www.elections.illinois.gov/CampaignDisclosure/ContributionsSearchByAllContributions.aspx)** it is not easy because the contributors can use many different names thereby making tracking more difficult if not impossible. Of course the various teacher union organizations do their best to confuse the public. For example the largest contributor ($15 million plus) the Illinois Political Action Committee for Education (IPACE) can be found using the following names: IPACE, I.P.A.C.E., 1 PACE, !PACE, IPACE PAC, IPACE-Il, IPACE-PAC, IPACE-ILLINOIS,

IPACE/ILLINOIS, LPACE, Ipage, IPACE-EDUC. In addition the various teacher organizations launder their contributions by sending money back and forth to each other in a manner befitting a Columbian drug cartel.

Therefore the $51 million total I have managed to come up with is probably low even though that is frightening enough. For example if you search for contributions from organizations containing the word "teach" in it you get $32 million, for the letters "ift" (Illinois Federation of Teachers) $14 million, the letters "aft" (America Federation of Teachers) $7 million plus the IPACE $15 million gives you $68 million including the money laundering amounts back and forth. And all of the money does not come from Illinois: over $4.6 million came from the American Federation of Teachers headquarters in Washington DC. In all, over $15 million in political contributions from the teacher unions have been fed into IL politics just since Jan 1, 2008.

Teachers Are Equal Opportunity Givers.
You will notice that although Democrats dominate the following list there are enough Republicans to make certain that the union's demands are met no matter which party is in power. I mean $487,000 to Republican House Minority leader **Tom Cross** is a fair piece of change. If there is a teacher-related bill on the agenda how do you think he is going to vote?

Teachers Give 510% More In Illinois Than Exxon Gives Nationwide.
Liberal Democrats are constantly complaining about "corporate" special interests such as the current corporate bad-boy Exxon. Federal contribution records show Exxon has made political contributions totaling $10 million since 1990.

So if you call $10 million contributed nationwide "special interests" what do you call $51 million contributed just in Illinois?

So if you are wondering why 14,000 plus public school employees have salaries over $100,000/yr., why 2,668 retired teachers have pensions over $100,000/yr. even though they average less than 33 years in-state work, and why the teacher pensions range from four to 8 times what Social Security would pay for the same years worked and salary earned just look at how much money changes hands.

Top political recipients:

Although most of the top recipients are Democrats many are notable Republicans. It doesn't matter, it is not an ideological position the IEA is taking it is a monetary one.

Source for the following 3 tables is the Illinois State Board of Elections.

Teacher Union Political Contributions thru 06/30/2011					
DEMOCRATS			REPUBLICANS		
Blagojevich	1,866,697	D	Cross T Total	487,438	R
Hynes D	1,379,580	D	Ryan G Total	289,506	R
Madigan L Total	929,996	D	Hassert B	213,486	R
Jones E Total	641,900	D	Bomke L Total	171,225	R
Quinn Total	640,199	D	Luechtefeld	158,369	R
Kilbride T Total	588,834	D	Saviano A Total	147,997	R
Demuzio D	533,882	D	Moffitt D Total	145,325	R
Madigan M Total	495,900	D	Mitchell J Total	132,777	R
Miller D Total	305,667	D	Eddy R Total	124,182	R
Forby G Total	285,861	D	Dillard K Total	122,050	R
Smith M Total	261,171	D	Kosel R Total	117,171	R
White J Total	243,450	D	Cronin D Total	115,000	R
Link T Total	232,907	D	Schock A Total	101,874	R
Netsch D Total	228,742	D			
Kotowski D	199,202	D	TOTAL>>>>>	2,326,400	
Hoffman J	193,606	D			
Schoenberg	188,523	D			
Hannig G Total	184,401	D			
Clayborne Total	182,631	D			
Crotty M Total	176,457	D			
Welch P Total	162,468	D			
Granberg K	154,806	D			
Bond M Total	144,014	D			
Harmon D Total	140,655	D			
Franks J Total	137,940	D			
Murphy H Total	137,394	D			

Turner A Total	126,794	D			
del Valle Total	126,200	D			
Elman S Total	126,055	D			
Halvorson Total	124,274	D			
Ronen C Total	122,300	D			
Garrett S Total	121,137	D			
Giles C Total	116,770	D			
May KTotal	111,171	D			
Scully G Total	107,407	D			
Myerscough	104,779	D			
Kelly R **Total**	103,175	D			
Flider B Total	102,620	D			
Delgado W	102,250	D			
Lang L Total	101,000	D			
Preckwinkle	100,000	D			
TOTAL>>>>>>	12,332,815				

Top one-check individual contributions by amount:

Not surprisingly the top contributions went to Democratic stalwarts Quinn and Blagojevich. But who is Thomas Kilbride? Well he was Democratic candidate for the Illinois Supreme Court in 2010 and the teachers, being worried about the constitutionality of the pension guarantee, were not about to let another Republican on the court.

Top One-check Contributions	
350,000	Quinn
300,000	Blagojevic
300,000	Blagojevic
250,000	Blagojevic
225,000	Blagojevic
200,000	Blagojevic
150,000	Kilbride T
150,000	Quinn

125,000	Hynes D
100,000	Blagojevic
100,000	Blagojevic
100,000	Hynes D
100,000	Hynes D
100,000	Miller D
100,000	Preckwinkle
100,000	Hynes D
100,000	Madigan M
100,000	Hynes D
100,000	Hynes D
100,000	Kilbride T
100,000	Kilbride T
100,000	Kilbride T

Top teacher union political contributions by organization:

Who would guess Peoria school teachers would contribute over $369,000?

Contributions by Teacher Organization	
14,220,141	IPACE Springfield IL
9,525,563	Chicago TU
6,245,530	IFT Westmont IL
4,664,347	AFT Washington DC
3,226,655	IFT Springfield IL
2,686,161	IFT Oakbrook IL
1,564,552	Lake County Fed. Of Teachers
1,538,190	AFT, Joliet IL
1,058,598	College Teachers
983,502	West Suburban Teachers Union
600,004	SW Suburban TU
369,012	Peoria IFT
292,269	North Suburban Teachers Union
152,514	McHenry County TU

Illinois teacher unions have $135 million per year revenue.

Where do they get it - from teacher union dues where else? Since there are 130,000 full-time teachers that's about $1,000/yr. in dues per teacher on average.

The teacher unions have a very good system of hiding contributions by spreading them out over many different organizations each with a different EIN (Employer Identification Number) used to report revenue and disbursements on IRS form 990 for non-profit organizations. I have found 50 (see below) that have annual revenue (union dues) in excess of $100,000/yr. adding up to total annual revenue of $134,970,812. And that does not include dozens more that have revenue of less than $100,000.

Total Teacher Union Revenue 2010		
SOURCE: IRS Form 990 www.guidestar.org		
Union	Location	Amount
ILLINOIS EDUCATION ASSOC.	Springfield, IL 62704	49,015,785
IL Federation of Teachers (AFT)	Chicago, IL 60654	30,088,035
IL Federation of Teachers (AFT)	Westmont, IL 60559	21,364,476
IL Federation of Teachers (AFT)	Crest Hill, IL 60403	5,486,268
IL Federation of Teachers (AFT)	Gurnee, IL 60031	3,955,667
IL Federation of Teachers (AFT)	Westmont, IL 60559	2,931,422
IL Federation of Teachers (AFT)	Chicago, IL 60654	2,686,653
IL Federation of Teachers (AFT)	Chicago, IL 60603	2,313,890
IL Federation of Teachers (AFT)	Orland Park, IL 60462	1,499,322
ILLINOIS EDUCATION ASSOC.	Rockford, IL 61108	1,461,485
ILLINOIS EDUCATION ASSOC.	Plainfield, IL 60586	1,101,361
IL Federation of Teachers (AFT)	Skokie, IL 60077	1,083,433
ILLINOIS EDUCATION ASSOC.	Naperville, IL 60563	862,072
IL Federation of Teachers (AFT)	Springfield, IL 62704	823,476
IL Federation of Teachers (AFT)	Schaumburg, IL 60173	774,113
IL Federation of Teachers (AFT)	Champaign, IL 61820	725,789
IL Federation of Teachers (AFT)	Peoria, IL 61603	668,269
ILLINOIS EDUCATION ASSOC.	Saint Charles, IL 60175	666,549
IL Federation of Teachers (AFT)	Oak Brook, IL 60523	455,198

IL Federation of Teachers (AFT)	Westmont, IL 60559	424,453
ILLINOIS EDUCATION ASSOC.	Belvidere, IL 61008	416,862
IL Federation of Teachers (AFT)	Woodstock, IL 60098	414,193
IL Federation of Teachers (AFT)	Chicago, IL 60607	401,844
IL Federation of Teachers (AFT)	MacHesney Park, IL	388,075
ILLINOIS EDUCATION ASSOC.	Evanston, IL 60202	381,243
IL Federation of Teachers (AFT)	E Saint Louis, IL 62204	363,936
ILLINOIS EDUCATION ASSOC.	South Holland, IL 60473	327,628
ILLINOIS EDUCATION ASSOC.	Moline, IL 61265	306,057
IL Federation of Teachers (AFT)	Dekalb, IL 60115	296,778
IL Federation of Teachers (AFT)	Kankakee, IL 60901	274,494
IL Federation of Teachers (AFT)	Chicago, IL 60604	273,607
IL Federation of Teachers (AFT)	Collinsville, IL 62234	236,137
IL Federation of Teachers (AFT)	Belleville, IL 62223	205,126
IL Federation of Teachers (AFT)	Springfield, IL 62705	195,607
ILLINOIS EDUCATION ASSOC.	Elgin, IL 60123	189,638
IL Federation of Teachers (AFT)	Troy, IL 62294	154,633
IL Federation of Teachers (AFT)	Peoria, IL 61603	147,167
IL Federation of Teachers (AFT)	Burbank, IL 60459	145,706
IL Federation of Teachers (AFT)	Moline, IL 61265	141,482
IL Federation of Teachers (AFT)	Westmont, IL 60559	140,229
ILLINOIS EDUCATION ASSOC.	Springfield, IL 62704	138,839
IL Federation of Teachers (AFT)	Chicago, IL 60643	133,557
IL Federation of Teachers (AFT)	Calumet City, IL 60409	133,422
ILLINOIS EDUCATION ASSOC.	South Elgin, IL 60177	126,181
ILLINOIS EDUCATION ASSOC.	Silvis, IL 61282	116,787
IL Federation of Teachers (AFT)	Westmont, IL 60559	113,477
IL Federation of Teachers (AFT)	Evergreen Pk, IL 60805	108,869
IL Federation of Teachers (AFT)	Belleville, IL 62221	106,038
IL Federation of Teachers (AFT)	Grayslake, IL 60030	104,317
IL Federation of Teachers (AFT)	Millstadt, IL 62260	101,167
	Annual Total	134,970,812

2.7) Teacher Unions Say Pensions Are Too Low.

Unions Think Top 25 TRS Pensions Should Be $82 Million Higher.

ONE OF THE top legislative priorities of the Illinois Education Association is a plan they call "80, 30 and out." It would allow teachers to retire after 30 years with a pension equal to 80% of their salary. This is in contrast to the current plan of 35 years at 75% of salary.

If implemented the "80, 30 and out" plan would mean a teacher (or administrator) could retire at age 51 with full pension equal to 80% of the average of his last four years salaries.

Here's the quote from the ift-aft website:
* An increase in the ceiling from 75% to 80% of earnings for all retirement systems
* A "30 years and out" with no penalty retirement option for all systems

NOTE: AS of 01/01/2011 this item has been removed from the IFT website. That doesn't mean they don't believe in 80-30 and out or that they have given up on achieving it someday.

Even the Teachers Retirement System, a state agency under the Department of Insurance, supports full retirement at age 55 with 30 years service credit which means 28 years work with 2 years sick-leave credit. If they haven't removed it from the TRS website take a look at what else these state employees think taxpayers should pay for at http://trs.illinois.gov/subsections/legislative/platform.pdf This should come as no surprise since 6 of the 13 members of the Board of Trustees is required to be a teacher or former teacher. Democratic governors appointed the other seven members of the board after receiving millions of dollars in political contributions from the teacher unions. Blagojevich alone received over $1.7 million from the teachers including checks for $300,000, $300,000, $250,000, $225,000 and $200,000.

Unions are out of touch but not out of money.
The teacher unions in Illinois have more money available to spend than any other Illinois political group. They have contributed over $51 million to Illinois politicians since electronic records

began in the 1990's. To see which politicians got how much see Appendix items 15, 16 and 17. Their 160,000 members keep sending in their dues every payday (they are deducted automatically and submitted to the local union by the school districts.) Since we know teachers' salaries go up every year by 7%, the union dues keep stacking up in the union's bank account. The IEA itself had revenue of more than $47 million in 2009.

The teacher unions are inherently political organizations because only by political means can they increase transfers of wealth from the private sector taxpayers to their members. Increases in teacher salaries, benefits and pensions come about by the political assignment of an ever-increasing percentage of available tax revenues to the benefit of the teachers at the expense of less powerful political groups such as the poor and the elderly. How can the poor and the elderly compete with the teacher union's $51 million in political contributions?

That is how teachers at Avoca District 37 can sign a contract for 35% salary increases (minimum) over the next five years with political approval while politicians, at the same time, cut $90 million from the Department of Human Services, money originally earmarked for the handicapped, mentally ill and poor seniors.

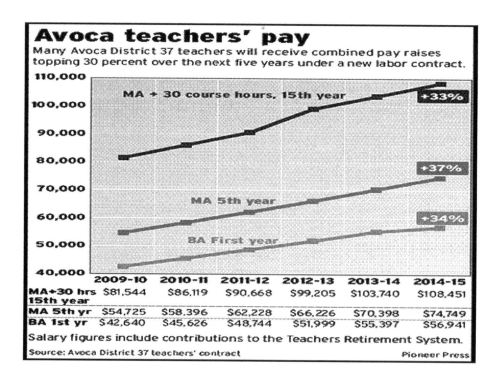

Avoca teachers' pay

Many Avoca District 37 teachers will receive combined pay raises topping 30 percent over the next five years under a new labor contract.

MA + 30 course hours, 15th year — +33%
MA 5th year — +37%
BA First year — +34%

	2009-10	2010-11	2011-12	2012-13	2013-14	2014-15
MA+30 hrs 15th year	$81,544	$86,119	$90,668	$99,205	$103,740	$108,451
MA 5th yr	$54,725	$58,396	$62,228	$66,226	$70,398	$74,749
BA 1st yr	$42,640	$45,626	$48,744	$51,999	$55,397	$56,941

Salary figures include contributions to the Teachers Retirement System.

Source: Avoca District 37 teachers' contract   Pioneer Press

Thanks to the Pioneer Press for above graphic.

This is how $51 million in political contributions begets $100,000 salaries for 9-month part-time public employees. Too bad the poor don't contribute more, maybe then they would get increases too.

Increasing pensions from 75% after 35 years to 80% after 30 years increases these 25 pension payouts by 36%.

At the end of this article there is a table showing how the pensions would change if the 80/30 plan had been in effect for just the Top 25 TRS pensions. As you can see the average pension payout would have increased by more than $82 million just for these 25 people. Note also the union plan does not include any increase in the teacher's contribution rate meaning the every extra dollar would be on the back of the taxpayer.

Also note number 7, Reginald Weaver actually works for the National Education Association but we lucky taxpayers get to pay his $10 million pension.

What the next governor should do:

First, instead of increasing pensions the governor should revert the pensions back to where they were when they were "guaranteed" by the state constitution in 1980. That would be 60% at age 60 growing to a maximum of 70% at age 66.

Second, he should also insist a sharing of risk between employees and employer. If the pension funds do not earn a rate of return assumed by the trustees then the cost should be split 50/50. Currently the entire investment risk lies with the taxpayers.

Third, the maximum pension any public employee could earn cannot exceed the average family income for Illinois currently about $75,000/yr.

Fourth, replace as many pension trustees as possible with accountants, actuaries and businessmen so we can have an honest, taxpayer friendly appraisal of investments and benefits.

Fifth, use Wisconsin's K-12 system as a model for pay and benefits reform in Illinois. See WI – IL comparison Chapter 4.5.

Illinois taxpayers are ready for comprehensive pension reform. Let's hope the next governor is ready too.

Teachers Retirement System Top 25 Pensions Increase by $82 Million						
If Pension Rules Changed						
From 75% of Salary After 35 Years to 80% after 30 Years						
Per Teacher Union Legislative Agenda						
	Name	School Dist.	Beginning Annual Pension @ 75%	Total Pension Payout 35 yrs. / 75%	Total Pension Payout 30 yrs. / 80%	Pension Increase 30/80 vs. 35/75	Years Worked
1	Murray, Laura L	Homewood-Flossmoor CHSD 233	238,882	10,799,837	14,709,091	3,909,254	36
2	Catalani, Gary T	Community Unit SD 200	237,195	10,723,597	14,605,254	3,881,657	35
3	Gmitro, Henry A	Community CSD 93	234,803	10,615,435	14,457,940	3,842,505	34
4	Hager, Maureen L	North Shore SD 112	231,703	10,475,275	14,267,045	3,791,771	34
5	Bangser, Henry S	New Trier TWP HSD 203	230,531	10,422,319	14,194,922	3,772,602	32
6	Curley, Mary M	Hinsdale CCSD 181	226,645	10,246,624	13,955,630	3,709,005	34
7	Weaver, Reginald L	National Education Association	226,485	10,239,376	13,945,758	3,706,382	42
8	Kelly, Dennis G	Lyons TWP HSD 204	213,693	9,661,039	13,158,078	3,497,039	30
9	Burns, Kevin G	Community HSD 218	206,495	9,335,619	12,714,865	3,379,246	34
10	Hintz, James S	Adlai Stevenson HSD 125	201,444	9,107,300	12,403,900	3,296,600	32
11	Bultinck, Howard J	Sunset Ridge SD 29	199,299	9,010,302	12,271,792	3,261,490	33
12	Johnson, Michael D	IL Assoc of School Boards	193,273	8,737,887	11,900,770	3,162,883	33
13	Kanold, Timothy D	Adlai Stevenson HSD 125	191,674	8,665,596	11,802,311	3,136,715	33
14	Gallagher, James J	Evergreen Park CHSD 231	190,848	8,628,254	11,751,453	3,123,199	39
15	Palermo, Joseph A	Berkeley SD 87	189,278	8,557,271	11,654,776	3,097,505	38
16	Van Clay, Mark	La Grange SD 102	186,496	8,431,482	11,483,455	3,051,972	34
17	Conyers, John G	Palatine CCSD 15	186,175	8,416,975	11,463,697	3,046,721	28
18	Baskin, Lawrence M	Glen Ellyn CCSD 89	185,365	8,380,344	11,413,806	3,033,462	33
19	White, James W	Queen Bee SD 16	184,548	8,343,404	11,363,495	3,020,091	40
20	McGee, Glenn W	Wilmette SD 39	184,119	8,324,015	11,337,087	3,013,072	32
21	Bridge, Susan J	Oak Park-River Forest SD 200	182,253	8,239,642	11,222,173	2,982,531	38
22	Mink, Jon L	Aptakisic-Tripp CCSD 102	181,524	8,206,678	11,177,278	2,970,599	34
23	Conti, Dennis R	Woodland CCSD 50	175,935	7,954,000	10,833,136	2,879,136	33
24	Patton, Ronald C	Bloom TWP HSD 206	175,818	7,948,721	10,825,947	2,877,226	35
25	Lueck, J Peter	Kane County ROE; Lisle CUSD 202;	173,918	7,862,835	10,708,972	2,846,137	34
						82,288,801	34

SOURCE: Teachers Retirement System of IL

2.8) "Average" State Pensions Are Far Above Average.

How much pension should be paid to part-time employees with partial careers?

Teachers lead the offensive against pension reform.

THE PUBLIC RELATIONS offensive by the IEA (Illinois Education Association) and other public unions is in full force here in Illinois. Virtually every day letters to the editors and op ed pieces regale the public with arguments suggesting average pensions of state workers as being "modest" and reasonable. Only the forces of darkness (like championnews.net for example) could propose cuts to what these public servants have "earned".

Like most public pronouncements by the IEA these tend to be disingenuous at best and outright deceitful at worst.

The "average" retired teacher is a part-time employee with a part-time career.

Let's review the basics regarding teachers vs. private sector employees:

1. Teachers work 170 days or 34 weeks a year or less.

This is calculated off of the standard teachers' contract that calls for 182 workdays per year. Subtract from that number at least 12 days for sick days and personal days per year and you come up with 170 days or 34 weeks a year in the classroom. The sick days are subtracted because if they are not used they are available as time-worked credit when they retire. And the time-worked credit at retirement is worth a lot more because it is based upon the final year's salary rather than the first year's salary.

In contrast the average private sector worker works 235 days or 47 weeks a year. This is based upon 260 days (52 weeks of 5 days) less an average 13 days' vacation, 8 holidays and 4 personal/sick days.

I think it is safe to say most people working 235 days per year would consider a 170-day work year to be part time employment.

2. For private sector employees with college degrees a career that begins when you are 22 would typically end at its earliest after 40 years at age 62 or more likely after 44 years at age 66.

Age 62 would be with early Social Security and age 66 would be with full benefits. Very few would be able to afford to retire prior to age 62 if then.

For teachers on the other hand less than 1% works 40 or more years before they retire and the average works only 25 years.

Twenty-five years is not a full career nor are 170 days a full time job. So the IEA's "average" is not the same thing that we private sector workers consider "average".

3. Teachers do not pay 9.4% for their pensions; they have paid on average 7.2%.

If you listen to the unions and read editorials and letters-to-the-editor you will hear this constant complaint: teachers' pay 9.4% for their pensions which is a lot more than private sector employees pay. While it is true teachers have 9.4% of their pay deducted from their pay and sent to TRS only 7.5% is used to calculate their pension and prior to 1998 it was 7%. So a teacher with 35 years has paid, on average, about 7.2% for their beginning pension over his career.

Here's the breakdown:

   7.5% pension (7% prior to 1998)
   0.5% annual 3% COLA (only since 1998)
   0.4% Early Retirement Option (only since 2004 and refundable)
   1.0% survivor benefits basically a life insurance policy (refundable).

The Early Retirement Option and the survivor benefit contribution are both refundable at retirement for those who do not want them. In 2010 76% of retirees received refunds of one or both of these non-pension contributions.

Pensions four to seven times Social Security are not "modest".

The ultimate test for "average" pension would be in comparison to most people's pension plan – Social Security. So what does the TRS "average" pension look like if that same person retired on the "average" pension the 95% of us who are not eligible for the state pension systems rely on? That pension system is Social Security.

Here are the stats for the "average" retired teacher:

1. Average TRS pension - $46,000.
2. Average age at retirement – 58.
3. Average years worked – 25.
4. Average teacher contribution - $58,000.

The Social Security calculation is a little complicated but basically it is a progressive one whereby those with the least incomes (about $8,000/yr.) get a higher percentage of that income (90%) and the percentage decreases as incomes go up ending with 15% of income above about $50,000/yr. The maximum Social Security at age 62 is $22,000 and at age 66 about $28,000. And by the way to get max Social Security you need to work at least 35 years which as we know 90% of teachers do not do.

So once the Social Security math is done, using the "average" teacher pension values given above (1 thru 4), we find that the "average" TRS retiree would be receiving about $12,000/yr. at age 62 rather than $46,000 at age 58. Since the "average" teacher retires four years earlier than the age 62 minimum for Social Security the value of his pension is more than 4 times the value if he was on Social Security.

If all teachers' pension' were limited to 2 times Social Security there would be a pension surplus not deficit.

Some teachers get more than 8 times Social Security.

If we look at our infamous Music teacher who retired after 33 years of work at age 54 with a beginning pension of $130,000, would receive about $6 million over his expected lifetime. If he retired at age 62 on the max Social Security of $22,000 he would receive about $780,000. So though he contributed on average over his career 7.2% to his pension for his $130,000 starting pension he actually contributed less than his self-employed peer in the private sector paid for his $22,000 Social Security pension.

So contribute less get 8 times more payout.

Only someone with their foot on the throat of the political class could suggest that 4 to 8 times Social Security is "modest".

How much pension should be paid to part-time employees with partial careers?

We know that the supposedly "modest" average teacher pension is 4 to 8 times greater than the equivalent Social Security pension for the same years worked and salary earned. So let's examine the other pension state systems: SURS (State University Retirement System), SERS (State Employees Retirement System), JRS (Judges Retirement System) and GARS (General Assembly Retirement System).

This being Illinois is it any surprise that the best pension deals by far go to Politicians and Judges?

SYSTEM	Avg. Age At Retire.	Avg. Pension	If Soc. Sec.	Avg Years Worked
Teachers	58	46,000	12,000	25
University	60	35,000	11,000	18
State	60	41,000*	10,000	24
Judges	63	117,000	20,000	19
General Assembly	60	52,000	10,000	15

* Incudes Social Security for 95% of state workers.

How do judges compare to max Social Security recipients?

Not surprisingly judges do very well when compared to maximum Social Security recipients getting $22,000 at age 62. Keep in mind the max Social Security recipients could have earned as much or more than their retired judge counterparts. The following chart shows all judges who have received more than $2 million in pension payments along with the amount they actually contributed to those pensions.

Then I add the similar values for Social Security at the bottom of the chart.

Judgse Pension Multiplier Vs. Social Security				

Retiree Name	Years Worked	Annual Pension	Total Pension Paid out to date	Total Contributions	Pension vs. Contrib. Multiplier
JONES, CHARLES	32	140,243	2,376,852	112,213	21
WRIGHT, PAUL	29	135,209	2,274,397	85,823	27
MAXWELL, FRANCIS	20	132,563	2,272,667	70,899	32
MASSEY, ROBERT	21	122,682	2,270,987	72,001	32
SCHNAKE, PAUL	18	129,471	2,219,652	68,118	33
IBEN, CHARLES	20	106,922	2,212,263	61,832	36
NASH, WILLIAM	21	138,802	2,168,385	93,559	23
SHERRICK, JAMES	20	119,481	2,161,131	53,479	40
STAMOS, JOHN	22	143,182	2,160,224	104,802	21
POLIKOFF, BERNARD	24	120,718	2,124,154	59,388	36
BASTIEN, ROBERT	27	131,271	2,119,634	92,260	23
STONE, CALVIN	20	131,271	2,118,897	82,737	26
PETRONE, FRANK	20	131,271	2,115,398	76,351	28
VERKLAN, JOHN	20	121,725	2,101,016	59,474	35
HECHINGER, JOHN	20	119,306	2,045,397	76,505	27
Average for Judges	22	128,274	2,182,737	77,963	29
Social Security max.	40	43,056	760,000	130,000	6
22,000 @ age 62 to					
age 85 assuming 3%					
CPI/yr.					

The stark contrast between pension systems is obvious. Just looking at the averages for the judges compared to the maximum Social Security recipient (an attorney in private practice perhaps) we see:

1. SS person works almost twice as long (40 vs. 22 years)
2. SS annual pension about one-third judges' pension (128,000 to. 43,000).
3. SS total pension paid out to age 85 about one-third judges' payout (2.1 million vs. 760,000).
4. SS person contributed 160% more to his pension than judges (130,000 vs. 78,000)
5. SS person received 6 times his contribution while judges received 29 times their contribution.

The difference is paid for by taxpayers.

Politicians arguably do best of all.

Of all politicians who have collected more than $1 million in pension benefits the average years worked is 20 and although there are none who have received more than $2 million former Gov. Jim Thompson and former state senator John Friedland will pass the $2 million mark this year.

Some of the retired politicians are still pulling down state salaries along with their hefty pension checks. Two that come to mind are former Gov. Jim Edgar whose substantial $135,000 pension is supplemented by $177,000 from the University of Illinois as a "Distinguished Fellow".

General Assembly Top 10 Pensions vs. Social Security				
Name	Annual Pension	Total Contrib.	Pension in Excess of Contrib.	Pension as Pct. Of Contrib.
Social Sec. Age 86	37,000	130,000	-93,000	26%
BERMAN, ARTHUR	203,428	109,293	94,135	186%
FRIEDLAND, JOHN	140,649	66,716	73,933	211%
THOMPSON, JAMES	127,215	84,996	42,219	150%
NETSCH, DAWN	121,720	87,778	33,943	139%
HOMER, THOMAS	120,021	78,093	41,927	154%
BOWMAN, H	115,447	73,377	42,071	157%
KARPIEL, DORIS	114,234	95,999	18,234	119%
DEGNAN, TIMOTHY	112,152	85,291	26,861	131%
MOLARO, ROBERT	112,074	109,860	2,214	102%
MCGREW, SAMUEL	110,407	76,963	33,444	143%

Less than 1 in a 100 state retirees work 40 years (age 62) before drawing their pension.
What is shown here is the vastly superior nature of the state pensions compared to Social Security, the truly "average" pension. State retirees work fewer years, work shorter years and get more in pensions than the average taxpayer. Why is that?

The forces for pension bankruptcy (aka the IEA) would have you believe the "average" state pension is modest when in fact they are valued at many times what that retiree would receive if he was on Social Security. They also do not take into account that indeed, the average state pension is based upon part-time employees working partial careers as can be seen in the following table:

State Retirees - Part-time Employees With Part-time Careers?					
	Total Retirees	Worked at Least 40 Years	Pct. Worked 40 Years	Worked at Least 35 Years	Pct. Worked 35 Years
TRS	87,744	870	0.99%	8,356	9.52%
SURS	42,213	19	0.05%	1,368	3.24%
SERS	48,637	731	1.50%	5,957	12.25%
GARS	288	-	0.00%	4	1.39%
JRS	730	9	1.23%	40	5.47%
	179,612	1,629	0.92%	15,694	8.74%
NOTE: Does not include disability or survivor beneficiaries.					

The problem: more than full pensions for part-time employees with part-time careers.
Less than 1 in a 100 state retirees worked 40 years or the equivalent of working from age 22 to early Social Security retirement at age 62.

Less than 1 in 11 even worked 35 years.

Over 72% of retirees are educators (TRS & SURS) and most of those worked only 9 months a year.

So part-time employees should have part-time pensions.

The solution: same plan as that of private sector workers - Social Security and 401Ks.
We can no longer afford to have two pension systems: a superior one for public employees and an inferior one for private sector employees. Public employees are not special. They do not have to be public employees if they don't want to. So let's level the playing field when it comes to retirement benefits.

Public employees should receive exactly the same benefits as private sector employees.

No more, no less. ⇐

2.9) Legal Corruption: Substitute Teach 1 Day get $108,000 Pension from TRS.

How many pigs can fit at the pig-trough?

STEVEN PRECKWINKLE, ILLINOIS Federation of Teachers lobbyist, made $93 substitute teaching for one day in 2007. However he made up for that rather modest payment by being made eligible for the Teachers Retirement System with 16 years service credit.

Preckwinkle is currently making $245,000 (2011) marking four years in a row over $200,000 all of which are used to calculate his pension. If he retires next year when he is 60 years of age his TRS pension will be in the neighborhood of $108,000/yr. At age 60 the total pension payout assuming an average life expectancy is about $3.8 million. Not bad for one day's work.

Steve Preckwinkle Salary History with IEA

Year	Title	Gross Salary	Total Compensation
2010	ADMIN STAFF	$223,939.00	$253,084.00
2009	ADMIN STAFF	$211,263.00	$241,763.00
2008	ADMIN STAFF	$210,322.00	$245,789.00
2007	ADMIN STAFF	$159,010.00	$186,094.00
2005	ADMIN STAFF	$142,251.00	$177,257.00
2004	ADMIN STAFF	$147,735.00	$173,659.00
2003	ADMIN STAFF	$140,621.00	$166,738.00
2002	ADMIN STAFF	$131,186.00	$155,465.00

SOURCE: Unionfacts.com

"A spokesman for the Illinois Federation of Teachers emphasized that the lobbyists' actions were legal."

That is the common response by those taking advantage of the legal corruption. For example former State Senator Arthur Berman pulling down over $203,000/yr. in pension payments responded to BGA's (Better Government Association) expose "Sticker Shock: Illinois' Public Pension Crisis" by saying "Everything I did was legal." Of course it was.

Likewise Roland Burris on being confronted about his $126,000 pension (over $1.6 million total collected so far) said "It's legal and the law allows it and that's all I've got to say". Note that Burris is an attorney also.

Another one-day worker, Dennis Gannon, union boss of the Chicago Federation of Labor went to work for the city of Chicago one day in 1993 and ended up with a city pension of $158,000. His response, no surprise, was "I always followed the pension laws." Sure you did Dennis.

Of course all of these corrupt practices were/are legal. This is Illinois after all. All the key decision makers are and have been attorneys. They will make absolutely sure that any legislation codifying corruption will be legal.

Illinois House Speaker Michael Madigan, Attorney General Lisa Madigan, Governor Rod Blagojevich, Governor Pat Quinn, Senate Majority Leader John Cullerton, Senate Minority leader Kirk Dillard and House minority leader Tom Cross attorneys each and every one.

This particular corrupt law was passed in 2007 shortly after the 2006 elections were held. During the calendar year 2006 teacher representatives gave Mike Madigan a total of $230,000 and Rod Blagojevich two checks totaling $500,000. And it is not just Democrats either. Republican Kirk Dillard received a nice juicy $250,000 from the teachers last year when he was running for Governor.

Let's see how much the most powerful attorneys in IL have received from the teacher's union.

Amounts Received from Teacher Union Sources

POLITICIAN	AMOUNT
Blagojevich, Rod	$1,866,697
Madigan, Lisa	$929,996

Quinn, Pat	$640,199
Madigan, Michael	$495,900
Cross, Tom	$487,438
Dilliard, Kirk	$372,050
Cullerton, John	$51,800
	$4,844,080

In fact Steve Preckwinkle's name appears on the contributors list as donating $25,000 to the Madigans' campaign war chest on June 24, 2006 although I am sure the money came from the Illinois Federation of Teachers. I mean why use your own money when you have access to tens of millions of dollars of teachers' money sitting in the IFT's war chest?

These people are neither teachers nor public employees so why do we have to pay them a "public" "teacher's" pension?
How many other non-public, non-teacher union officials are gorging at the TRS pig trough?

Looks like 34 union officials pulling down more than $4 million total per year in pensions at taxpayer expense. That is an average of more than $119,000 per year each and a total payout over their expected lifetimes of $121 million including the 3% annual Cost Of Living Allowance.

Note the average union retiree only worked 28 years about 2/3 the average of the rest of us. One of them only worked 8 years in IL as a teacher and is pulling down almost $100,000 per year in pension payments.

Preckwinkle will soon join these illustrious recipients at the pension pig-trough:

TRS Teacher Union Officials Pensions in Excess of $100,000	Column1	Column2	Column3	Column4	Column5
Name	Employer	Annual Pension	Pension Paid out to date	In-state Years Service	Highest Salary
AVERAGE FOR GROUP>>>>>>>>>>		119,023	834,753	28	164,325
Geppert, Edward J Jr.	IFT	185,851	1,081,079	25	260,038
Smith, Glenn P	IFT	160,348	898,826	31	226,069
Drum, Kenneth J	IFT	159,348	2,056,286	31	165,058
Davis, Anne P	IEA	148,295	760,178	41	197,037
Abrahamson, Barbara J	IFT	142,466	721,949	29	203,700
McKenzie, Karen S	IFT	142,466	721,949	27	203,700
Baird, Andrea	IFT	140,742	805,127	16	197,173
Amato, Thomas J	IFT	136,354	1,214,090	31	189,204
Koster, Lanita	IFT	132,739	567,058	31	193,341
Betterman, Lieselotte N	IEA	130,899	1,780,120	31	118,654
Turley, Terry W	IFT	129,905	658,023	34	184,051
Peickert, Robert	IFT	127,461	1,036,936	32	163,281
Bron, James L	IFT	126,483	182,347	29	211,053
Zinn, Dennis	IFT	126,048	1,093,398	33	155,865
Haisman, Robert W	IEA	125,985	1,051,766	32	116,589
Wright, Tavey L	IFT	125,145	534,614	34	182,280
Bell, Michelle R	IFT	123,129	82,086	33	203,911
Miller, Gerald	IFT	121,504	688,860	31	203,700
Arterburn, Laura L	IFT	116,377	543,092	28	193,341
Penca, James F	IFT	114,967	1,412,541	32	119,082
Deboer, Virgil W	IFT	112,668	1,386,984	34	117,193
Ewing, Bertram	IFT	109,263	1,423,247	26	126,393
Blackshere, Margaret R	IFT	107,868	1,407,423	30	110,607
Bowman, Martha V	IEA	100,090	513,074	37	143,556

Mackey, Raymond M	IFT	97,239	260,446	8	220,898
Shea, Susan R	IEA	93,183	436,782	22	107,895
OKeefe, Raymond	IFT	92,982	1,144,643	26	117,193
Manering, Donna L	IEA	92,559	215,970	25	143,336
Weil, Oscar	IFT	88,848	1,400,312	35	96,599
Jones, Dianne R	IFT	76,119	1,123,997	31	85,859
Breving, Robert J	IFT	44,803	268,030	7	120,921
Walther, Daniel O	IEA	41,738	211,480	13	69,767
Allen, John W	IFT	30,264	119,648	13	130,932

Reform the pension systems by "retiring" the pension systems.

When all public employees are on a 401K type system there will be no way to game the system because it will be just like the rest of us have. And God knows we can't game the system.

So let's adopt Tom Cross' SB 512 proposal with the 401K option only.

Then and only then will the legal corruption end. ✐

CHAPTER 3:

PENSION MYTHOLOGY.

"For the greatest enemy of the truth is very often not the lie – deliberate, contrived and dishonest – but the myth – persistent, persuasive and unrealistic."

— John F. Kennedy, 1962

3.1) Pension Crisis: Politicians and Unions Lied To Us in 1995 and Have Been Lying to Us Ever Since.

There has never been a "skipped payment".

As most Illinois citizens know IL passed a law in 1994 (Public Act 88-0583) that required the state to make required pension contributions that would provide 90% funding by 2045. Those required payments would start July 1, 1995 and thus this was a 50-year funding plan.

Over the past few years publicity has been negative in regards to the state meeting the 1995 funding mandate. Politicians of both parties, the news media of every shape and size and especially union honchos have repeatedly bombarded us with claims of shortfalls in taxpayer (state) contributions. Of course they never use the word "taxpayer" they always use the euphemism "state". After all the "state" is a commonly disliked, amorphous entity held in high disregard by virtually everyone. The "taxpayer" on the other hand is something to be courted and protected. The last thing unions and politicians want is to anger the "taxpayer" since they ultimately control the purse strings.

But when you say the state is in arrears on its pension payments you are saying the taxpayer is in arrears. When you say it is the state's fault you are saying it is the taxpayer's fault.

But based upon the payment schedule presented to us in 1995 that is absolutely not true which makes the $17 billion pension bond authorizations (2004, 2010, 2011) and the entire pension system a complete scam.

Very simply put: is $40 billion more than $30 billion?

If the answer is "YES" then taxpayers have overpaid into pensions not underpaid.

Lie #1 in 1995: We need taxpayers to contribute $9 billion from 1995 to 2003.

Taxpayers paid in $9.6 billion over that period so what's the problem?

If we paid more than we agreed to pay in 1995 why in 2003 were we considered to be behind in our payments?

In fact why is there a problem at all? Did someone else perhaps not pay their fair share?

State Contributions 1995 to 2003			
State Payments as Projected in 1995			
Versus			
Actual State Payments			
Year	Projected in 1995	Actual Taxpayer Payments	Overpaid or (Underpaid)
1996	627	682	55
1997	749	761	12
1998	881	932	51
1999	1,022	1,190	168
2000	1,173	1,313	140
2001	1,339	1,434	95
2002	1,516	1,549	33
2003	1,705	1,702	(3)
	9,012	9,563	551
SOURCE: State Actuarial Reports 1995-2003			

Lie #2 in 1995: We need $18 billion in pension assets in 2003 to be on schedule. (1)

At the end of fiscal year 2003 we had $23 billion in pension assets, five billion more than required in 1995. So what's the problem?

How can accumulating 27% more assets than needed be the cause of a shortfall?

Lie# 3 in 2003: It's 2003 and the state (taxpayer) is behind on its payments and we need to borrow $10 billion and charge it to the taxpayers' credit card.
How can that be when we have over-contributed and accumulated more assets than we supposedly needed for 2003 when we were told about the 50-year funding plan in 1995?

So in spite of over-contributing and over accumulating assets the taxpayers of Illinois have to pay out another $22 billion (including interest).

Since the taxpayers over-contributed and over accumulated shouldn't the people who benefit directly from the pension system i.e. the public employees and public retirees pay any excess amounts due? Why is this a taxpayer liability?

Lie #4 in 1995: We need taxpayers to contribute $31 billion from 1995 to 2011.
Taxpayers paid in $36 billion ($40 billion including interest) over that period so what's the problem?

If we paid more than we agreed to pay in 1995 why in 2011 are we considered to be behind in our payments?

In fact why is there a problem at all? Did someone else perhaps not pay their fair share?

State Contribtuions 1995 to 2011			
State Payments as Projected in 1995			
Versus			
Actual State Payments			
Year	Projected in 1995	Actual Taxpayer Payments	Overpaid or (Underpaid)
1996	627	682	55
1997	749	761	12
1998	881	932	51
1999	1,022	1,190	168

2000	1,173	1,313	140
2001	1,339	1,434	95
2002	1,516	1,549	33
2003	1,705	1,702	(3)
2004	1,906	9,111	7,205
2005	2,107	1,767	(340)
2006	2,337	1,048	(1,289)
2007	2,573	1,474	(1,099)
2008	2,824	2,105	(719)
2009	3,099	2,831	(268)
2010	3,377	3,991	614
2011	3,527	3,848	321
	30,762	35,738	4,976
Plus bond interest>>		4,056	
SOURCE: State Actuarial Reports 1995 - 2011			

Lie #5 in 1995: We need $31 billion in pension assets in 2011 to be on schedule. (1)
At the end of fiscal year 2011 we had $37 billion in pension assets, $6 billion more than required in 1995. So what's the problem?

How can accumulating 19% more assets than needed be the cause of a shortfall?

Lie# 6 in 2010/2011: The state (taxpayer) is behind on its payments and we need to borrow $7.2 billion more and charge it to the taxpayers' credit card.
How can that be when we have over-contributed and accumulated more assets than we supposedly needed for 2011 when we were told about the 50-year funding plan in 1995?

So in spite of over-contributing and over accumulating assets the taxpayers of Illinois have to pay out another $9 billion (including interest). That's $31 billion total in pension bond payments.

Since the taxpayers over-contributed and over accumulated shouldn't the people who benefit directly from the pension system i.e. the public employees and public retirees pay any excess amounts due? Why is this a taxpayer liability?

Lie #7 in 1995: If between 1995 and 2011 taxpayers contribute $31 billion and accumulate $31 billion in assets then taxpayer contribution from that point forward will be 21% of payroll. (1)

OK since we the taxpayer contributed $5 billion more than the $31 billion required ($40 billion counting interest on Pension Bonds) and accumulated $6 billion more in assets than the $31 billion required why is our annual contribution going forward 50% more than we were told it would be in 1995 (32% vs. 21% of payroll)? And why is the average employee contribution less than 7%?

And the Big Lie in 1995: The state payments over the next 50 years will be modest because the amount we owe for pensions going forward will be modest. (1)

Each year actuaries are required by accounting standards to provide for each pension fund a number call PBO (Pension Benefit Obligation). PBO is the amount of money we owe i.e. need to have in the bank in order to pay all the pensions due as of the date of the report assuming the funds earn the assumed interest rate (ROI). Like a mortgage the higher the PBO the higher the annual payments have to be. So lower PBO lower payments, higher PBO higher payments.

As with everything else we were told in 1995 concerning the 50 year payment plan, the projected PBO's for each of the 50 years was much lower than what actually happened. That is because the pension benefits due to be paid out turned out to be much higher than projected therefore even though we paid in more than we were told we needed and we accumulated more assets than we were told we needed neither was enough. The reason for that is the taxpayer is obligated to pay all increases in benefits. The burden is not shared by the employees actually receiving the increased benefits.

As you can see from the following chart the differences in projected PBO and actual PBO were significant. The difference has to be paid solely by the taxpayer. So the taxpayer (state) is being castigated for not paying amounts that should never have been assigned to us. We never agreed to these higher payments.

It's as if your mortgage payment was $1,200/mo. and you (over) paid the bank $1,700/mo. for 10 years you would think you had paid down your balance. But then the bank called and said "You know what your payment was really $2,000/mo. and now you owe us back payments plus interest at 8.5% on the past due amount." This kind of illogic is impossible anywhere except in Illinois pension politics.

Note the $10 billion difference in 2003 was exactly the amount of the bonds issued in 2004. In other words we were forced to borrow $10 billion to pay for increased benefits for teachers not including the other pension funds. They are not included because they do not have data going back to 1995.

TRS - 1995 Projected Pension Benefits			
Vs. Actual Pension Benefits in Billions of $			
	1995 Projected	Actual	Benefits Increase
1996	24	26	2
1997	26	27	1
1998	27	30	3
1999	29	33	4
2000	31	36	5
2001	33	39	6
2002	35	43	8
2003	37	47	10
2004	40	51	11
2005	42	56	14
2006	45	59	14
2007	48	66	18
2008	50	69	19
2009	53	73	20
2010	56	77	21
2011	59	81	22
SOURCE: TRS Actuarial Reports 1995-2011			

So if the taxpayers have done more than their share why are we $85 billion unfunded?
Mainly it is because of new benefits handed out to public employees like Christmas candy as can be easily seen in the above chart.

Here are just a few of the benefit enhancements. The "Conversion from Step Rate to Flat Formula" passed into law in 1998 for all state pension systems resulted in pension increases of up to 30% guaranteed by the taxpayers. Employee contribution for these and other increased benefits were free to SURS and SERS members and cost TRS members only .5% increased contribution. On average members of the state pension systems pay less than ½ of 1 percent of their salaries for all the pension benefit increases passed since the 1995 50-year funding law went into effect. All the other costs are paid and guaranteed by the state (taxpayer).

1. 1995 – ERI (Early Retirement Incentive) for teachers.
2. 2005 – ERO (Early Retirement Option) for teachers.
3. 1997, 1998 – Increase in pensions by up to 30% by changing from a stepped rate to a fixed rate.
4. 1998 - For certain state employees (troopers for example) change pension calculation from average salary over last 4 years to final year salary only. This change allowed 13 state troopers to retire in 2009 with pensions over $100,000/yr. at age 50 by including overtime in the final year's salary.
5. 2002 – For state employees rule of 85 was instituted meaning someone who started working for the state at age 19 could retire at age 52.
6. 2002 – University employees 30 years and out meaning someone who started working for the university at age 19 could retire at age 49.
7. 2002 – State employees working in highway maintenance would be on same plan as troopers and could retire after 27 years at age 50 with pension based upon their last year's salary including overtime.
8. 2003 – State employees have Early Retirement Incentive (ERI).
9. 2004 - Allow up to 2 years of sick leave to be applied as service credit meaning if you worked 33 years you could receive a pension as if you had worked 35 years.
10. 2005 - Allow teachers automatic 6% salary increases in each of the last 4 years, boosting pensions by 25%, without any additional pension payments from schools.

Why were the "experts" wrong in their estimates?

By "experts" I mean all of those with something to gain: teachers, union bosses, pension trustees, consultants, actuaries, lawyers, bond salesman, investment advisors, various and sundry boot lickers (Rezko, Levine, Cellini et al) and, of course, politicians.

They were wrong because there was no price to pay for being wrong. When they are wrong the taxpayers are expected to pay the price; meaning ever increasing taxes into perpetuity.

So what should be done about it?

If the "Liar's Club" of politicians and union bosses had told us in 1995 that we would see a retired U of I professor with a $120,000 pension after 5 years employment or high-school music teacher retire at age 54 with a pension of $130,000 or a retired superintendent with a $225,000 pension after paying $29,000 for $75,000/yr. pension increase and only working 18 years in Illinois or the $108,000 pension for a the Illinois Federation of Teacher's lobbyist who received his pension after working one day as a substitute teacher or that 20,000 public employees would have pensions in excess of $100,000 by 2020 would we have agreed to it? Of course not.

Let's go back to the rules originally presented to us in 1995 by rolling back all the pension enhancements passed into law since 1995 and watch the unfunded pension liability and taxpayer pension taxes drop like a rock. We never agreed to these increased pension benefits and should not be obligated to pay for them. Let those who received the increased benefits pay for them.

1. TRS data was used for these items because other funds do not have data for the entire time period. TRS serves well as a proxy because it is the largest fund by far representing about 60% of the total cost. ⇐

3.2) Pension Mythology: When The Going Gets Tough, Just Make Stuff Up.

Just because you read it in the papers doesn't mean it's true.

THERE ARE MANY supporters of the current pension system including union members, union leaders, state bureaucrats, investment advisors not to mention various and sundry politicians. Between and among them is a long history of misinformation and lack of transparency when it comes to disclosing real facts about the Illinois state pension systems.

Here are three of the most egregious examples.

No, the pension system is not unfunded by $85 billion because of short payments by the state.

This particular myth is especially popular with teachers and their union bosses and subsequently by their lackeys in the media. The myth goes something like this: over the years, the state has not made payments in full, has skipped payments etc. and that is the cause of the funding shortfall. In other words it's the taxpayers fault.

Unfortunately for the mythmakers we have numbers to dispute that claim. Each year state actuaries are required to calculate an amount called the Net Pension Obligation (NPO). It is defined as follows:

"NPO represents the cumulative difference between the annual pension cost and the actual contribution to the plan".

In layman's terms the NPO is the state's "Past due" amount accumulated over the years.

As of 2009, the NPO for the state pension funds represents about 25% of the $85 billion shortfall. In other words 75% of the unfunded is NOT "past due"; it is the result of other factors including $29 billion for investment return shortages and excess employee compensation since 1996.

And by the way, over the last 10 years the tightwad taxpayers have paid more than twice as much into the system, including interest, as the employees have paid in. How much more than 100% more should we be obligated to pay?

Average pensions seem low because they include all the retirees who worked only part time. For K-12 teachers you can receive a pension with as little as 5 years work. Pensions are also available to substitutes, part time teachers and hourly paid teachers. For state employees more than 80% also receive Social Security. This lowers the average pension substantially.

So the $46,000/yr. average pension for teachers that is constantly being hawked by union leaders and reporters should be compared to the average Social Security pension of $12,800 not to the pensions of private sector workers who work full time for more than 40 years to receive their pension. That's because the average teacher only works 25 years and retires at age 57.

In fact over 13,000 members of the TRS (Teachers Retirement System) currently have pensions of over $75,000/yr. which means in 10 years, because of the 3% COLA, every one of them will have pensions in excess of $100,000. That means by 2020, with the ever escalating salaries, there will be about 20,000 members of TRS with pensions over $100,000 paid for by the generous taxpayers of Illinois.

There is a huge surplus of teachers not a shortage.
One of the oldest and most persistent myths is that we have to pay teachers more and let them retire early and make them millionaires when they retire because there is an acute shortage of them. This is patently false.

Every year the Illinois State Board of Education (ISBE) produces a report titled: "Educator Supply and Demand in Illinois". This report lists in detail how many teachers are needed and how many the state actually produces. In 2010 for example we produced 30,000 certificated regular teachers and 14,000 substitute teachers or 44,000 total.

How many do we need? About 12,000. So last year alone we created 18,000 more teachers than we needed and if you include the substitutes we created 32,000 more than we needed. Since a teaching certificate in Illinois is good for five years we have at least 80,000 certified teachers not teaching in public schools. And if certified substitutes only make $100/day why do we have to pay the people they are substituting for $1,000/day?

And no, teachers are not leaving in droves because the job is so difficult. In fact they are staying in record numbers. The ISBE report also calculates the retention rate of teachers. It is about 95%, higher than any other white- collar job. You would have to be nuts to walk away from the huge salaries and pensions handed out by Illinois public schools.

And by the way, ISBE says the number of students is decreasing and will continue to decrease in the future. Doesn't that mean we will need fewer teachers as we go forward?

What the next governor should do.
The next governor should use the power of the executive branch to demand more transparency and accountability. We need all pensions on the Internet, sortable by amount, department/ school, number of years worked, total employee contributions made, etc. We need quarterly, timely financial statements from each pension fund.

We need summaries of actuarial reports in layman's language with key items like who contributed how much, and what are projection costs 5, 10, 15, 20 and 30 years out etc.

Since the pension systems operate under the Dept. of Insurance, appoint taxpayer friendly people to the board of trustees instead of those benefiting from the pensions. For example, 6 of the 13 members of the TRS board are former teachers, an obvious conflict of interest, and hardly impartial taxpayer oriented decision makers.

And most importantly use the bully pulpit to demolish the pension and salary myths that permeate the bureaucracy and media.

Be like Chris Christy. Tell it like it is and let the chips fall where they may. ≈

3.3) With 80,000 Unemployed Teachers in Illinois, Why Don't We Just Replace Any That Go On Strike?

THERE IS PERHAPS no more frustrating action against the public than teachers' strikes. While teachers have the advantage of being home with their kids every day after school, school holidays, and summer vacations and even during strikes non-teacher parents have to scramble for kid-coverage during those very same periods.

Unfortunately here in Illinois the news is replete with stories of strikes by teacher unions against IL school districts. And no wonder teachers strike since they cannot be fired for going on strike and if they do strike they get back-pay for any time missed.

Here are just a few of the most recent examples.
1. Nokomis School Dist. 22 has threatened to go on strike if its salary demands are not met.
2. Lake Forest Dist. 115 has authorized a strike if a new contract cannot be reached by Dec. 7. Note that LF 115 employee's average over $106,000/yr. salary.
3. Altamont Dist. 10 has filed an "intent to strike" in October over new contract salaries.
4. North Boone, Galesburg and Sullivan schools have recently signed contracts barely avoiding strikes.
5. Zion Benton HS teachers recently voted to strike.

The Avoca District 37 example.
Avoca District 37 is a prime example of how the teacher unions use strikes or the threat of strikes to completely control the public education system. By previously threatening a strike in 2002, Avoca's teachers' union paved the way for big contracts every year since.

In a democratic society public schools should be controlled by parents and taxpayers not by unelected public employees. But in Illinois the system is held hostage by a political process that has allowed teacher unions to make political contributions in excess of $50 million dollars thus assuring themselves guaranteed jobs (tenure) at above market prices. They can't lose their jobs by striking so why not do it? It is better that students, parents and taxpayers suffer than teachers not get what they want.

Avoca's September 2010 contract included 35% raises for teachers over the next 5 years as shown below.

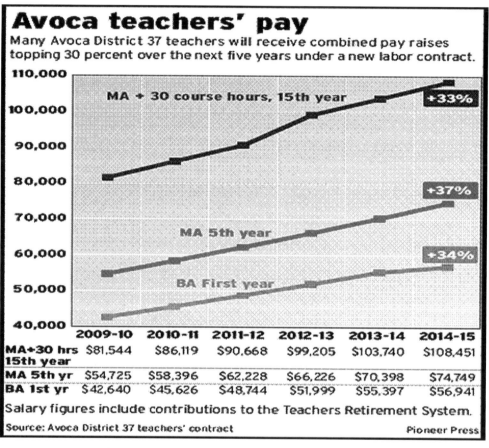

Avoca teachers' pay

Many Avoca District 37 teachers will receive combined pay raises topping 30 percent over the next five years under a new labor contract.

	2009-10	2010-11	2011-12	2012-13	2013-14	2014-15
MA+30 hrs 15th year	$81,544	$86,119	$90,668	$99,205	$103,740	$108,451
MA 5th yr	$54,725	$58,396	$62,228	$66,226	$70,398	$74,749
BA 1st yr	$42,640	$45,626	$48,744	$51,999	$55,397	$56,941

Salary figures include contributions to the Teachers Retirement System.

Source: Avoca District 37 teachers' contract   Pioneer Press

Thanks to Pioneer Press for the above graphic.

One of the complaints from the union is teacher salaries at other districts are higher therefore District 37 salaries should match or exceed those. Let me suggest a different solution: teachers should go and apply at any school district they perceive would be a better place to work. Of course the teachers know that every suburban school district has 100's of resumes from those 80,000 unemployed teachers and they would have little or no chance of getting hired. So teachers leaving one school to go to another for a higher salary are an empty but effective threat.

Let's put to rest the myth that teacher turnover causes teacher shortages.

The ISBE (Illinois State Board of Education) just released their latest report on teacher retention called "Educator Supply and Demand in Illinois, 2011 Annual Report". This report shows a retention rate of 95%, meaning only about 12,000 new teachers are needed each year. The report also shows 767 "unfilled" positions in all of Illinois including Chicago District 299. That means out of more than 160,000 K-12 jobs in IL about ½ of 1% were unfilled. And out of that 767 less than 80 were in the 6 county area exclusive of Chicago District 299.

Here is the number of new certified teachers for 2010 for 12,000 new jobs:

New Teacher Certificates Issued 2010		
NEEDED: 12,000 per year		
Type	Issued in 2010	Issued in Last 5 Years
Elementary	10,308	49,961
Early Childhood	1,427	6,362
Secondary	6,631	34,671
Special Teaching	5,041	16,284
School Service Emp.	1,506	7,101
Administrative	2,912	13,628
Provisional Cert's	3,130	10,000
Substitute	13,322	65,225
Total New Certs	44,277	203,232

So it is easy to see that in 2010 we created 30,000 new certified teachers (44,000 counting substitutes) when we only need about 12,000 leaving 18,000 unemployed but eager to teach.

Over the last five years we created about 140,000 certified teachers (not counting substitutes) for about 60,000 available jobs leaving 80,000 unemployed.

So much for the "myth" that teacher turnover leads to teacher shortages.

How much do other teachers make?

And the 80,000 unemployed teachers doesn't count the pool of experienced private sector teachers making an average of $38,000/yr. 40% less than the $65,000 average for Illinois teachers and 55% less than the $101,000 average at District 211 in Palatine. And private sector teachers have neither tenure nor multi-million dollar pensions.

Here we compare the salaries of certified teachers working for the Archdiocese of Chicago compared to Avoca District 37. If the Chicago Diocese can hire teachers with dual master's degrees and 15 years experience for $40,000 why does Avoca have to pay $81,000 for the same credentials?

Elementary School Teachers: Lay Certified - Lane I							
2011- 2012 Salary Scale							
							Avoca 37
Step	BA	BA + 15	MA	MA + 15	2nd MA	Ph.D.	*MA +30*
1	$27,387	$28,387	$28,887	$29,387	$30,387	$31,387	
2	$27,900	$28,965	$29,470	$30,000	$31,025	$32,050	$51,129
3	$28,367	$29,449	$29,954	$30,484	$31,509	$32,534	$53,462
4	$28,504	$29,587	$30,123	$30,664	$31,787	$32,837	$55,794
5	$28,993	$30,142	$30,697	$31,249	$32,394	$33,464	$58,127
6	$29,550	$30,764	$31,360	$31,923	$33,168	$34,264	$60,460
7	$30,108	$31,386	$32,022	$32,595	$33,942	$35,063	$62,793
8	$30,665	$32,009	$32,684	$33,267	$34,716	$35,863	$65,125
9	$31,223	$32,631	$33,347	$33,941	$35,490	$36,662	$67,457
10	$31,781	$33,254	$34,009	$34,615	$36,263	$37,461	$69,791
11	$32,338	$33,876	$34,672	$35,289	$37,037	$38,261	$72,123
12	$32,896	$34,498	$35,334	$35,963	$37,811	$39,060	$74,456
13	$33,453	$35,120	$35,997	$36,637	$38,585	$39,860	$76,788
14	$34,011	$35,742	$36,659	$37,311	$39,359	$40,659	$79,122
15	$34,568	$36,364	$37,322	$37,985	$40,133	$41,459	$81,454
16	$35,126	$36,986	$37,984	$38,659	$40,907	$42,258	$83,786
17	$35,684	$37,609	$38,646	$39,333	$41,681	$43,058	$86,119
18	$36,241	$38,231	$39,309	$40,007	$42,455	$43,857	$88,242

19	$36,799	$38,853	$39,971	$40,680	$43,229	$44,657	$93,966
20	$37,356	$39,475	$40,634	$41,354	$44,003	$45,456	$95,631
21	$37,914	$40,097	$41,296	$42,028	$44,777	$46,256	$97,298
22	$38,472	$40,719	$41,959	$42,702	$45,551	$47,055	$98,965
23	$39,001	$41,341	$42,621	$43,376	$46,325	$47,855	$100,631
24	$39,531	$41,921	$43,284	$44,050	$47,099	$48,654	$102,297
25	$40,061	$42,499	$43,946	$44,724	$47,873	$49,453	$103,963
26	$40,591	$43,078	$44,608	$45,398	$48,647	$50,253	
27	$41,121	$43,658	$45,271	$46,072	$49,421	$51,052	
28	$41,650	$44,237	$45,904	$46,746	$50,195	$51,852	
29	$42,180	$44,815	$46,493	$47,420	$50,969	$52,651	
30	$42,710	$45,394	$47,082	$48,094	$51,743	$53,451	

Overpaying public employees does not serve the common good.

It makes no sense to pay a Phys-ed teacher $203,000/yr. and a pension of $6 million like we did in 2011 (see Chapter 4.8 "Top 100 Teacher Salaries for 2011") when the certified teacher unemployment rate is over 33% (80,000 out of 240,000 total). Obviously a lot of people would like to have a teacher's job and would be willing and able to do it for much less than $203,000. Why should taxpayers have to pay a premium for a service that is available in the private sector for a fraction of what the government supplies it for? If taxation's purpose is to provide for the common good then what common good ensues from overpaying for a public service?

In recent years we have also seen a $196,000 art teacher salary, $100,000 annual salary increases for superintendents and 40 administrators whose salaries increased more than the median income of a full-time Illinois worker. By the way, that $196,000 art teacher salary was a 22% increase over his 2007 salary of $161,000, which was an 18% increase over 2006's $136,000 which was a 16% increase over 2005's $117,000 for a total of $81,000 in increases over 3 years.

This Art teacher's pension will start at $114,000/yr. and during the 27 years of his expected lifetime he will collect more than $4.4 million in pension payments. How do those numbers compare to your salary increases over the last 3 years? And how does that $4 million pension stack up to your 401K?

Make teacher strikes illegal.

The right to strike by any public employee should be limited. Perhaps the teachers should lose their tenure if they strike. How many of the 19,000 K-12 employees making more than $10,000/mo. would go on strike with the threat of tenure loss hanging over their heads? Not many would be my guess.

Let's take back the schools from the teacher unions. Or alternatively let's give more of our students to the Diocese of Chicago via vouchers and save more than 50% of our education costs.

CHAPTER 4:

YOU CANNOT CONTROL PENSIONS UNLESS YOU CONTROL SALARIES.

"We should stop swatting flies and go after the manure pile."

— General Curtis Lemay, 1944

4.1) You Cannot Control Pensions Unless You Control Salaries. Illinois taxpayers deserve reasonable limits on public salaries.

A s Illinois taxpayers face the impossible task of how to pay at least $400 billion worth of pension taxes over the next 35 years, the question arises: how did we get to this point?

The villains have been many but as we have discussed before the biggest culprit has been excessive, out of control salaries. If public salaries had increased at the same rate as Social Security wages over the last 20 years there would be no pension deficit.

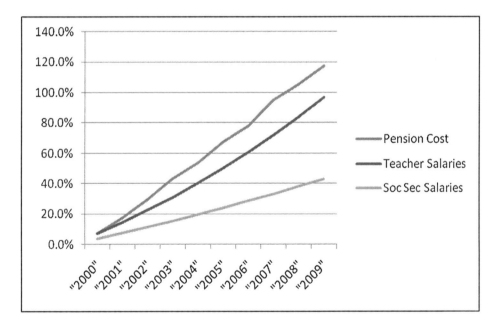

Top line = Pension Cost increases, Middle line = Teacher salary increases, Bottom line = Social Security wage increases

Option 1: If it's non-academic why don't we outsource it?

In 2009 the top teacher salary was $189,434 but he is just one of many overpaid so-called "teachers". If we look at the Top 10 Teacher Salaries for 2009 we see something unusual:

Salary	Subject	Name	School District
$ 189,434	Instrumental Music	Kimpton	Hinsdale Twp HSD 86
$ 189,248	Speech and Language Impaired	Dahlstrand	Lake Forest SD 67
$ 184,029	Physical Education	Parpet	DuPage HSD 88
$ 183,182	Guidance Counselor	Roeing	Leyden CHSD 212
$ 181,795	Learning Behavior Specialist I	Lendraitis	Cons HSD 230
$ 179,468	Librarian/Media Specialist	Masura	Lake Forest SD 67
$ 177,928	Physical Education	Heuerman	Niles Twp CHSD 219
$ 176,504	Physical Education	Mitz	Adlai E Stevenson HSD 125
$ 175,093	Instrumental Music	Moan	Cons HSD 230
$ 174,689	Physical Education	Knepler	Northfield Twp HSD 225

Notice none of the Top 10 teach an academic subject despite averaging a mind-boggling $181,137 or $20,000/mo. No English teachers, no history teachers, no physics teachers or algebra teachers. These are school employees who have been added to the "teacher" list over the years even though they don't really teach anything important. There is no reading, writing or arithmetic in the whole group. Four phys-ed teachers but no physics teachers

So part of the problem is adding more and more school employees to the "teacher" list (nurses and librarians for example), allow them to work only 9 months a year, pay them high wages and allow them to retire as part of the lucrative Teachers Retirement System even though they don't really teach anything.

One money-saving possibility is outsourcing as many subjects as possible. Instead of adding new categories of teachers let's start subtracting them. Certainly we can find skilled musicians to teach our children trombone and how to march at half-time of the football games for less than $189,000/yr. plus pension plus fringe benefits plus tenure.

Other obvious outsource possibilities include: Drivers Ed, Art, Drama, Phys Ed, Librarians, Nurses, Language and Behavioral.

Option 2: Limit pay for non-academic teachers to the 90th percentile nationwide.
The BLS (Bureau of Labor Statistics) puts out data by job title. Expanding on the previous paragraph if we are going to keep the non-academic workers then let's limit their pay to what other people with their skill set make in the private sector.

In the case of the two instrumental teachers in the Top 10 the BLS has a title called "Conduct, direct, plan, and lead instrumental or vocal performances by musical groups, such as orchestras, choirs, and glee clubs. Include arrangers, composers, choral directors, and orchestrators." Sounds about right.

So what do people in this category make in the real world the rest of us non-teachers live and work in? According to BLS the average is $53,410 and the 90th percentile for this occupation is $85,020 – and that's for a 12-month work year.

So let's make a rule that no public employee can make more than the 90th percentile of what his peers in the private sector make as defined by the BLS statistics. There are few taxpayers who would think $85,020 for a music teacher working 9 months a year with tenure and an extravagant pension available at 55 is inadequate pay for that particular job.

The constitution guarantees pensions not salaries.
The Illinois constitution states that pensions cannot be "diminished". However it does not say that salaries cannot be "diminished" and since pensions are directly correlated to salaries the one legal way to "diminish" pensions is to diminish salaries. And from the look of the salaries of the so-called "teachers" in the above table their salaries could and should be diminished by a significant amount.

If we had the "90th percentile" rule in effect, Illinois taxpayers would save $2.6 million pension tax dollars just from that one music teacher.

What the next governor should do.
The next governor needs to forcefully put salary limits into play at every level of government. One place to start is the high end. No public employee, including school administrators and college professors, can make more than the governor ($177,000).

149

Every other job should have a limit of the 90th percentile for that job description. Overtime should be limited to those making less than the average household income in Illinois or about $65,000/yr. If you make more than that you work overtime as part of your job description. Over a certain amount of overtime you could get comp time off. Comp time off would not add to pensions.

The governor must emphasize the need for public sector pay, pensions and benefits to match those in the private sector. It is not only an issue of fairness but also the only way to avoid bankrupting the state.

The 5% of Illinois workers that are in the state pension system cannot continue to have better pay, pensions and benefits than the 95% who pay for them. ⇐

4.2) Anatomy of a Teachers Contract: Blueprint for a Taxpayer Mugging.

One More Reason Why Illinois Needs A "Fairness In Compensation Act".

I RECENTLY RECEIVED, VIA a Freedom of Information Act request, a copy of the most recent teachers' contract with Illinois High School District 214 in Arlington Heights, IL. What I found was 67 pages of gifts for the teachers at the direct expense of the taxpayers. This document represents the definition of "special interests".

As you review each of the following eight items ask yourself this simple question: is this element of compensation available anywhere in the private sector? My answer is "No"; this is political payback for $50 million in political contributions by the teachers unions.

Contract Salaries:
1. For 2009, $48,062 (no experience) to $113,907 (18 years or more). See contract page 31.
2. Plus additional amounts for non-classroom activities (see below).
3. Increase each year by the CPI plus the normal step increase.
4. If CPI is 3.5%/yr. then average increase for 18 years will be about 8.5% per year not including at least three new contracts which will certainly drive the percentage increase even higher. If new contract increases average 3% every 5 years then average salary increase goes to 9.3% per year. Compare this with the average worker increase of 3.9% (including inflation) as calculated by Social Security.
5. Average teacher salary 2011 is $95,333 or over $10,000/month.
6. Automatic salary increases of 6%/yr. each of last 4 years before retirement.

Fringe benefits:
1. School district pays the teacher's pension contribution of 9.4% or $8,500 for average teacher. That cost is included in the salary.
2. Average family insurance paid for by district approx. $15,000.
3. Four personal days off.

4. Fourteen sick days to be taken or accrued for retirement (see below).
5. Up to $300,000 Early Retirement Option payments (see below).

Average compensation: $110,333 or $12,600/mo. ($95,333+$15,000).

Average years worked: 13

Other Payments: Co-Curricular Pay.
1. Head coaches $10,400, Pom-pom $7,100, Chess Club $4,300 per year. See contract pages 35-39 for other examples.
2. Ushers, timekeepers, scorers, etc. at sporting events - $ 74 (You thought they were volunteering didn't you?)
3. Summer school, $54/hr.
4. All of the above payments accrue pension benefits too.

Teachers Work Schedule (see contract pages 17-19):
1. Contract year: 185 days.
2. Less 4 personal days and 14 sick days = 167 work days.
3. Work day: 8 hrs. including lunch (7 hrs. and 10 minutes if you subtract lunch period)
4. Work day = 480 minutes broken down as follows:
   Five classes/student support = 300 minutes
   Fifty (50) minute lunch or free period
   Fifty (50) minutes "unassigned"
   Eighty (80) minutes "other"
5. Total hours worked per year = 1,197 (167 days times 7hrs and 10 minutes per day).

But as they say in the TV ads, "That's not all folks." As bad as the above examples are of unearned largesse, I have saved the two worst examples for last.

Buy Sick Days for $20 Each.
Under Illinois law teachers may, at retirement, use up to 340 unused sick days as 2 years service credit i.e. it is just as if they worked those 2 years. Under this contract teachers can buy extra sick days for $20 each up to the maximum (see page 54 of contract). So for $3,400 a teacher

could buy an extra year of "work" and receive about $3,000 in extra pension each year for the rest of their life. How does that compare to the return on your 401K?

And it leads to this perverse incentive: Why not take your sick days while you are working (while being compensated in excess of $700/day) and then buy them back for $20 when you retire? That would only be rational. And in fact in 2009 a retiring English teacher did exactly that. Her $6,800 payment for 340 sick days increased her pension payout by $4,800/yr. and over her expected lifetime by $178,000.

Should that extra $178,000 giveaway be guaranteed by the Constitution? Teachers think so.

School District Could Pay $300,000 or More to Allow Teachers Early Retirement.
Under Illinois law teachers may use ERO (Early Retirement Option) to retire early without penalty. The plan is very complicated but basically involves large lump sum payments from the school as well as the retiree to the Teachers Retirement System at the time of retirement. For example a teacher wanting to retire 5 years early would pay 57.5% of her highest salary and the school district (the taxpayer) 117.5% in order to retire penalty free.

Under this contract, page 53, the school district pays both the employer's portion and the employee's portion up to a maximum of 175% (57.5%+117.5%) of the teacher's highest salary.

The school also pays for excessive raises or when they give teachers sick-leave without them actually earning it.

The following table shows only those K-12 employees from District 214 who received over $100,000 in ERO (Early Retirement Option) payments. Also note the district paid for excess salaries and excess sick-leave. Do you think $188,000 payment by your school to allow an employee to retire early is a good use of tax dollars?

Township HS Dist. 214 ERO Payments Over $100,000	Employers' Contribution Amount for ERO	Employers' Contribution for Excess Salary Increase	Employers' Contribution for Excess Sick Leave	Total D-214 ERO Payments
Knuth, Martin J	175,385	13,454	-	188,839
Bratta, Joanne M	183,417		-	183,417
Hastings, Kendall R	168,097		-	168,097
Kerwin, Richard A Jr.	143,539	3,337	18,019	164,896
Cheatham, Karen J	160,614		-	160,614
Mann, Keith B	158,154		-	158,154
Thieman, Jeffrey S	156,140		-	156,140
Brennan, Lynne D	146,343		-	146,343
Hruska, Penny J	143,697		-	143,697
Blair, Kimberly R	119,965	201	17,973	138,139
Rosenstein, Marianne J	135,540	2,473	-	138,013
Koehl, Philip C IV	107,459	880	27,855	136,193
Bole, Edward C	132,448		-	132,448
Rosenbaum, Jill A	131,943		-	131,943
Steigerwald, Ronald C	129,222		-	129,222
Schmohe, Kathleen A	128,883		-	128,883
McDonell, Daniel A	128,847		-	128,847
Richards, Robert C	127,200		-	127,200
Cuevas, Alma R	108,434		17,277	125,710
Gwardys, Bronislaw H	121,876		-	121,876
Rubly, James T	121,179		-	121,179
Amelio, Catherine M	120,471		-	120,471
Rano, Denise R	120,205		-	120,205
Kowall, Susan F	120,140		-	120,140
Duellman, Michael J	118,977		-	118,977
Rhodes, Anita R	118,604		-	118,604
Connolly, Michael D	118,491		-	118,491
Vanhuele, Denise M	116,445		-	116,445
Prejna, Patricia W	115,921		-	115,921

Binder, Susan P	115,427		-	115,427
DeGiorgio, Vera M	113,428		-	113,428
Blustein, Carol L	113,220		-	113,220
Lilleeng, Michael D	113,040		-	113,040
Bellito, Michael J	112,318		-	112,318
Sutherland, Beth A	112,063		-	112,063
Mueller, Glenn A	111,598		-	111,598
Bieber, Catherine R	110,782		-	110,782
McCormick, Jo Anna	110,304		-	110,304
Ratay, Gregory W	110,156		-	110,156
Peterson, Neal C	110,121		-	110,121
Markshausen, Kim G	109,608		-	109,608
Vongerichten, Paula A	108,822		-	108,822
Peters, Bonnie S	107,487		-	107,487
Wesolowski, Sally B	106,949		-	106,949
Hausheer, Julie R	105,770		-	105,770
Tantillo, Susan H	105,751		-	105,751
Solar, Esther Garret	105,721		-	105,721
Turasky, Richard P	104,880		-	104,880
Perica, Esther P	104,044		-	104,044
Stoltz, Robert S	102,585		-	102,585
Wolfinger, Stephen M	102,202		-	102,202
Nash, Jane	101,857		-	101,857
McGinnis, Mark B	100,472		-	100,472

SOURCE: Teachers Retirement System of IL

Conclusion – We Need "Fairness in Compensation" Legislation.

What justification is there for private sector workers to be forced to pay higher taxes so that their peers in the public sector can be compensated at levels 50%, 100% or even 300% more than their own compensation?

There is no rational or reasonable explanation; there is only a political one. Since public sector pay, fringe benefits and retirement benefits are determined by politicians only politicians can change them. It will take courageous politicians (an endangered species here in Illinois) to confront the most powerful special interest in the country: public sector workers and their unions. But it must be done.

The purpose of a "Fairness in Compensation Act" would be to bring public employee total compensation into reasonable alignment with their peer groups in the private sector. In order to do this fairly we need to determine the value to the employee of each of the following compensation elements:

... Salaries
... Health, life, disability and dental insurance
... Vacation days
... Holidays
... Work day/week
... Sick leave policy
... Retirement health care
... Employee Pension contribution
... Employer Pension contribution
... Age at retirement
... Job security provisions such as tenure.
... Unemployment rates private vs. public
... Promotion schedules and policy

Once this determination has been made then public workers who are considered to be under-compensated (there are not many that I have found) will be granted compensation allowances over some period of time to bring them up to par. On the other hand, public employees who are considered to be over-compensated will have a menu of compensation cuts over a period time to bring them into alignment with their peers in the private sector. Any employee unhappy with this plan is certainly welcome to find other employment.

In a time of budget crisis at every level of government, now is the time to begin this process. Since 80-85% of government operational expenses are employee compensation elements it can be shown that if "compensation fairness" had been implemented years ago there would be little or no budget crisis at this time. For example if Illinois public employees had been on Social Security plus 401K for the last 30 years there would be no $100 billion unfunded pension and retiree health care liability. What could be "fairer" than Social Security and 401K for ALL employees public and private?

Fairness in compensation: how can that possibly be unfair?

Sources:
Illinois School Board - Teacher Service Records 2008-2009
Illinois School Board – School Report Cards 2009
Township High School District 214 – "Cumulative Agreement 2009-2014"
Teachers Retirement System of Illinois website ═

4.3) The Four Rules of "Too"
The Real Reason Why Illinois Pensions Are in Trouble.

I F YOU LISTEN to union representatives and their lackeys in the media you will hear this constant refrain: Illinois pension problems are the direct result of the taxpayers not paying their fair share over the last 15 years. This is patently false.

The problem with Illinois public pensions is the result of the "Four Rules of "Too":
1. Public employee salaries are "Too" high
2. Public employee contributions are "Too" low
3. Public employee pensions are "Too" high
4. Public employee retirement is "Too" early.

Public employee salaries are "Too" high.
Teachers' salaries rise twice as fast as private sector salaries.

This particular chart is related to the Teachers Retirement System (TRS) but it could apply to other state workers too. For example, 35% of Illinois State Troopers make more than $100,000/ yr. with a high salary of $185,000.

Over the last 10 years teachers' salaries have risen by 7% per year or 96% compounded and the pension cost (Pension Benefit Obligation) taxpayers are responsible for paying has gone up 116%. If we look at the rest of us, those working within the Social Security Retirement System, our salaries increased by an average of 3.65% or 43% compounded, less than ½ of the teachers' increases. Thus although our income has gone up less than half as fast as teachers' salaries and pensions we have had to pay more taxes (out of our lesser incomes) to pay the for higher teacher salaries and the higher pensions associated with those higher salaries.

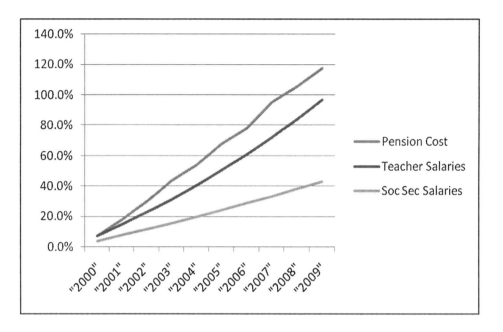

Top line = Pension Cost increases, Middle line = Teacher salary increases, Bottom line = Social Security wage increases.

On what exact basis is it justified for teachers to receive annual raises almost twice as high as Social Security employees? What exactly makes them special? Did we, the employer/taxpayer, ever vote for or approve these high salaries? Is $189,000/yr. a reasonable salary for a 9-month public employee teaching Music? What justification is there for 14,688 public school employees to be making over $100,000/yr.?

Let's take our $189,000 Music teacher and work backwards by 7%/yr. to find his beginning salary 33 years ago. That number would be about $23,000/yr. If we then move forward from $23,000 at 5% per year rather than 7% we end with a salary of about $104,000, still excessive in my estimation for 9 months work but certainly better than $189,000. Why aren't 5% raises and a $104,000 9-month salary enough for a 54 year-old Music teacher? If his top salary was a very fair $104,000 instead of an outrageous $189,000 his total pension payout would be reduced by about 45% or $2.7 million.

Public employee contributions are "Too" low.

Teachers contribute less but get 4 to 7 times more pension than Social Security workers.
Next let's compare our $189,000/yr. public school music teacher with a self-employed music teacher. Let's assume the self-employed person begins his career at the same time as the teacher and ends up making $189,000/yr. at his earliest retirement date of 62 vs. 56 for the teacher. The public school music teacher pays in 8% and works 9 months per year for 33 years while the self-employed person pays both the employee and the employer portion of the Social Security tax or 12.4% and works 12 months per year for 40 years.

Here are the disturbing results:

Pension Comparison		
Public Sector Employee vs. Private Sector Employee		
	Music Teacher Public Employee	**Music Teacher Self-Employed**
Years Worked	33	40
Ending Salary	189,000	189,000
Current Contribution Rate	8%	12.40%
Total Contributions	194,000	268,000
Pension At Age 54	130,000	zero
Pension At Age 62	150,000	22,000
Total Lifetime Pension Paid Out	5,800,000	800,000

This simple table shows the stark difference between the public sector pension system and the private sector pension system. Those in the private sector pay more, work longer and get 1/7th as much pension in return. That is an overwhelming argument that teachers (and other public employees) do not pay nearly enough into their plans. How is it possible that they pay less yet receive 7 times as much benefit?

In this example the public teacher has accumulated pension payments by age 62 that total as much as the self-employed teacher will receive over his entire lifetime.

The 5% Solution.

If since 1995 teacher raises had been limited to 5% (35% more than Social Security raises) and they had contributed 5% more of their salary there would be no contribution deficit for TRS although there would still be an investment-loss deficit of about $15 billion. So the so-called taxpayer "shortage" is a simple function of paying employees too much and asking them to contribute too little.

Combine the "5% Solution" with a reasonable limit on public pensions of the median family income in Illinois (about $66,000) and there is no pension deficit at all.

The Union-Politician Industrial Complex leads to unsustainable costs.

Why do the 5% of Illinois workers who are in the state pension system get a special deal while the 95% of workers who are not in the pension system pick up the tab?

That's a rhetorical question of course. We all know that in Illinois politics he who pays gets. And the teacher unions alone have contributed more than $50 million to Illinois politicians over the last 15 years. The unions give millions and the politicians give back billions. That's how it works.

And the taxpayers continue to pay, decade on decade, in a form of generational theft no one wants to talk about. ⬿

4.4) Illinois Pays an Average of 30 Times More Per Student for Superintendents than Arizona

FORMER DISTRICT 200 Superintendent **Gary Catalani** recently signed a contract with an Arizona school district worth $195,000/yr. plus benefits. That's about $20,000 less than his $214,000 retirement from Illinois. And it is a whole lot less than his Illinois salary of $380,000 in 2006 in fact about twice as much for five times as many students.

And, by the way, we calculated his total Illinois pension take at over $9 million.

As you can see from the following table, AZ highest paid superintendent salaries are much lower than Illinois. Why is that do you suppose?

District	Superintendent	Students	Base salary
Phoenix Union	Kent Scribner	25,200	$200,000
Scottsdale Unified	Gary Catalani	26,600	$195,000
Mesa Public Schools	Michael Cowan	72,600	$180,000
Chandler Unified	Camille Casteel	37,000	$174,865
Paradise Valley Unified	James Lee	33,400	$159,000
Gilbert Public Schools	David Allison	36,700	$150,000
Peoria Unified	Denton Santarelli	38,800	$150,000
Deer Valley Unified	Virginia McElyea	36,700	$150,000

You can see that the Mesa Schools chief with 76,000 students makes less than an Art teacher made in Illinois last year. In Illinois only Chicago school district has more students than Mesa. As for Illinois superintendent salaries here's a table of the highest paid in 2008. Overall these 9 IL school districts average $112 per student for superintendent salaries alone.

Name	School	Salary	Students	Cost Per Student	Times AZ
Codell, Neil C	Niles Twp. CHSD 219	411,511	4800	86	21
Murray, Laura L	Homewood Flossmr	402,331	3000	134	34
Gmitro, Henry A	CCSD 93	348,113	4500	77	19
Kelly, Dennis G	Lyons Twp HSD 204	342,075	3800	90	23
King, Eric A	ESD 159	340,267	2000	170	43
McKanna, Robert	Palatine CCSD 15	327,596	12400	26	7
Hager, Maureen L	North Shore SD 112	317,268	4400	72	18
Gallagher, James J	Evergreen Park HS	299,866	950	316	79
			IL AVERAGE		30

So Illinois taxpayers pay superintendents 6 to 78 times more per student for their superintendents than AZ does. Why can't Illinois School Boards find these less expensive people when they are recruiting new superintendents? By the way, the pension payout for those 8 Illinois superintendents will total about $60,000,000.

In 2011 there were also 129 teachers in Illinois who made more than the 6th highest paid superintendent in AZ.

This is more evidence of the unholy alliance between Illinois politicians of both parties and the public school employee political organizations. Illinois taxpayers pay more for public education because Illinois politicians take more money from school employees.

Illinois politicians should take AZ as an example of how to hold down education costs by paying reasonable salaries for school employees. There is no reason Illinois taxpayers should pay 78 times more for school management than AZ. One place to start would be to consolidate Illinois 900 plus school districts into 300 thereby saving the need for 600 over paid superintendents.

In the end, what is the purpose of taxation?
If the purpose of taxation is providing for the common good, what common good is provided by a $130,000 pension for a 54 year old public employee who has worked 9 months a year for 33 years? And in fact what important public good is not being provided by that $130,000 pension?

Taxing for Fire and police services are for the common good, taxes for highways and sewer and water are for the common good. But $130,000 pensions for 54-year old public employees serve no common purpose only a political one. And that represents a political system we can no longer afford or tolerate. ⟞

4.5) Wisconsin: Top Teacher Salary $95K Less Than IL Top Teacher, Top Superintendent $103K Less.

More evidence that Illinois taxpayers pay too much for education not too little.

IF ILLINOIS WANTS a model of how to run a public school system for a reasonable cost they would do well to emulate what Wisconsin is doing. When it comes to education everything costs less in WI.

Let's look at some of the key facts about school salaries in WI vs. IL.

Key Comparisons Illinois vs. Wisconsin 2011				
	Wisconsin	Illinois	Difference	IL Higher By
Top Teacher Salary	108,000	203,000	95,000	88%
Teachers with Salaries over $100K	8	7,856	7,848	99%
Average Salary Top 100 Teachers	84,142	160,679	76,537	91%
Top Superintendent Salary	265,000	368,000	103,000	39%
Average Salary Top 100 Admin.	150,000	261,000	111,000	74%
Education Salaries over $100,000	1,161	14,866	13,705	Infinity
Education salaries over $200K	2	222	220	Infinity
Education Salaries Over $300,000	0	7	7	Infinity

Teachers' salaries WI vs. IL.

WI has exactly 8 teachers with a salaries over $100K and the highest one at $108,000 is barely over half of Illinois' highest. IL on the other hand has 7,848 and with the built in 3% compounding pension COLA every one of those 7,848 will have a pension over $100,000 by the time they are 65 and most of them long before 65.

Even more telling is the average salary of Il Top 100. In WI there are only 8 education salaries, all superintendents, in the entire state higher than the average of IL Top 100 teachers.

Illinois has 2 music teachers, 3 phys Ed teachers and a librarian all making more than the superintendent of the 85,000-student Milwaukee Public School District.

And by the way it is not just WI teachers. Missouri has 11 teachers making over $100,000 and Kentucky has zero, none, nada teachers making more than $100,000 compared to IL 7,848.

Administrators' salaries WI vs. IL.

What does IL get in exchange for the incredible $103,000 difference in salaries between the top WI ($265,000) and IL ($368,000) superintendents? Well, for a lot more money the IL superintendent supervises a school with less than 4,000 students while the much lower cost WI superintendent supervises more than 24,000 students. So we pay a lot more and get a lot less. As we have reported earlier the same is true in AZ where the top superintendent salary is $200,000 for a 25,000-student campus. On a per student basis, IL superintendents often earn 30 times more than their peers in other states.

Wisconsin has big savings in pensions too.

In WI the maximum pensionable age is not reached until age 65 and it is 70% not 75% of salary as it is in Illinois. That's because the annual pension increment is 1.6% per year worked instead of 2.2% per year in IL. In addition, any post-retirement increase is based upon investment return being greater than 5%. And there are no $300,000 Early Retirement Options (ERO) or sick leave pension credits like IL. In all likelihood there are no $100,000 teacher pensions in WI nor will there be any in the foreseeable future.

Teachers in WI can retire as early at age 57 with 30 years but their pension would then be 48% of a lower but reasonable salary as opposed to 75% of a much higher and unreasonable salary for Illinois teachers at age 54. This may explain why WI has more than 7,000 teachers over the age of 60 and 1,100 over the age of 65 still working. So much for the argument put forth by IL teacher unions that having teachers work beyond age 60 is cruel and unusual punishment.

We know that the top paid teacher in IL in 2009, an $189,000 music teacher, retired last year on a pension starting at $130,000/yr. that will require a pension payout of about $6 million over his expected lifetime. If we apply Wisconsin's pension rules, including a 1.5% annual increase, to their top teacher we end up with a pension payout of about $1.7 million, still substantial but 70% less than the payout to the Illinois teacher. Including WI teacher's Social Security the savings are over $3 million.

What the next governor should do.
The next governor needs to use the bully pulpit to point out these huge salary and pension disparities between the education systems in WI vs. Il. If WI can find and keep teachers at a fraction of the cost of IL teachers then why are we forcing IL taxpayers to cough up an additional $4 billion/yr. to make millionaires out of public employees?

He needs to explain that the cost of IL public sector salaries and pensions makes IL uncompetitive when it comes to recruiting new business. What business in their right mind would move to IL rather than WI knowing that public employee costs are far higher and on the horizon is a trillion dollar pension and retiree health care cost which will almost certainly be thrown onto the shoulders of IL business via higher taxes?

And while Pat Quinn wants to raise taxes to pump even more money into an already bloated education system, the new governor should ask why the IL education system costs $4 billion more than WI and what can we do to make our system more competitive.

And finally he should ask why IL's higher cost system results in a 78% graduation rate while WI's much lower cost system has an 85% graduation rate? ⇐

4.6) IL School Administrators Make 67% More than Wisconsin's.

IL could save $500 million/yr. by adopting WI administrator compensation plan.

WE ALL KNOW Wisconsin is in trouble financially and that they have trouble with their public sector unions just like Illinois. But as bad as things are in WI things are much worse here at home in IL.

One reason WI is better off is the much lower cost of K-12 education expenses specifically salaries and pensions. If IL had WI salary and pension system our K-12 costs would drop by $4 billion/yr.

WI vs. IL Top 25 Administrator salaries:

The most striking thing you notice is in this table is the huge difference in cost with each of the Top 7 IL administrators costing more than $200,000 more than their WI counterparts.

The 2nd is the almost $5 million per year in added cost just for these 25 public employees.

Top 25 Admin Salaries 2010	IL Vs. WI						
Illinois	Illinois		Wisconsin	WI	WI	WI	WI
School	Salary	#	School	Salary	Salary Diff.	Annual Pension Cost Diff	Total Cost Diff.
Yorkville CUSD 115	350,154	1	Madison Metropolitan	198,500	151,654	83,561	235,215
Schaumburg CCSD 54	341,748	2	Green Bay Area Sch Dist	184,000	157,748	82,684	240,432

Lincolnshire-Prairieview SD	334,912	3	Racine Sch Dist	180,000	154,912	81,067	235,979
Riverside SD 96	318,325	4	Milwaukee Sch Dist	175,062	143,263	76,591	219,854
Bloom Twp HSD 206	307,471	5	Whitefish Bay Sch Dist	170,850	136,621	73,776	210,397
Kildeer Countrys CCSD 96	299,600	6	New Berlin Sch Dist	166,089	133,511	71,932	205,443
Plainfield SD 202	297,606	7	River Falls Sch Dist	165,626	131,980	71,379	203,358
Marquardt SD 15	292,157	8	Whitnall Sch Dist	164,779	127,378	69,818	197,196
Wheeling CCSD 21	288,564	9	Greendale Sch Dist	163,256	125,308	68,901	194,209
Mannheim SD 83	282,648	10	Eau Claire Area Sch Dist	162,000	120,648	67,246	187,895
Schaumburg CCSD 54	282,121	11	Marathon Co CDEB	159,299	122,822	67,399	190,221
Park Forest SD 163	281,950	12	Franklin Public Sch Dist	157,926	124,024	67,506	191,531
Skokie SD 68	279,670	13	Edgerton Sch Dist	156,783	122,887	66,945	189,832
HomewoodFlossmoor CHSD 233	276,014	14	Cedarburg Sch Dist	154,993	121,021	66,040	187,061
Batavia USD 101	274,935	15	Hamilton Sch Dist	154,895	120,040	65,722	185,762
Thornton Twp HSD 205	274,593	16	Monona Grove Sch Dist	154,652	119,941	65,646	185,587
Indian Springs SD 109	272,413	17	Wausau Sch Dist	154,463	117,950	65,005	182,955

Valley View CUSD 365U	271,241	18	Cooperative Ed Serv Ag 01	153,681	117,560	64,739	182,299
Glenview CCSD 34	271,142	19	Elmbrook Sch Dist	153,466	117,676	64,734	182,410
DuPage HSD 88	270,635	20	Wisconsin Rapids Sh Dist	152,256	118,379	64,720	183,099
Lemont Twp HSD 210	270,198	21	Shorewood Sch Dist	152,250	117,948	64,587	182,535
Joliet Twp HSD 204	269,343	22	Fond du Lac Sch Dist	152,000	117,343	64,356	181,698
Twp HSD 113	269,336	23	Mukwonago Sch Dist	150,800	118,536	64,493	183,028
New Trier Twp HSD 203	266,420	24	Kenosha Sch Dist	150,000	116,420	63,698	180,118
Leyden CHSD 212	265,724	25	Janesville	150,000	115,724	63,486	179,211
Average>>>	288,357		Average>>	161,505		Total Diff	4,718,114

The salary cost difference is obvious, why are the IL pensions so much higher?
The pension cost difference is due to several reasons one of which is, of course, the much higher salaries in IL compared to WI since in both cases pensions are a percentage of final salary. But other reasons pay a big part too.

1. Retirement age:
In WI full retirement age is not reached until age 65. In IL it is at age 54. Total pension payout for a 65 year-old Wisc. native would be about 50% less than the payout for his 55 year-old IL counterpart assuming their salaries were the same. Since IL salaries are much higher the difference in total pension payout for the WI teacher is 1/3 of the total pension payout for the IL teacher.

2. Maximum payout:

In WI the maximum is 70% of final salary at age 65 compared to IL 75% at age 54 and of course that lower percentage (70% vs. 75%) is calculated against a much lower salary.

3. Annual accrual towards pension:

In IL the accrual is 2.2% of final salary (avg. last 4 years) for each year worked compared to WI's 1.6% meaning for example that an IL employee with 27 years of service (the average for TRS) would receive 59% of a much higher salary compared to 43% of a much lower salary for his counterpart in WI.

4. Cost-of-living-adjustment (COLA):

In IL the COLA is always 3%/yr. even if the Social Security COLA is zero as it has been for the last 2 years. In WI pensions only increase if investment returns are above a certain amount. So for the last few years there has been no increase. The highest COLA increase in IL for 2010 was $12,120, just slightly less than the $13,000 average Social Security annual payment.

5. No early retirement or sick-leave credits.

In IL, teachers and administrators can accrue up to 2 years of sick leave and apply those to retirement meaning, for example, they can work 33 years, use 2 years sick leave credit and retire at 55 on full pension. That means taxpayers have to pay for 2 more years of pension. Wisconsin has no pension credit plans: your pension is based upon years actually worked.

Wisconsin vs. Illinois		
Highest Salaried Teacher 2011		
Total Pensions Paid Out Earliest Full Retirement		
	Illinois	Wisconsin
Salary	203,000	108,000
Age At Retirement	55	65
pension % of Salary	75%	70%
Life expectancy	30 yrs.	21 yrs.
COLA	3%	1.50%
Beginning Pension	128,000	67,000
Total Pension Payout	$6 million	$1.9 million

Annual pension cost for administrators (adjusted for population): IL = $353 million, WI $89 million.

According to IL state actuaries, taxpayers' pension contribution for 2012 fiscal year beginning July 2011 will be 30.44% of teachers' payroll. This compares to WI 11.3%, which includes 6.2% for Social Security and 5.1% for pension. Employees match the 11.3% compared to IL teacher's average pension contribution of 8%.

It's not complicated: Wisconsin's lower salaries, later retirement age, higher employee contributions and lower pension accruals add up to a fair and affordable pension plan. It is obvious when comparing IL to WI that Illinois' pension plans are neither fair (to the taxpayer anyway) nor affordable.

If we add the savings in salary and pensions to teachers and administrators IL could save $4 billion/yr. by using the Wisconsin plan even with the state's Social Security payments.

Here's a comparison between WI and IL that shows the depth of IL's problem:

Key Comparisons Illinois vs. Wisconsin 2011				
	Wisconsin	Illinois	Difference	IL Higher By
Top Teacher Salary	108,000	203,000	95,000	88%
Teachers with Salaries over $100K	8	7,856	7,848	99%
Average Salary Top 100 Teachers	84,142	160,679	76,537	91%
Top Superintendent Salary	265,000	368,000	103,000	39%
Average Salary Top 100 Admin.	150,000	261,000	111,000	74%
Education Salaries over $100,000	1,161	14,866	13,705	Infinity
Education salaries over $200K	2	222	220	Infinity
Education Salaries Over $300,000	0	7	7	Infinity

Gov. Quinn should put on a cheese-head hat and go recruiting in Wisconsin.
Certainly the teachers and school administrators in WI could do a bang up job here in IL. Why not give them a chance?

Of course Quinn won't do anything (well maybe don a cheese-head hat) about Illinois over-blown and out-of-control education cost because he is a captive of the teachers unions as are most state Democrats and far too many Republicans. But it does show how IL bloated $30 billion K-12 education costs could be cut by billions if only a little common sense prevailed.

Wisconsin has taken a big step in controlling its out-of-control public employee costs and Illinois' need is much, much greater. The financial time bomb is ticking while IL politicians sit on their hands refusing to recognize the depth of the problem.

In the meantime moving vans are speeding towards IL borders, carrying taxpayers and employers to other states including Wisconsin. Rome is burning and Springfield is fiddling.

So what's new? ⚊

4.7) If Public Employees Received Raises Equal to Yours There Would Be No Pension Deficit.

Excess public salaries are the main driver of pension deficits.

T HE DIRTY LITTLE secret of pension funding problems is the huge salaries public employees earn compared to their peers in the private sector. Take a look at the following chart where the upper line represents the Pension Cost due to public employees from Illinois taxpayers, the middle line the Teacher Salary increase compounded over 10 years at 7% per year and the bottom line representing the average Social Security salary increase compounded over 10 years at an average of 3.65%.

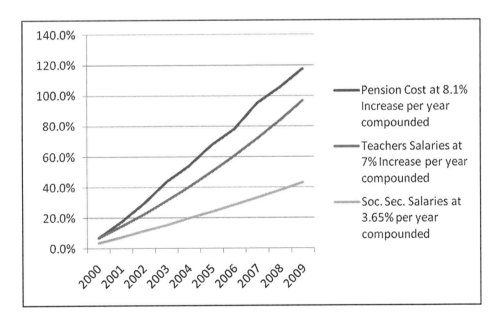

Notice that the upper "Pension Cost" line, with its huge corresponding pension deficit, is correlated to the middle "Teacher Salaries" line. This is because as salaries increase pensions increase at approx. the same rate or a little more because you are adding more people to the retirement list each year and they are retiring at higher salaries and they are getting their 3% COLA.

So how do we bring down pensions to the point where they are in a surplus position rather than a deficit position? Simple: lower the Teacher Salary down from the current 7% increase per year to where the Social Security Salary increase is: 3.65% increase per year. Voila – pension deficit suddenly becomes surplus as the Old Pension Cost (top line) drops by more than half to the New Pension Cost (bottom line). See the chart below for details.

If teacher's salaries increased at the same rate as Social Security earners there would be no pension problem.

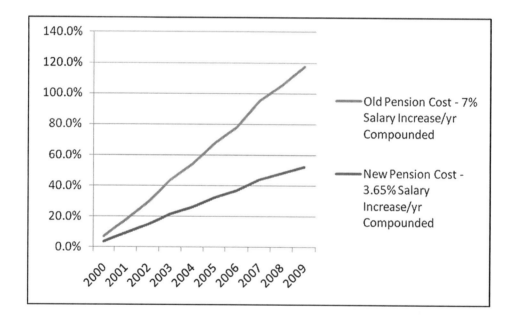

This shows how the 95% of Illinois workers who are not in the lucrative state pension system are obligated to pay outsize pensions to their peers in the public sector even though their own salaries are not increasing nearly as fast.

Every excess tax dollar required by the state pension system to pay for the privileged 5% is a dollar less the 95% have for their own retirement.

What the next governor should do:

The most obvious solution is to lower salaries. In Ireland when the financial crisis hit they lowered public salaries by 13% across the board. The governor could do that with the employees under his control and would save $1.5 billion if he followed Ireland's lead.

However there is a huge swath of salaries that the governor does not control – public schools K-12. At the local school district level, where the soccer moms and soccer dads on the school boards are routinely taken advantage of by well trained and politically supported teacher union reps, salaries continue upward to ridiculous levels. How else do you get $189,000 music teachers, $138/hr. 2nd grade teachers and $100,000 plus one-year salary increases?

An easier way to achieve the same goal is to expand on legislation already in effect namely Public Act 94-0004 enacted in 2005 that limits the state's pension obligation to a certain percentage increase in annual salary over a certain time period; in this case 6% per year for each of the last four years before retirement.

Since PA 94-0004 has established a precedent for limiting annual salary increases over a certain number of years then let us just change the parameters. For example would it be legal to limit increases to say 5% over 5 years? Certainly if we can do 6% over 4 years we can do 5% over 5 years.

So why not 3.65% salary increases over 35 years? In other words tie the state's pension obligation to the Social Security rate of wage increase with the excess going to where it should have been at the beginning – to those who control the salaries. The local school district would then have to collect more taxes from the local property owners, a much more difficult task than just passing it on to the state. How do you justify higher property taxes to make multi-millionaires out of part-time Drivers Ed and Drama teachers?

For state departments their budgets would be unchanged but if average salary increases exceed 3.65% then other parts of their budget would have to be cut in order to fund the excess pension costs.

This approach has precedent and would serve the dual purpose of lowering pension costs and salaries across the board. ⇐

4.8) Top 100 Teacher Salaries for 2011: Phys. Ed Teacher Heads List with $203,154.

You can't control pensions if you don't control salaries.

As ILLINOIS CITIZENS struggle with the severe economic downturn plaguing the state, Illinois public school employees enjoy another record year of salaries, fringe benefits and pensions. In 2011 an amazing 14,866 public school employees made more than $100,000 up 18% from 2010's 12,588.

Apparently there is no tax money for the barren shelves at food pantries or the lack of beds at homeless shelters or to support for the handicapped but there is enough tax money to pay for:

- A Phys. Ed teacher $203,154 for a 9 month work year.
- The 7,576 teachers made more than $100,000 in 2011.
- The 21 teachers who made more over $1,000/day ($170,000/yr.)
- A Drivers Ed teacher whose salary is $18,222/month to teach teenagers how to parallel park.
- The 13 teachers who make more than the Governor's $177,500.
- Top 100 Teachers average $18,169 per month salary ($163,579/yr.).

And all of that is for a 36-week work-year (182 day contracts).

These Top 100 Salaries Do Not Include Massive Amounts of Fringe Benefits.

Add about $48,000 each for state pension contribution (30% of salary) and at least $7,500/yr. health insurance benefits. Then include 12-15 days sick leave payable at retirement if not used, 2-4 personal days/yr. and up to $300,000 payment to the Teachers Retirement System by the local school district if they decide to take early retirement.

And what is the value of a guaranteed $100,000 job (called "Tenure") for as long as you want it?

$100,000 Teacher Salaries By Subject		
Fiscal Year Ending June 30, 2011		
Subject	2011 High Salary	Greater $100K 2011
Art	179,660	213
Automotive Repair	175,122	24
Cabinet maker	146,295	21
Clothing/Apparel	131,620	8
Drama	179,660	30
Drive Ed	166,658	143
Elementary Education	161,104	1006
English	174,300	545
Foodservice	135,997	17
French	176,600	55
Latin	135,912	10
Librarians	155,546	53
Music	182,686	284
Nurse	136,166	35
Phys Ed	203,154	760
Radio and TV Broadcasting	154,413	15

Nineteen (19) of the Top 100 teachers retired with pensions in excess of $100,000.
Should public employees who average a mere 32 years of 9 month work retire at an average age of 57 with an average payout of $3.7 million? On average these people will receive their entire contribution back in less than 20 months.

No one in their right mind thinks this kind of public payout is fair, reasonable or guaranteed by the constitution.

Here's the list:

	Name	School District	Age	First Year Pension	Years Work in IL	Sick Leave Service	School ERO Contrib.	School Excess Sick Leave Contrib.
2011 Teacher Retirees With Beginning Pensions Over $100,00								
1	Sebald, David F	Leyden CHSD 212	57	127,875	32	2.000		-
2	Oddo, Linda L	New Trier TWP HSD	58	122,260	32	2.000		-
3	Kay, Bruce	Community HSD 155	56	117,765	32	1.909		-
4	Filippo, Anthony	Lake Forest CHSD 115	56	117,038	34	2.000		-
5	Gasper, Kip E	Highland Park 113	57	116,838	32	2.000		-
6	Kirwan, James P	Hinsdale TWP HSD 86	56	113,930	32	2.000		-
7	Nihells, Robert A	Lake Park CHSD 108	55	111,929	33	2.000		-
8	Kaplan, Susan	Highland Park 113	65	111,529	29	2.000		
9	Lagesse, Gary L	Thornton TWP HSD	58	109,231	34	2.000		13,326
10	Scahill, Joseph	DuPage HSD 88	56	108,801	33	2.000		29,168
11	Ratajczyk, Bruce	Highland Park 113	57	107,576	32	2.000		-
12	Fischer, Steven	Lake Park CHSD 108	57	107,409	32	2.000		-
13	Richards, Evan	Lake Forest CHSD 115	57	106,299	35	2.000		-
14	Vanko, James S	Leyden CHSD 212	55	106,234	32	2.000		-
15	Blazevich, R.	Northfield TWP 225	60	105,936	36	2.000		-
16	Zizzo, Gary A	Lake Park CHSD 108	58	104,925	27	2.000	62,072	-
17	Vogel, Debra C	Lake Park CHSD 108	58	103,546	33	2.000		-
18	Cantor, Iris L	Niles TWP CHSD 219	60	102,746	28	2.000		-
19	Koval, Karen J	Lake Park CHSD 108	55	100,220	31	1.776	188,837	-

Notice several things about this list:

1. The years actually worked in IL, boots on the ground, only averages 32 years as compared to the private sector, working 40 years and retiring at age 62 with a maximum $22,000 Social Security pension. That is not even mentioning the fact that these multi-millionaires only worked 9 months a year for those brief 32 years.

2. The sick leave column shows how teachers accumulate sick-leave years and use them as actual work years. This taxpayer scam adds up to about 157,000 free pensionable years.

3. The "School ERO Contrib." column shows the amounts local taxpayers pay to allow the teacher to retire on full pension before she is eligible. Note number 19, Ms. Karen Koval, a dance teacher, received a taxpayer funded $188,837 so she could retire early. That is in addition to her salary of $165,888 for a taxpayer total of $354,725 which allows a dance teacher to retire with a pension payout of $3.4 million over her expected lifetime.

4. The last column shows two teachers (numbers 9 and 10) with amounts in the "**School Excess Sick Leave Contrib.**" Column. This is paid by the taxpayers for sick-leave days GIVEN to the teacher as part of the contract. Because that increase pension costs for absolutely no reason the local taxpayer must send money to TRS to partially (not fully) cover the ensuing pension costs.

Public education in IL is of the teachers, by the teachers and for the teachers.

Why do taxpayers have to pay these outrageous salaries and benefits?

Since the purpose of taxes is to "provide for the common good", please explain to me what common good is "provided for" by making public employees millionaires? I would suggest that school districts that can afford to pay compensation of this magnitude should be paying for their own pensions rather than throwing it on the backs of all the state taxpayers. Doing that would save the state $1.6 billion a year. We cannot control teacher pensions unless we control teachers' salaries.

The "wealth transfer" progressives' talk about is not from the rich to the poor but from everyone to the public employees. There would be billions more dollars available for the poor if public employee compensation were equal to the private sector – and without raising taxes.

SOURCES: Teacher Retirement System, Illinois State Board of Education. ⇐

4.9) $800,000/yr. for Superintendents Past and Present at Just One School District.
Retirement at 55 instead of 65 increases pension payout by 69%.

A FEW WEEKS AGO Jack Roeser, publisher of the Championnews, asked me how much taxpayers were paying for the job of superintendent at each school district if we included the current employee and all those who preceded him in the job but were now retired and pulling down a state pension. Intrigued, I sent out a sampling of FOIA's (Freedom Of Information Act) requesting that information to 7 of the approximately 220 school districts in the six-county area. Of those 7 Bremen District 228 in the south suburb of Midlothian came up with the biggest number: $800,537 per year.

District 228's pay and pensions may seem outrageous to most of us (including a $142,000/yr. phys ed teacher) but they are relatively modest compared to many other districts in the state so I am certain there are districts with bigger numbers than D228. For example, D228's average salary is $87,000 compared to Niles District 219's $96,000 and their superintendent's $220,000 salary does not even make it to the Top 100 school administrators in Illinois although it is $20,000 higher than the highest superintendent's salary in Wisconsin. More about WI pay and pensions later.

Early retirement means more retirees and more pension cost per job.
In Illinois the retirement age is 55 for maximum pension whereas in Wisconsin it is 65.

Since superintendents average about 5 years on the job before they retire, a retirement age of 55 will leave two more retired superintendents (and two more pensions) than a retirement age of 65. In our Bremen D228 example this will result in an additional cost of about $300,000 per year on average. Of course that number is just an estimate since all superintendents do not retire at 55 in IL or 65 in WI. See Chapter 4.6 for comparison of IL vs. WI superintendent's salaries.

Here is a table of Bremen's superintendent costs, current and retired.

Bremen Dist. 228	Annual Pension	Pensionable Salary	Employee Contribution	Pension Paid To Date	In-state Years Service
Wheat, Robert M	110,268	69,400	-	1,991,404	35
Riordan, James E	178,490	193,275	-	1,458,735	31
Evans, Frank H Jr.	123,252	136,939	142,865	703,446	32
Reiplinger, Raymond	168,339	185,971	175,988	1,007,413	39
Kendall (Salary)	220,188				
TOTALS>>>>>>>>>	800,538			5,160,998	

Several things jump out here besides the $800,000 annual cost.

1. Within four years or so every one of the retirees will have a pension greater than their original pensionable salary due to the automatic 3% per year COLA.

2. Also within that time frame they will all have an annual pension greater than the total amount they individually contributed to their pension. Social Security would be a max of about 25% of employee contribution in the best case.

5. Over $5 million has been paid out already and that is increasing by about $600,000/yr.

6. They average about 34 years worked compared to 44 to reach full Social Security in effect a six-figure pension for what most people would consider to be less than a full career.

Bremen's total annual pension cost is over $20 million/yr. paid for by the state not the local district. Here is just the Top 10:

Bremen District 228 Top 10 Pensions as of 03/01/2011					
	Mo. Pension	Annual Pension	Employee Contribution	Pension Paid To Date	Years Worked
Riordan, James E	14,874	178,490	Unknown	1,458,735	31
Reiplinger, Raymond M	14,028	168,339	175,988	1,007,413	39
Coleman, Geraldine	11,663	139,959	166,642	598,215	36
Beishuizen, Robert A Sr.	11,161	133,931	133,263	859,558	33

Welch, Patricia J	10,984	131,811	174,908	482,784	33
Glenn, Marianne	10,843	130,110	164,759	477,793	32
Evans, Frank H Jr.	10,271	123,252	142,865	703,446	32.2
Meyer, Vita J	10,249	122,990	-	1,095,316	33.7
Moy, Edward S	10,040	120,479	135,209	728,388	31.2
Carter, Richard R	9,973	119,674	138,543	511,514	37
Social Security at 66	2,350	28,200	161,000		45
		1,369,037	1,232,178	7,923,161	33.8

Note the short careers and modest employee contributions considering the huge payouts. For comparison a person working on Social Security for 45 years until full retirement (11 years more than the above average) at age 66 and earning the same wages as above would pay about $130,000 into Social Security for a $28,000 pension.

The pension system is in trouble because teachers retire too early and do not contribute nearly enough.

Should part-time, 34 week/yr. employees with partial careers get full pensions?
TRS (Teachers Retirement System) members who retired in calendar year 2010 averaged $47,000 pension for 25 years work. Since 90% of K-12 employees are 9-month employees (TRS defines a work year as 170 days or 34 weeks) there is a valid argument that these are, by and large, part-time employees.

In the private sector if you graduate from college at 21 you have to work 45 years to reach full Social Security age 66. So how many TRS members who retired in 2010 meet this definition of a full career? An infinitesimal 11 out of 4,735 or two-tenths of 1%.

OK let's make it a little easier. If you graduate from college at 21 and work 41 years you will reach the earliest Social Security retirement age of 62. So how many TRS members who retired in 2010 meet this less-strict definition of a full career? A giant, humungous 1.3% of them.

OK let's grade on the curve here and use the TRS definition of a full career i.e. years needed for full 75% of salary pension. – 34 years. How many TRS members who retired in 2010 meet this only-in-the-government-is-this-possible definition of a full career? A still measly 12%.

A much higher percentage 30% actually had 35 years "Service Credit" allowing full 75% of salary retirement. Although they only worked 33 or 34 years, under TRS rules they can accumulate unused sick-days up to 340 days or two years and then use those as if they actually worked them. In 2010 alone retiring teachers used almost 5,000 years of sick-leave credits to boost them from 33 or 34 years actual work to 35 years "Service Credit" and therefore a full pension. In effect TRS pretended these members worked 5,000 years when they really didn't.

Of course that's 33 years of 34 weeks work for a teacher compared to 47-week years for private sector workers. Therefore actual boots-on-the-ground teaching for 33 years is the equivalent of 24 years in the private sector.

If we limited pensions to 2 times Social Security there would be no pension crisis.
How could anyone argue that a state pension two times Social Security is not enough? State, university and k-12 employees contribute about 15% more on average (6.9% vs. 6.2%) to get 100% more 11 years earlier (55 vs. 66). Why exactly is that a hardship?

Our average TRS retiree with 25 years and a pension of $47,000 would have a Social Security value of $17,000 at age 66 ($12,000 at age 62). So under our new system her pension would be $34,000/yr. instead of $47,000. And it would increase annually at the Social Security rate.

Savings at higher pension levels would be even greater. For the 18,000 or so public employees making more than $100,000/yr. their max pension would be 2 times the Social Security maximum at 66 or $57,000. By the way $57,000 is the median family income in Illinois, why should any public employee get more than that?

As an option we could offer retirees a very generous cash buyout equal to 5 times their contributions.

For those school districts that think 2 times Social Security is not enough, they could always add retirement annuities to the contracts. My guess is taxpayers would not stand for it. The only reason outrageous pensions are available today is because local property taxpayers don't have to pay for them. Prior to 1998 when TRS pensions were increased across the board by up to 30%

local property taxpayers paid the pension cost. Starting in 1998 pension costs were transferred to the state where they remained hidden, breeding huge deficits, for the next decade or so.

So let's solve the pension crisis by amending the state constitution to read "pensions shall not be diminished or impaired below two times Social Security."

Problem solved. ⇐

4.10) $138 per hour 2ⁿᵈ Grade Teachers Will Bankrupt the State.

To Avoid Financial Armageddon Salaries, Pensions and Benefits Must Come Down

THE CITY OF Des Plaines has some very expensive part-time employees working at CCSD District 62 including a second grade teacher who makes a salary of $153,466 per year for a six hour day, 37 weeks a year. That adds up to 1,110 hour a year or about 22 hrs. Per week. Of course she doesn't really work 185 days because she gets 3 personal days and 15 sick days off per year so if we subtract those she only works 990 hrs. Per year and makes $154/hr.

So how are these ridiculous wages possible? Let's take a look at the teachers' contract involved.

Contract school day: of the teachers, by the teachers and for the teachers:
The contract calls for a workday from 8:50AM to 3:40PM or 6hrs and 50 minutes

But wait there is more. Teachers get a 50-minute lunch break so that puts the day down to 6 hours.

Except on Mondays and other "Early Release Days" when the workday ends at 3:25PM instead of the harsh, slave-like 3:40PM. Those days are 5 hours and 45 minute days.

And except for first day and last day of school when students are released at 11:30 and 9:30 respectively. Those days are 1 hr. and 40 minutes, and 40 minutes respectively.

Insurance and pension benefits.
The school district pays 100% of her health insurance cost and 2/3's of her families cost. She also gets district paid life and dental insurance.

And over her last 3 years she received salary increases totaling an absolutely incredible $51,518. This increased her pension payout by $600,000 over her expected lifetime.

By definition she, and every Illinois teacher, is a part time employee.
In 1996 Illinois passed a law Public Act 89-170 which defined a policeman as part-time if he worked less than 1,560 hours a year. This teacher's 1,110 hours, and that is a generous calculation, is less than half the hours the average white-collar works at 9 hrs./day, 240 days per year.

Her salary is $19,000/yr. more than what the Bureau of Labor Statistics says the average Illinois Pediatrician makes ($134,000). Obviously, any government that pays part-time employees more than MD's is headed towards financial oblivion.

And, geez, I wonder if pediatricians work more than 6 hours a day, 9 months a year?

Just one of many.
She is not alone either. There actually were two other grade school teachers who made more than her last year. Here are the highest paid K-5th grade teachers for 2009 and the salary increase they received their final year:

K-5th Grade Teacher Salaries 2009

NAME	SCHOOL	2009 Salary	2008 Salary	1 Year Increase	Per cent Increase
O'Hara	Lake Forest D 67	158,699	134,224	24,475	18%
Hiler	North Shore D 112	158,515	120,420	38,095	32%
Ehnert	Des Plaines D 62	153,466	127,691	25,775	20%
Jannusch	Des Plaines D 62	151,932	126,857	25,075	20%

What is the purpose of taxation?
The purpose of taxation is to provide for the common good. What common good is provided for by paying part-time public employees these kinds of salaries, benefits and pensions? None that I can see.

And in fact, the question must be asked: what common good is being denied by allowing these kinds of personal and political benefits to be funded by taxes intended for the common good? If these 4 people alone had been paid $50/hr. plus extremely good benefits, $400,000 would be available to help the poor, the sick, the homeless and the hungry. Which of the above are "common" good versus "personal" good and which should taxes be used for?

The teacher union – politician industrial complex must end.
Teacher unions have donated more than $50 million to Illinois politicians since 1995 and the politicians in return have given them free reign over contracts like the one outlined above. That is how 19,000 public school employees now make more than $10,000/mo.

In addition politicians have continually enhanced teacher pensions to the point where every teacher with 33 years service-credit retires a multi-millionaire at the expense of every other common societal good.

It will only end when we vote out of office every politician who has taken money from the teachers union – and that is most of them. ⇐

4.11) Unsustainable: $15,000/month Average Teacher Compensation.

Public Sector Pay & Benefits Soar While Private Sector Languishes.

IT IS BECOMING more obvious every day that government spending for public employee compensation is well beyond what is available in the private sector. What is more, because the tax dollars being allocated to pay public compensation comes from the private sector, taxes are being increased at the very time when taxpayers can least afford it.

How Big Is The Difference between Public and Private Sector Compensation?

When we talk about compensation we mean the total cost of an employee to an employer. This would include not only wages and salaries but fringe benefits such as retirement pay (or pensions), retirement health care, vacations and other time off with pay, and insurance (health, life, disability).

There are several ways to look at the disparity between public employee compensation and private sector compensation. Previously we have written about the huge difference between federal workers compensation and the average private sector employee, $120,000/yr. vs. $60,000/yr. per the BEA (Bureau of Economic Analysis).

We can also look at the BLS (Bureau of Labor Statistics) and see the comparison according to their statistics:

	Total Hourly Compensation	Wage Portion	Benefits Portion
State and local government workers	$39.66	$26.01	$13.65
Private Sector all workers	$27.41	$19.39	$8.02
Difference in dollars/hr.	$12.25	$6.62	$5.63
Difference in percentage	45%	34%	70%

Those numbers are stunning: 45% more in total compensation for state and local workers and an amazing 70% in fringe benefits. And public employee unemployment is ½ of private sector unemployment. So government workers are compensated more and have more secure jobs. Not a bad deal if you can get it.

Many Illinois School Districts Are At The $15,000/mo. Level of Compensation.
On October 30, 2009 the Daily Herald printed a report showing the highest average teacher salaries by school district:

2009 teacher salaries

highest average salaries	Avg. salary 2008	Avg. salary 2009	Amount change	Percent change	Adequate yearly progress* in '08	in '09
Maine Twp. H.S. D207	$88,539.00	$94,205.00	$5,666.00	6.40%	no	No
Palatine-Schaumburg H.S. D21 1	$88,022.00	$92,811.00	$4,789.00	5.44%	no	No
Fenton H.S. D100	$84,696.00	$92,373.00	$7,677.00	9.06%	no	No
Stevenson H.S. D125	$86,932.00	$90,555.00	$3,623.00	4.17%	yes	No
Libertyville-Vernon Hills D128	$83,690.00	$90,273.00	$6,583.00	7.87%	no	Yes
Northwest Suburban H.S. D21 4	$87,457.00	$90,112.00	$2,655.00	3.04%	no	No

Keeping in mind that teachers in Illinois only work 9 months (182 day contracts) these 6 schools average more than $10,000 per month in salary for each of their teachers. But they also receive superior benefits including pension, insurance and days off.

If we look at just one of these schools, Stevenson High School District 125, we can come up with a total compensation package in excess of $143,000/yr. or more than $15,000/mo.

Here's the calculation:

Illinois School District 125 Teacher Compensation

Average Salary	90,555
Pension Contribution - State 30.5%	27,619
POB - Pension Obligation Bonds 3%	2,717
OPEB - Retiree Health Care 3.25%	2,943
Pension Contribution - Local and Federal 1%	906
Insurance Family Coverage	19,125
TOTAL COMPENSATION>>>>>>>>>>>>>>>>	143,865
Average Monthly Compensation>>>>>>>>>>>>	15,985

The same calculation could be made for the other five $90,000/yr.-plus districts with similar results.

It Would Be Cheaper To Hire Full-time Consultants Than Teachers.
According to the teacher contract teachers receive 2 personal days off per year and 16 sick days. Of those 16 sick days 10 may be accrued each year towards 340 days which can then be used at retirement as two worked years. That puts the actual work days per year at 170 (182 minus 12). In addition there are sabbatical leaves, professional leaves, family and medical leave and by contract the school day is 8 hours or less. Then there are the additional costs of tenure, up to $3,000/yr. tuition reimbursement and disability insurance. So the true cost of a teacher at District 125 is far more than the $143,000/yr. we have documented here.

If we take $143,000 annual compensation and divide it by 170 days and 8 hours/day we get $105/hr. So in effect taxpayers are paying consulting rates for teachers but, because of tenure, without the right to fire them as they would have with consultants. And of course you don't pay consultants when they are sick, you don't reimburse them for tuition and you don't provide disability insurance.

Private Sector Workers Get 1.5% Raises, While Teachers Get 9.06% Raises.
The Labor Department reported this week that for the 12 months ending Sept. 30, 2009 wage increases averaged 1.5%. If you look at the teacher salaries in the table above you will see annual increases up to 9.06%.

Below is a chart showing the monthly compensation of state and local workers, federal workers and Illinois teachers compared to the average for private sector workers.

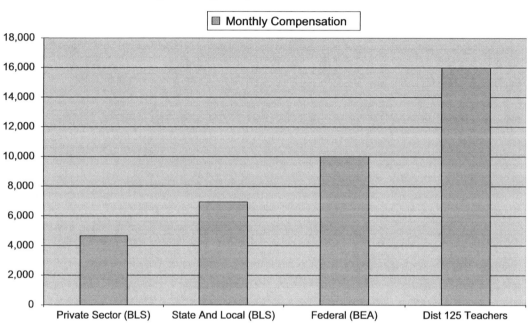

Please notice how those of us in the squashed left column are being taxed to pay for the vastly higher compensation of our public sector peers in the 3 right-hand columns. The distorted 1.5% to 9.06% wage increase explains how this can happen.

The Huge Disparity between Public and Private Compensation is a Form of Political Corruption.

The publically available data outlined above shows the unsustainable nature of current public policy. More and more income is being redistributed from private sector wages to public sector wages via taxes and this can only happen with political approval.

Not only is this policy financially unsustainable, it is patently unfair.

Sources:

Bureau of Economic Analysis

Bureau of Labor Statistics

Illinois Commission on Government Forecasting and Accounting

Chicago teachers' Pension Fund

Teachers Retirement System Actuarial Report June 30, 2008

4.12) Why Is Illinois's Top Teacher Salary $108,000 More Than Kentucky's?

And $95,000 more than WI and $92,000 more than IA and $83,000 more than MO?

OR TO PUT it another way why is IL top teacher salary more than twice as much as Kentucky's ($203,000 vs. $95,000)?

The answer the above questions is simple: because the National Education Association (NEA) and its spawn, the Illinois Education Association (IEA) completely control the political process in Springfield and in every local school district.

What other reason could there be?

Are IL teachers twice as good as KY teachers? I don't think so.

Are IL teachers twice as smart as KY teachers? I don't think so.

Are IL teachers twice as deserving as KY teachers? I don't think so.

Are Illinois test scores twice as good as KY? No they are actually lower.

As you can see from the following table Illinois test scores are generally lower than the adjacent states with much lower teacher salaries confirming what everyone already knows: teacher salaries have nothing to do with student achievement.

Notice how IL scores last in 4 out of the 7 categories and is 4th in two others. Only in "8th Grade Writing" does it outscore all of its neighbors.

2011 National Assessment of Education Progress						
SOURCE: National Center for Education Statistics						
	Illinois	KY	IA	WI	MO	IL Place
Scale Score, Grade 4 Math	238	239	243	244	241	**LAST**
Scale Score, Grade 8 Math	282	279	284	288	286	**4th**
Scale Score, Grade 4 Reading	219	222	225	223	221	**LAST**
Scale Score, Grade 8 Reading	263	262	267	264	263	**4th**
Scale Score, Grade 4 Science	148	158	N/A	158	158	**LAST**
Scale Score, Grade 8 Science	148	153	N/A	158	154	**LAST**
Scale Score, Grade 8 Writing	160	151	155	158	153	**First**

The high salaries in IL are not anomalies.

As can see from the following chart of the Top 10 Salaries in each state the differences are widespread.

	Top 10 Teacher Salaries Illinois and Adjacent States				
	IL	KY	IA	WI	MO
	203,155	95,179	111,188	108,152	119,909
	199,887	95,179	105,700	108,150	116,771
	198,667	93,518	104,213	104,986	112,657
	195,437	88,574	99,979	101,018	112,515
	186,364	88,574	95,924	99,209	109,767
	185,993	87,247	94,462	99,203	108,369
	185,736	87,247	92,725	98,871	104,898
	185,451	87,247	92,471	98,871	103,293
	183,777	85,638	91,389	97,534	102,180
	182,686	85,019	91,227	97,457	101,692
Average	190,715	89,342	97,928	101,345	109,205

And if we look at the number of teachers making more than $100,000 per year the differences between the states are even more pronounced: Illinois has 445 times more $100,000 teachers that the other four stets COMBINED.

Number of teachers with salaries in excess of $100,000/yr. ($11,000/mo.):

Illinois = 7,576
Kentuck y = ZERO
Iowa = 2
Wisconsin = 4
Missouri = 11

Here are the top Illinois teacher salaries for various subjects. Notice how many high salaries are in non-academic subjects.

$100,000 Teacher Salaries By Subject Fiscal Year Ending June 30, 2011		
Subject	**2011 High Salary**	**$100K Salaries 2011**
Phys Ed	203,154	760
Music	182,686	284
Art	179,660	213
Drama	179,660	30
French	176,600	55
Automotive Repair	175,122	24
English	174,300	545
Drive Ed	166,658	143
Elementary Education	161,104	1006
Librarians	155,546	53
Radio and TV Broadcasting	154,413	15

Cabinet maker	146,295	21
Nurse	136,166	35
Foodservice	135,997	17
Latin	135,912	10
Clothing/Apparel	131,620	8

Excessive salaries lead to excessively high pensions.

With pension payouts in the $5 million range for the last four years top earners one needs to ask if this is the best use of taxpayer dollars.

Top Teacher Salaries 2008 - 2011 and Their Current Pensions							
Year	Name	Final Salary	Subject	Current pension	Years Taught in IL	Age At Retire.	Est. Total Pension Payout In Millions
2008	Vanderschoot	196,000	Art	125,852	38	58	$4.80
2009	Kimpton	189,000	Music	130,472	33	54	$5.89
2010	Mitz	191,000	Phys Ed	113,616	31	55	$4.87
2011	Sebald	203,000	Phys Ed	127,875	32	57	$5.31

And it is not just the top earners either. Just in 2011 alone nineteen 9-months a year teachers retired with pensions in excess of $100,000. In total the TRS (Teachers Retirement System) has 3,499 retirees with pensions over $100,000 and the number is growing by 25% per year.

Here's a list of the nineteen 2011 teacher retirees with $100,000 plus pensions. Note there are no 40 year careers here in fact they are as low as 27 years and the average is only 32 years. Compare this with a private sector worker starting work at age 22 and working 40 years to get the maximum $22,000 Social Security pension at age 62. There are no administrators in this list just teachers.

	Name	School District	Age	First Year Pension	Years Work in IL
2011 Teacher Retirees With Beginning Pensions Over $100,000					
1	Sebald, David F	Leyden CHSD 212	57	127,875	32
2	Oddo, Linda L	New Trier TWP HSD 203	58	122,260	32
3	Kay, Bruce	Community HSD 155	56	117,765	32
4	Filippo, Anthony	Lake Forest CHSD 115	56	117,038	34
5	Gasper, Kip E	Highland Park 113	57	116,838	32
6	Kirwan, James P	Hinsdale TWP HSD 86	56	113,930	32
7	Nihells, Robert A	Lake Park CHSD 108	55	111,929	33
8	Kaplan, Susan	Highland Park 113	65	111,529	29
9	Lagesse, Gary L	Thornton TWP HSD 205	58	109,231	34
10	Scahill, Joseph G	DuPage HSD 88	56	108,801	33
11	Ratajczyk, Bruce	Highland Park 113	57	107,576	32
12	Fischer, Steven D	Lake Park CHSD 108	57	107,409	32
13	Richards, Evan	Lake Forest CHSD 115	57	106,299	35
14	Vanko, James S	Leyden CHSD 212	55	106,234	32
15	Blazevich, Richard	Northfield TWP HSD 225	60	105,936	36
16	Zizzo, Gary A	Lake Park CHSD 108	58	104,925	27
17	Vogel, Debra C	Lake Park CHSD 108	58	103,546	33
18	Cantor, Iris L	Niles TWP CHSD 219	60	102,746	28
19	Koval, Karen J	Lake Park CHSD 108	55	100,220	31

Obviously in the other four states there are no teachers with $100,000 pensions since there are only 11 with salaries over $100,000. This means in 2011 there were more teachers who retired with pensions greater than $100,000 (19) than four other states had teachers with salaries over $100,000 (11).

All of these statistics show that IL pension deficit is due more too excessive salaries than it does to lack of state payments. If Illinois had salaries similar to our neighbors in KY, IA, WI and MO our pension problems would be much less worse than they are.

If IL salaries and pensions were the same as WI we would save $4 billion per year in education costs.

High pensions are due to high salaries and high salaries are due to the NEA. Unless we control the NEA and their undue influence on IL politicians the pension problem will never be solved.

CHAPTER 5:

WHAT WE NEED TO DO TO SOLVE THE PROBLEM.

"Arithmetic will overwhelm wishful thinking sooner or later."

– Bill Zettler

5.1) Illinois Pensions and Intergenerational Theft.

How union bosses and politicians protected themselves at the expense of our children and grandchildren.

WHEN IT COMES to pensions, it is easy to manipulate public expectations, and therefore public beliefs, because the whole process is so complicated and esoteric almost no one on the outside understands it. Therefore a few very knowledgeable insiders can make an improbable financial future look like a sure thing, unthreatening and moderate when in fact it is disaster waiting to happen, the Titanic with the lifeboats reserved for the politically connected and their minions. The only casualties are the taxpayers, three generations of them in Illinois' case.

It is an example of a new breed of corruption – legal corruption. Why do you think most politicians are lawyers? So they can pass laws mealy-mouthed enough to escape any courtroom punishment yet flexible enough to be manipulated for political purpose.

Theft #1: How to keep pension contributions low and everybody happy – for a while.

If you are a union boss it is a plus if you can tell your members "We have a great pension plan and it won't cost you much." Ditto if you are a politician except you keep two groups happy – unions contributors and taxpaying voters.

How is this low-cost legerdemain accomplished – justifying $130,000 pensions at age 54 for public employees as reasonable while having to admit $22,000 pensions at 62 for Social Security paying private sector employees is on an unsustainable course?

It is accomplished by abusing the actuarial term "Assumed Interest Rate" (AIR) at the very beginning of the process. This serves more than one purpose but the key one is it is the Assumed Return On Investment (ROI). Meaning they assume the assets in the pension fund will increase by 8.5% per year for 35 years. As we all know that is not likely to happen going forward.

Under government rules (GASB) 8.5% is the highest interest rate allowed. Of the hundreds of public pension funds only a handful use 8.5% and that handful includes the TRS pension funds. As a comparison, public companies (such as IBM) must by IRS rules use 6.1% and Social Security uses 4.5%.

The Pension Benefit Guaranty Corp. (PBGC), the company chartered to fund all bankrupt public corporations (United Airlines was the biggest company to transfer its pension obligations to PBGC) uses 4% to come up with their $35 billion unfunded pension liability. If IL used 4% as their AIR the unfunded balance for IL pensions would be $220 billion six times PBGC.

Simply put the higher the Assumed Interest Rate the lower the contribution rate so Illinois, by assuming the highest rate allowed is able to tell both employees and employers (that's us the taxpayers) their contribution rate is so low there is no reason not to keep increasing salaries and pension benefits. It's as if everything is free.

The key word though is "assumed". What if the assumption is too high as it was the last 10 years when Illinois pension funds averaged about 3% ROI? Well in that case the contributions must go up to make up for the investment losses and in Illinois' case that means all the extra contribution comes from the taxpayer not the employee. He keeps his phony low rate while our rate skyrockets.

How high does it go? Right now the actuaries say we must pay about 30% of every public employee's salary into his pension fund in order to make sure he's a multi-millionaire when he retires and we must do this for the next 35 years. So state employees (teachers, university and state) pay an average of 6.9% and taxpayers pay 30%.

And keep in mind this is a "Best Case Scenario." If they do another 3% average return over the next 10 years like they did the last 10 years we will be looking at taxpayers paying 55% of public employees' salary into the pension system to keep them on their multi-millionaire track. That's compared to your employer's 6.2% pay-in for Social Security.

How does this affect the next two generations? Because contribution rates were knowingly too low at the beginning, actual pensions granted were too high to be supported by the artificially low contribution rates originally granted. This has guaranteed future generations would pay extra billions in cost to support a pension payout structure that was based on false assumptions and illegitimate from day one.

Here is the "Best Case Scenario" Payout:
(It will most certainly be much worse)

$ 78 billion	- 2009 Unfunded Pension Liability
$ 230 billion	- 2009-2034 Pension taxes paid in
$ 142 billion	- 2034 Unfunded Pension Liability up $64 billion from 2009.
$ 4.5 billion	- 2010 Pension Tax Payment
$ 15 billion	- 2034 Pension Tax Payment
$ 24 billion	- 2044 Pension Tax Payment

When does the current $78 billion unfunded decrease? Not until 2044. Best case.

Yes, under the "best case" we pay in $230 billion in taxes to the pension system over the next 25 years and leave a $142 billion Unfunded Pension Liability to our children, almost twice what it is today. We will also leave them with a $15 billion pension tax payment, four times what ours is today. And that's the "best case" – heaven helps us if we see the worst case.

This, ladies and gentlemen, is Intergenerational Theft Example 1.

Theft #2: Actuarial methods can rob our children too.
The two most common methods of determining pension liability are PUC (Projected Unit Credit) and EANL (Entry Age Normal Level). For accounting reasons PUC is almost always used by private sector employers and EAN is almost always used by public sector employers. So why did Illinois chose PUC instead of EAN for calculating its pension costs?

Because PUC allows you to legally move most of the pension costs to future generations.

Here is a simple example. Assume you have a 30 year-old employee who is going to work 35 years and will start at $50,000 and get 5% increases each year for 35 years and then he will retire on his pension. The following are the pension costs associated with each method:

	EANL Pension Cost	PUC Pension Cost
Year 1	930	166
Year 5	930	386
Year 10	930	787
Year 15	930	1,464
Year 20	930	2,682
Year 25	930	4,954
Year 30	930	9,281
Year 35	930	17,849

Notice how early on, while the politician is still in office, the costs for the chosen PUC method are low compared to what they would be if they had chosen EANL. Then as they approach year 15 they begin to exceed EANL costs until at year 35 PUC pension costs are more than 100 times what they were in year 1. Of course if you are a politician or a union leader, who cares? You are either dead or retired by then.

However you are, in effect, stealing $17,849 from future generations 35 years after you initiated the plan.

This, ladies and gentlemen, is Intergenerational Theft Example 2.

Theft #3: Pension Obligation Bonds and Interest Only sub-prime loans have something in common.

One of Rod Blagojevich's greatest sales jobs (and there were many) was in 2003 when he convinced the state legislature to saddle the Illinois taxpayers with a $10 billion financial millstone called Pension Obligation Bonds. Of course we didn't get the whole $10 billion, about $900,000 or so went to various and sundry Blago hangers on, contributors, sycophants and boot-lickers including the well know Kjellander, Kelly, Rezko and Levine. But I digress.

The nature of the bonds was like sub-prime lending because they were sold as interest only in the first four years and interest only plus .5% of principal in the next four years.

The end result is 76% of the principal of the 2003 Pension Obligation Bonds are due in the last 10 years of the 30-year bond from 2024 to 2033 just when your kids will be paying taxes.

This, ladies and gentlemen, is Intergenerational Theft Example 3.

Three strikes and our children's future is out.
Notice how all three items ending up costing a lot more during the period 2025 – 2040. This means if you have teenagers now they and their children will be picking up these huge tabs left to them by the politicians of the last decade or so.

More pension obligations, more pension payments and more bond payments, all funds going into the insatiable maw of the Illinois public pension system.

This, ladies and gentlemen, is Intergeneration Theft of the first magnitude.

What the next governor should do.
The last political generation's malfeasance will cost the next generation of taxpayers their financial freedom unless there is fundamental pension reform

Real pension reform will save our children's financial future. That is the purpose of the reform and that is how you generate support for the reform.

The need for reform and the support for reform are there; it only requires courage and political leadership.

So who will lead? ⇐

5.2) Illinois' $30 billion/yr. K-12 Cost Can Be Reduced Significantly.
St Libory Public School District 30 shows us how to do it.

THE MOST COSTLY government function in Illinois, by far, is K-12 education funding. Few realize how much we spend because that is information that could reflect badly on those who benefit the most from the $30 billion namely teachers and politicians. Therefore their goal is to obfuscate, fight transparency every step of the way and use cost information that conveniently leaves out billions of dollars of cost in order to make taxpayers think cost per student is really less than it is.

The ISBE (Illinois State Board of Education) provides a report called "Total Expenditures, Operating Expense Per Pupil" from costs collected for each of the 870 school districts. Those local school reports are in a standard, virtually undecipherable format based upon what looks like a 44 page Excel spreadsheet. Even someone who is experienced in reading financial reports will have their eyes glaze over as they plow through pages of column totals without a combined or "Grand Total". That is because schools do everything by fund (Education Fund, Transportation Fund, Operations Fund etc.) and no one (except us taxpayers) cares how much they spend in total.

If you are up to it take a look at Stevenson High School Dist. 125's report on their website.

Note that important information that taxpayers really want to see such as salaries, fringe benefits and pensions for teachers are nowhere to be found on Stevenson's web site. In another example of obfuscation and lack of transparency the few administrative salaries they did post to their website showed Superintendent Eric Twadell with a salary of $181,800, a seemingly modest amount considering Stevenson reported a salary of $191,124 for a Phys Ed teacher last year. The problem is they reported Twadell's salary to ISBE as $248,243. So why is the reported salary local taxpayers see on Stevenson's website $67,000 less than the salary reported to the state? Is this the transparency Gov. Quinn talks about?

Average cost per student is actually $16,000 not the well-advertised $11,000.
The end result of this fiscal legerdemain is an ISBE report that shows average expenditures per student for all 870 districts at $11,196.

But that number conveniently ignores the following costs:
1. "Other Expenditures". In Stevenson's case this is $21 million out of $86 million.
2. Pension cost. Since pensions are paid at the state level school districts conveniently ignore these $3.9 billion costs (2010) as not part of education expense.
3. Pension bond interest cost. This is another $600 million/yr. that does not get added into "education Expense".
4. State and regional education costs of about $50 million.

When we include all of these costs as part of "Education Expenses" we come up with $30.1 billion spread over 1,881,000 Average Daily Attendance (ADA) students for an average cost of $16,002 per ADA student fully 43% higher than the number commonly thrown around by politicians and union honchos. In Stevenson's case their website says $15,191 per student while the "Real" all inclusive education costs comes out at $23,303.

Here are the Top 10 Schools by "Real" cost per pupil including all pension and other costs. Note Chicago District 299 is above average in expenditures. It is not a poor district having 1,735 employees making over $100,000/yr.

SCHOOL	Expenditures	Real Cost/Pupil
Lake Forest CHSD 115	61,155,240	43,061
Northfield Twp. HSD 225	124,452,468	32,993
Bannockburn SD 106	5,241,924	32,630
Winnetka SD 36	49,558,549	32,043
Highland Park HSD 113	89,347,548	29,945
Niles Twp CHSD 219	109,226,136	29,204
Kenilworth SD 38	12,462,450	27,288
Sunset Ridge SD 29	10,740,763	26,038
Avoca SD 37	14,882,835	25,939
New Trier Twp. HSD 203	88,609,582	25,740

City of Chicago SD 299	5,548,468,036	18,090
Average All 870 Schools		16,026

St. Libory District 30 shows the way to hold down costs.

Meanwhile down in St. Clair county 30 miles from St. Louis lies the small town of St. Libory with the aptly named school St. Libory School District 30. Here the all-inclusive "Real" cost per student is $10,711, less than ½ as much as Stevenson.

If you go to the St. Libory website you will see the teachers' contract and the superintendent's contract right at the bottom of the page. Teachers' contract is 15 pages (still too long) vs. 47 pages for Stevenson's. The St Libory's superintendent's contract is 5 pages. I was unable to find Superintendent Eric Twadell's contract for $181,000 on the Stevenson website. Or was it $248,000?

There are interesting comparisons between Dist. 30 and Stevenson salaries. The superintendent's salary, with a PhD, is $76,570 in the contract and $76,570 reported to the state as opposed to Stevenson's $181,000 and $248,000 respectively. Highest teacher salary at Dist. 30 is $44,294 while lowest salary at Stevenson is $52,454. Forty-seven percent of Stevenson's employees make more than $100,000 and fully 77% make more than Dist. 30's superintendent. In fact the 26 part-time teachers at Stevenson average more than the highest paid teacher at Dist. 30.

And St. Libory's teachers are doing an excellent job too – the school rates at 92 on a 100- point scale for standardized state tests vs. a state average of 78. In addition St. Libory spends 56% of its budget in the classroom compared to the state average of 46% and Stevenson's 47%. If all schools would cut overhead until classroom costs matched St. Libory's 56% of budget instead of 46% state taxpayers would save $5 billion/yr.

Even taking into account the difference in cost-of-living between the two areas it is obvious that the hiring of good teachers and superintendents does not require making them millionaires.

Stevenson High School has the right to pay their employees whatever they want as long as they pay all the other costs associated with them too.

Let's make school districts pay their own pension costs including interest on the Pension Obligation Bonds. This would add $11 million to Stevenson's budget and $157,000 to St. Libory's.

Why should the hard-working people of St. Libory be stuck with paying taxes for the outrageous pensions for Stevenson's employees?

To show you the magnitude of the problem here is a side-by-side comparison between Stevenson's Top 10 pension payouts and St. Libory's Top 7. Why 7? That's all the retirees they have.

Note that all 10 of Stevenson retirees *individually* have annual pensions that exceed the entire property tax income of St. Libory's Education Fund $117,330. Additionally, the top five Stevenson pensions combined exceed the entire St. Libory budget of $742,481.

This wealth transfer from the poor to the rich should outrage St. Libory taxpayers, and indeed all Illinois taxpayers.

The time for massive pension reform is now. Transferring pension to the schools where they belong would save the state $3 billion/yr. until reform is complete.

Those who cause the pension problem should pay for it.

Stevenson HS Dist. 125 High Pensions				St Libory Dist. 30 High Pensions		
NAME	Mo. Pension	Annual Pension		NAME	Mo. Pension	Annual Pension
Hintz, James S	16,787	201,444		Brickey, Carol S	2,864	34,366
Kanold, Timothy D	15,973	191,674		McCormack, Carol	2,578	30,936
Dufour, Richard P	15,751	189,015		Diecker, Charlotte	2,423	29,082
Martin, John D	12,199	146,386		May, Ruth	2,172	26,068
Galloway, Dan A	11,636	139,634		Mueth, Marian L	1,893	22,715
Giglio, Beth	10,778	129,340		Kellerman, Rebecca L	1,349	16,193
Green, Richard P	10,578	126,934		Compas, Celeste	740	8,881
Karhanek, Gayle A	10,512	126,141				
Gallenberger, Catarina V	10,497	125,968				
Raffaelli, Philip N	9,918	119,021				

5.3) Pension Reform Plan: Taxpayer Costs Must Be Fixed Not Unlimited.

Pension costs must be part of total compensation not separate and apart.

THE BIGGEST SINGLE problem that needs to be addressed as part of any comprehensive pension reform in Illinois is the idea that taxpayers are responsible for every shortcoming of the current system whether it is investment returns, benefit increases or 8.5% interest charges on assets that do not exist. Currently this is accomplished by having the state pay pensions separate from the operating budgets of each government unit. Thus one party determines salaries, fringe benefits, vacations, sick leave etc. and the pensions are paid by the state regardless of the cost.

What needs to be done is to fix the taxpayer portion of the cost and assign all pension costs above that amount to the operating budgets of each government unit whether State Police, community colleges or K12 school districts. Total compensation paid to each public employee should include the costs of pensions and when that is not the case salaries automatically rise to fill the gap left by pension cost not being part of total compensation. This is exactly what happens in Illinois now because those who determine salaries and fringe benefits are not assigned pension cost responsibility. This results in Illinois taxpayers paying more both for salaries and pensions.

This pension proposal assigns pension costs to operating entities and shows how to pay for them. It fixes taxpayer pension cost at 15% of payroll and all pension cost in excess of that must come out of departmental budgets and employee compensation costs.

The goals of this pension reform proposal are as follows:
1. Fix taxpayer pension costs at a reasonable figure similar to what would be paid in a Social Security/401K plan.
2. Force managers to manage by assigning all compensation and health care costs to their budgets. Freeze those budgets for 5 years.

3. Make employees understand that there are only so many dollars available and that pension contributions are part of their pay and if pensions go up then salary or fringe benefits must come down. A compensation dollar can only go towards one compensation element.

4. Give employees some flexibility by allowing them to switch compensation elements around as long as the total does not exceed their assigned total compensation value. More insurance and less pension or less insurance and more salary for example.

5. Give employees more cash-out options than they have now as long as it does not increase pension costs. This can be done by adjusting pension payouts down slightly and will make pensions more portable similar to 401K's.

6. Attempt to get reform buy-in from all groups by emphasizing the draconian cuts (including employment itself) that will and must be made if taxpayer pension costs are not reduced substantially.

7. Quick resolution is mandatory and a legal resolution will take years to resolve. Amending the constitution will also take years unless we can round up 300,000 signatures.

We need to get Illinois Open for Business by solving the problem quickly and efficiently. As it stands now no business in their right mind would open shop here and many are leaving. We must be competitive or we will wither and die on the vine. We can either be the next Indiana or the next Michigan.

The bomb is ticking and time is running out. ═

5.3.1) Pension Reform Plan Part 1: Purpose, reasoning and implementation. State of Illinois Pension Reform Outline:

PURPOSE: Limit taxpayer liability to 15% of state employee payroll.

REASONING: As the pension law is currently constituted, taxpayers are required to pay all shortages in the pensions' short and long-term liabilities plus interest at 8.5%. Employees' liability is limited to their current contribution rates (4% to 8%). Thus whatever the unfunded pension liability is ($85, $150, $200 billion?) 100% of it must be paid for by the taxpayers via higher and higher taxes.

(Argument for: why do the 95% of Illinois workers who do not belong to the state pension system have to contribute via taxes 4 times as much as the than the 5% who do?)

JUSTIFICATION: The very best private sector pension system costs about 14% of employee payroll - 6.2% for Social Security and 8% matching 401K contributions. Therefore this bill, at 15% of payroll, would provide the highest paid employer pension/retirement contribution in Illinois.

(Argument for: What could be fairer than the highest contribution in the state?)

A. IMPLEMENTATION:

Step 1: Define "Total compensation" for every job description as consisting of the following elements for budget purposes:

1. Salary
2. Plus overtime cost
3. Plus pension contribution cost (local, state, federal)
4. Plus health insurance cost
5. Plus other insurance (life, disability, dental, vision) cost
6. Plus sick days accrual cost
7. Plus personal days cost

8. Plus vacation days cost

9. Plus holiday days cost

10. Plus education reimbursement cost.

(Argument for: every one of these costs is paid for by the taxpayer therefore the taxpayer must control each of them as part of the total employee cost.)

Step 2: For state and university employees freeze that compensation cost at 2010 levels thru 2015 at which time it will be reviewed. For K-12 employees see below.

(Argument for: they probably should be cut not frozen.)

Step 3: State and university departmental budgets are frozen at 2010 level plus pension contribution (equal to 15% of payroll) and health care costs from state. Then from this point forward the managers of each state/university department/unit-of-government are now responsible for allocating costs for all 10 elements of "Total Compensation" as listed above. Thus pension costs over 15% of payroll would have to come out of the rest of the budget see "Allowable Pension Budget Adjustments" below.

The state would no longer accept responsibility for funding pension and health-care costs on an unlimited, ad-hoc basis. Costs would be allocated to the departments that generate and control those costs by their hiring and promotion policies. It is up to the managers who are being paid to manage to control and allocate costs just like in the private sector. No more "we don't care because the state picks up the cost". Their pay will depend upon how well they manage their costs as well as the execution of their business plan. For health insurance multiple lower-cost options would be provided including HSA's.

(Argument for: it's time to make managers manage.)

Step 4: Schools K12 are independent units with independent sources of elected control and revenue sources therefore it is only proper that they too be responsible for controlling all of their costs including pensions. Therefore pension cost equal to 15% of payroll would be paid by the state but all amounts in excess of 15% would be allocated back to the schools based upon average certified full-time salary. Thus schools that paid the highest salaries would be allocated the highest portion of excess pensions to pay, formula to be determined. Salary increases in excess of 5% or the average of other workers in the pension system (whichever is lower), as determined by state actuaries, would also be the responsibility of the local district with that portion in excess being allocated to school districts under the average thus lowering pension costs for schools who control salaries. In addition if non-classroom costs are above a certain level (50%) then districts would be liable for all pension costs. Alternatively, state funds could be withheld from high pension cost districts in lieu of pension payments.

(Argument for: those that create the pension problem with excessive salaries should pay for the pensions.) ═

5.3.2) Part 2: How pension costs can be allocated.

B. ALLOWABLE PENSION BUDGET ADJUSTMENTS – State and University: Once a "Total Compensation" value is arrived at adjustments could be made by the managers annually to fit their budget needs.

Currently state pension costs are about 33.3% of payroll (including interest on pension bonds) and change every year according to multiple assumptions used by state actuaries. Health care costs are about 20% of payroll.

As an example let's use a department with a $10 million budget in 2010 with a $6 million payroll. The budget for 2012 would be $12.1 million because the state would kick in $900,000 (15% of payroll) for the state's share of pensions. It would also provide the health insurance cost of $1.2 million (20% of payroll). That leaves 18% of payroll or $1.1 million for the department's share of pension costs that the department must come up with out of its budget of $12.1 million. In effect the manager must squeeze 9% out of his budget to pay for pensions.

Here are some cuts that can go towards the 9% (all %'s approximate):
1. One day a month furlough – 2%
2. Health Savings Accounts instead of the state insurance plan – 4%
3. Change maximum vacation days to 3 weeks from 5 weeks – 1%
4. Sick day accrual 10 days to 5 days – 1%
5. Layoff 4% of employees – 3%
6. Lower final pension by 5% - 2%
7. Allow employees with needed skill sets to work as sub-contractors at a rate lower than their total compensation. College faculty and administrators would excellent recruits for this type of privatization. They would then be responsible for their own pensions and fringe benefits. See "If It's in the Yellow Pages Privatize It" below. Savings variable.

As mentioned before K-12 are independent of the state and must determine their own cuts but all of the above apply to them also.

Note that in the above example if employees agreed to take 8% less in pensions no layoffs would need to be made. Since the current pensions are 3 to 10 times better than Social Security this might be an agreement all employees could agree on. In fact state employees, who have Social Security and the best dollar for dollar pension plan in the state, could cut their pensions and still retire with take home pay greater or equal to their final working take home.
(Argument for: One, state employees have a pension system far superior to anything in the private sector and therefore they should pay more for it; secondly taxpayers MUST have a limited liability.)

C. CHANGE IN PENSION RULES THAT COULD LESSEN CUTS:
1. Increase employee pension contributions by 4% (2% for those on Social Security). This would be the equivalent of lowering the pension Interest Rate of Return to 6% from 8%; which is more realistic (recalculate the Normal Cost.)
2. Eliminate all "Spiking" by restricting final year's salary increase (auto 6%/yr. increase for 4 years for teachers for example). Salary increases limited to cost of living last 4 years and only base salary can be used for pension calculations.
3. Use last 8 years salaries for average not last four or last one as in the case of legislators and Illinois State Police.
4. Reverse all benefit enhancements since 1998 including Early Retirement Option for teachers and sick leave accrual used for pension credit.
5. Tax state pensions over $50,000 and earmark money for pension payments.
6. Revert COLA to 1970 pension rules: 1.5% not compounded and earmark money for pension payments.
7. Pay off pension bonds thus eliminating interest costs.
(Argument for: this eliminates many "gimmicks" that have been added just to enhance what was already an outstanding pension plan. These are items that are especially irksome to taxpayers.)

D. EMPLOYEE REFORM ENHANCEMENTS:
1. Sell State Assets and use the money to pay off pension bonds. Anything left would be added to pension assets.

… Tollway

… Lotto

… Real estate including but not limited to: buildings, Thompson Correctional, parks

… Oil/ gas leasing rights to the New Albany shale gas fields covering most of eastern IL.

2. Allow employees at any time to take their contributions with interest actually earned plus state's 15% contribution without interest and leave the system. Actuarial adjustment to pensions would be required for this option to be implemented.

3. Allow employees to adjust their compensation according to their needs as long as the total cost remains the same. For example they could reduce pension and increase insurance coverage or cut vacations and increase salary

(Argument for: providing enhancements for employees would help sell the plan. If the cost to the state is neutral why not do it? The goal is to reduce state pension costs to manageable levels, end economic uncertainty and avoid long, drawn out legal action.) ⸺

5.3.3) Part 3: What happens if agreement is not reached?

E. IF IT IS IN THE YELLOW PAGES PRIVATIZE IT:

THIS WAS FORMER FL Gov. Jeb Bush's rule on reducing state costs and influence. All we would need to do this is hire one of his former assistants to head up the program in IL. Some functions that come quickly to mind are janitorial services, trucking, IT services, phone banks, corrections, Tollways, Lotto etc. Illinois State Police functions could be outsourced to county sheriff's departments if the sub contract cost is lower. Education credits for home schooling and private schools are another area ripe for savings in direct payroll as well as pensions and fringe benefits. Make teachers of non-academic subjects (Drivers Ed, Music, Art etc.) and non-tenured college faculty sub-contractors rather than employees. Sub-contracting is already done at the community college level why not at K-12 and at 4-year institutions?

(Argument for: the ultimate solution to high pension costs is to eliminate employees. Once an employee is fired or sub-contracted your pension costs go to zero.)

F. COST SAVING OPTIONS IF AGREEMENT NOT REACHED:

The following items are NOT guaranteed by the Constitution and therefore can be "diminished and impaired" at will.

1. Salary cuts, furloughs and layoffs.
2. Health insurance contribution increased substantially including retirees.
2. Vacations cut.
3. Sick days retirement accruals eliminated completely.
4. Holidays cut from 12 to 8.
5. Life insurance eliminated.
6. Outsourcing begins including Drivers Ed back to private sector.
7. 100% of pension costs transferred to local school districts.
8. Tenure law opened for revision including elimination or severe limits.
9. Collective bargaining law reopened for revision.

10. Open Meetings Act expanded to include public participation in all labor contracts.

11. New law requiring voter approval of all contracts increasing costs more than the Cost-of Living.

12. End of career (last 5 years) raises limited to cost-of-living.

13. Option to pay all pension amounts over $75,000/yr. with state IOU's.

14. Education funding frozen or cut.

15. Allow Community Colleges to offer 4-year degrees thus lowering state costs by cutting enrollment at high cost state universities.

16. Initiate change arbitrarily and let the courts decide if it's legal (see LEGAL OPTIONS BELOW).

17. Begin Constitutional Amendment process (300,000 signatures or 60% vote in House and Senate).

(Argument for: if pension costs cannot be limited then they must come out of current budgeted items. Legal changes must be made to minimize liability.)

G. REVIEW OF LEGAL OPTIONS:

Legal opinions are varied. The Chicago law firm Sidley Austin has studied the issue and are convinced in-place changes to pension rules (higher contribution rates, later retirements, etc.) can be made without abrogating the Constitutional guarantee. Their reading of the law says that employee's pension accruals are guaranteed but only up to the day changes are implemented. From that point forward, the new rules apply.

On the other hand Professor Amy Monahan of the University of Minnesota Law School says no, whatever the rules were in place when they were hired are guaranteed until they retire. Therefore interim changes cannot be made.

They both agree that a Constitutional Amendment can make serious changes including eliminating the guarantee and imposing draconian limits including reverting to the previous legal framework called "gratuity pensions" which were not and are not guaranteed at all. Texas and Indiana have "gratuity" pension systems. Social Security is a "gratuity" system so why shouldn't they all be "gratuity"?

There is also the question of changes being made against the constitutional contract guarantee if it is "to serve an important public purpose" or if the original contractual obligation "had effects that were unforeseen and unintended by the legislature". One would think state de facto or de jure bankruptcy was "unforeseen and unintended."

CONCLUSION:

The electorate is angry and much more knowledgeable of pension abuses now than they were just a few years ago. A constitutional amendment should be put forward sometime between now and 2015 if a reasonable limit is not established soon for taxpayer pension liabilities. We need a plan similar to this, severely limiting taxpayer liability going forward or a serious conflict will arise and it will be ugly and drawn out.

If in 1970 politicians had told us that at some time in the future pension tax payments would reach 82% of state employees pay would we have voted for the constitutional amendment? Of course not. And that 82% is what we are currently paying for – hold on – the politicians pensions in the General Assembly Retirement System.

Ironic? No, infuriating.

Just because something is legal does not mean it is not corrupt. The state pension system is corrupt and needs to be changed. If it isn't Illinois will see an exodus unlike anything it has seen before. And it won't be the poor people leaving either. It will be the taxpaying public.

At that point the only way to pay Illinois bills will be to tax moving vans. ═

5.4.1) Pension Solution: Retire the Pension Systems.

401K Plans For All Employees in the State Pension System.

I L HOUSE LEADER Tom Cross has suggested a new plan to resolve the pension funding issue.

It has three new options for current employees (not retired employees):

1. Employees could stay in the current plan but contribute more. Increased amount would vary by system but average about 5% of salary more. This is known as "Tier 1".

2. Employee could transfer to new plan introduced in March of 2010 whereby workers must work until 67 to get full retirement. This is known as "Tier 2" and includes everyone hired after Jan 1, 2011 and all those in "Tier 1" who chose to change to "Tier 2" under the new system.

3. Employees and the state would both contribute 6% to a 401K/401A Defined Contribution type plan. Anyone from Tier 1 or Tier 2 could select this option.

Below we will look at each of these options in detail. But before we do that we must accept the following caveat:

THE $85 BILLION LIABILITY TALKED ABOUT CONSTANTLY IS A PRETEND NUMBER AND IS ALMOST CERTAINLY TOO LOW.

Tentative contribution rates (of salary) for each of the five pension systems as outlined in IL Senate Bill 512 (SB512).

System Plan	Current Rate (Tier 1)	Rate to stay in Tier 1	Tier 2 Rate	401K Defined Contrib. Rate
1 SERS (State) with Social Security	4%	9.29%	4.04%	4.04%
2 SERS (State) alternative without Social Security	12.50%	18.91%	6%	6%
3 SERS (State) alternative with Social Security	8.50%	16.65%	4.46%	4.46%
4 TRS (Teachers)	8%	13.77%	6%	6%
5 SURS (University)	7%	15.31%	6%	6%
6 GARS (General Assembly)	11.50%	24.89%	6%	6%
7 JRS (Judges - maybe?)	11%	34.04%	6%	6%

NOTE 1: Items 2 & 3 are security personnel such as State Troopers and represent a less than 5% of SERS members

NOTE 2: JRS (Judges) as of now will not be required to change.

Why would anyone switch to a new plan? Only because they have no other choice.

People in the current Tier 1 category representing 99% of current active members, i.e. current employees not retirees, would have no choice but to switch to one of the three alternatives. In other words under Cross's plan Tier 1, as currently constituted, is going away never to return. So Cross's plan is to force people into plans that would be more affordable to the state.

Under the new TRS plan (170,000 active members) teacher's contribution would be upped from 8% (9.4% with ERO and death benefit but only 8% for pension) to 13.77%, a minor increase of a little more than 4%. If you compare to WI teachers whose pension contribution just went up 5% and MO teachers who pay 14% that seems reasonable considering the value of the pension. I don't see many teachers, except perhaps very young ones with few years in the current system switching over. If I am right, the biggest potential state savings from teachers will not occur in any significant amount because the state's contribution rate will only drop from 31% to 27% for all those remaining in the current system.

After taxes teachers would only be paying about 3% more for membership in what is arguably the best pension system in the country.

Ditto for SURS (85,000 active University employees). Although their rate would go up about 5% after taxes no one is going to want to work until 67 when they are retiring at an average age of 59 now. In 2009 the retirees with $100K pensions only averaged 29 years work. Think they are going to hang in there for another 8 years and get less just to save 5%?

As for State Employees (SERS – 64,000 active members) over 95% have Social Security and with that as a base some may switch to Tier 2 since they can't take Social Security until 62 or they may take the 401K so they will have cash when they retire. They also on average make considerably less than teachers or university employees so the jump in contribution rate from 4% to 9% may be more difficult for them to do.

GARS (182 active members) and JRS (966 active members) do not even rise to the level of a rounding error so we will ignore them completely even though looking at the percentage increases they are impressive. Ho hum.

<u>None of these options will diminish the $85 billion ($200 billion?) unfunded.</u>
That's the $85 billion that might really be $200 billion but why quibble.

The unfunded amount calculated each year is based upon what's owed as of June 30 to every active employee (employed as of June 30), every retiree and every inactive member (those that are vested but not working or taking retirement yet) minus what we have in the bank. It does not include any changes that may occur in the future.

What SB512 might do is lower the rate of increase in the unfunded each year. Under current law from 2011 thru 2031 the pretend-projected unfunded is projected to grow from pretend $85 billion in 2010 to pretend $160 billion in 2032. Based upon most members staying in their current system even with the increased employee contributions that number may drop somewhat but again the $85 billion is a pretend number and if the 8% ROI between now and 2031 is really 4% the funds will be effectively bankrupt before 2032 and it won't make any difference which plan they are in.

So the Tom Cross plan does not address the key issue affecting the state pensions, which is the Interest Rate assumption (ROI) of the pensions systems. If that number is wrong the increase in unfunded will overwhelm any minor savings induced by the three Tier plan. It is another case of IL politicians being too meek and too beholden to public employees to really effect the massive changes needed from top to bottom.

Here's how we retire the pension system.
Why is the government in the retirement business anyway?

Political control is the only reason. If the state controls the future retirements of the state employees then they control a huge block of voters and donors. They also can hand out favors to powerful commercial interests such investment bankers, advisors, consultants, brokers and, of course, attorneys.

So the solution to those massive sources of special interest and ethical conflict is to retire the pension system now. Free up public employees from being dependent upon politicians for their wellbeing. Free up taxpayers from being stuck with the bill for pension special interests.

Eliminate Tier 1 and Tier 2 and just convert all employees to 401K type plans.
Whatever plan you put forward is going to trigger a lawsuit so why not go with the plan that will permanently solve the problem: all employees, current and future on 401K plans.

Besides if you are going to take the heat and generate a lawsuit anyway why not really do something significant and implement only the 6% 401K plan for all employees, no other option available? If the 3 point Cross plan is legal then the 6% 401K would be legal by itself. So get rid of Tier 1 and Tier 2 altogether.

And if they put the 6% 401K state contribution back on the employers where it belongs (school districts would pay it directly and state entities would have it forced into their current budgets) all increased pension costs over the next 35 years would be eliminated because no new employee salaries would be entering the system, whether raises or new hires. This would retire the pension system almost completely over the next 35 years as every year the states funding obligation would be getting smaller and smaller as current members retire and no new members enter. And keep in mind all the current members pensions would be frozen at the rate earned as of the conversion date. So a teacher with 10 years would get 22% when they retired (plus their 401K), 5 years would get 11% etc.

Why converting everyone to 401K/401A plan would save approx. $200 billion.

Under the current plan taxpayers have to build up assets in the pension plan from $50 billion now to about $300 billion in 2045 all the while paying current and future pensions. That's required to support the 90% plan i.e. have enough money in the bank to pay pensions going forward from 2045 with mostly investment returns.

Under the new plan we would use the $50 billion we have now to subsidize the current pensions we have to pay-off over what in effect is the next 65 years (new employees hired this year work for 35 years and retire for 30 more). We don't have to raise $300 billion by 2045 or pay for any newly accrued pensions and therefore our annual payments will be much less. By 2045 there will still be a lot of pensions being paid out but they will be at a very low rate since by 2045 no new people would have entered the pension system in 35 years and those that did (those working in 2011 who are vested) would be paid off at an ever lower percentage of their salary (as low as 2.2%).

The following table is just an estimate or "model" of future savings. I have complained about "models" before as not being definitive since they have an infinite number of possible outcomes based upon the assumptions made. And some of my assumptions could be wrong. So these numbers are one estimate but Cross could get the state actuaries (who have more info than I do) to do a similar estimate.

Why not do that right now?

Pension Reform That Saves $200 Billion
_All numbers in billions of dollars.

	Pension Payout	Assets	ROI @8%	New State Contribution	6% SURS&SERS 401K	Total New State Con-trib.	Old State Contrib	Savings New vs Old
2010	7.2	51.0	4.1	2.8	0.4	3.2	4.0	0.8
2011	7.4	50.6	4.0	2.9	0.4	3.3	4.5	1.2
2012	7.7	50.0	4.0	3.0	0.5	3.5	4.9	1.4
2013	7.9	49.3	3.9	3.1	0.5	3.6	5.3	1.7
2014	8.0	48.5	3.9	3.3	0.5	3.8	5.8	2.0
2015	8.2	47.5	3.8	3.4	0.5	3.9	6.2	2.3
2016	8.3	46.6	3.7	3.5	0.5	4.1	6.4	2.3
2017	8.4	45.6	3.6	3.7	0.6	4.2	6.7	2.5
2018	8.5	44.5	3.6	3.8	0.6	4.4	7.0	2.6
2019	8.6	43.5	3.5	4.0	0.6	4.6	7.3	2.7
2020	8.6	42.5	3.4	4.1	0.6	4.8	7.6	2.8
2021	8.6	41.6	3.3	4.3	0.6	5.0	7.9	2.9
2022	8.6	40.8	3.3	4.5	0.7	5.2	8.2	3.0
2023	8.6	40.1	3.2	4.7	0.7	5.4	8.6	3.2
2024	8.6	39.6	3.2	4.8	0.7	5.6	8.9	3.3
2025	8.5	39.2	3.1	5.0	0.8	5.8	9.3	3.5
2026	8.5	39.1	3.1	5.2	0.8	6.0	9.7	3.7
2027	8.4	39.1	3.1	5.3	0.8	6.1	10.1	4.0
2028	8.3	39.1	3.1	5.2	0.9	6.1	10.5	4.4
2029	8.2	39.1	3.1	5.1	0.9	6.0	10.9	4.9
2030	8.1	39.1	3.1	5.0	0.9	5.9	11.3	5.4
2031	8.0	39.2	3.1	4.9	1.0	5.9	11.6	5.7
2032	7.9	39.1	3.1	4.7	1.0	5.7	12.0	6.3
2033	7.7	39.1	3.1	4.6	1.0	5.6	12.5	6.9
2034	7.6	39.0	3.1	4.3	1.1	5.4	13.8	8.4
2035	7.4	38.9	3.1	4.2	1.1	5.3	14.0	8.7
2036	7.3	38.8	3.1	4.1	1.2	5.3	14.6	9.3
2037	7.1	38.7	3.1	3.9	1.2	5.1	14.6	9.5

2038	6.9	38.6	3.1	3.7	1.3	5.0	15.0	10.0
2039	6.7	38.5	3.1	3.5	1.3	4.8	15.4	10.6
2040	6.5	38.4	3.1	3.3	1.4	4.7	15.9	11.2
2041	6.3	38.3	3.1	3.1	1.4	4.5	16.4	11.9
2042	6.1	38.1	3.0	2.9	1.5	4.4	16.9	12.5
2043	5.9	38.0	3.0	2.7	1.5	4.2	17.3	13.1
2044	5.7	37.9	3.0	2.6	1.6	4.2	18.4	14.2
2045	5.6	37.9	3.0	2.5	1.7	4.2	18.9	14.7
			TOTALS:	142.0	32.6	174.5	388.4	213.9

Assumptions for above:

1. 25% of employees in the 5 state pension systems are not vested (2010 numbers). They would be due return of contributions not pensions.
2. 3% COLA is eliminated. Colorado, SD and MN have recently won lawsuits on this matter.
3. Salary increases are limited to 3%/yr. Increases above that number for vested employees would require additional contributions from employers/employees.
4. Mortality rate are assumed to be 2%/yr. from age 58.
5. Original $2.8 B state contribution increased by 4%/yr. until 2032 when it would revert to an amount needed to pay remaining benefit.
6. If assumed 8% ROI is not accomplished additional contributions would be made by employers and/or employees not the state.
7. School districts pay entire 6% 401K/401A employer contribution not the state.
8. Assumes $42,900 as average current payout and $78,000 average salary at retirement (TRS numbers).

The new system would be better for employees too.

The new system would be better for employees and release IL politics from the death-grip that politicians and unions have over not only taxpayers but public employees. Employees could quit and move on taking their retirement funds with them without being penalized. No one would have to remain a public employee in a dead-end job because they were afraid of losing their pension. Every penny of the contributions and investment gains is theirs to do with as they wish both their contributions and the states. And there is no vesting period – if you leave after a year you take employee and employer contributions with you as well as all investment gains.

Currently if you leave the system before you retire and want to take your money with you, you only receive your contribution back without interest. You get none of the state's contribution. In effect you are a slave on the pension plantation.

And employees could make additional tax free contributions above the 6% if they so choose.

Do IL politicians have enough courage to propose this plan?

The word "courage" and "IL politician" are seldom found in the same sentence and for good reason. I am hopeful but not optimistic.

The 401K plan is already on the table and this new approach is actually much simpler and easier to implement than the original bill. No confusing tiers and give backs. Just a simple solution everyone understands and which in my opinion will save the pensions already committed to without bankrupting the state and threatening all pension systems.

So Tom Cross, step up and take IL into a new and prosperous future. After all it's right there sitting in front of you.

The 95% of IL workers not in the state pension system are waiting for your courage. But we are not going to wait forever. ⇐

5.5) IL Professors Pension Reform Plan: More of the Same. Was this project part of their state salary or did it cost us extra?

THE INSTITUTE OF Government & Public Affairs (IGPA) recently released a report titled "Public Pension Policy in Illinois – An Introduction to a Crucial Issue." In it five University of Illinois professors from a variety of disciplines presume to educate us, once more, about the problems with the Illinois State Pension Systems. And, once more, they ignore or refuse to recognize the basic issues surrounding this "Crucial Issue." Some of their examples and many of their generalizations are disingenuous at best, deceptive at worst.

So let's just go from front to back of the study and point out problems we see in assumptions and outcomes. Keep in mind as we go thru this material that educators K-12 represent about 60% of the pension debt and the State University Retirement System (SURS), of which these authors are members, another 20%. So if we don't reform these two systems we have no chance of reform at all. It is also of interest that 99 of the Top 100 state pensions come from these two systems.

Page numbers refer to pages from the report "Public Pension Policy in Illinois – An Introduction to a Crucial Issue."

Part 1: Jumping all over the claim jumpers claims.

CLAIM: Employees who receive higher benefits receive lower salary (Page 8).
Not in Illinois. As we have pointed out in multiple cases Illinois salaries, pensions and benefits have all risen in the last decade or so especially since 1998. This uncontrolled spending on public employees has far outstripped any similar gains in the private sector.

Here is a simple example of how pension payouts and salaries for teachers have far outstripped Social Security employees (a proxy for private sector workers i.e. taxpayers). It is impossible to claim **higher benefits receive lower salary** after looking at this chart – where exactly is evidence of salary give-backs for any of the increased benefits handed to teachers since 1998? In fact according to state actuaries teacher salaries increased by $961 million above the 7% estimated increase since 2000.

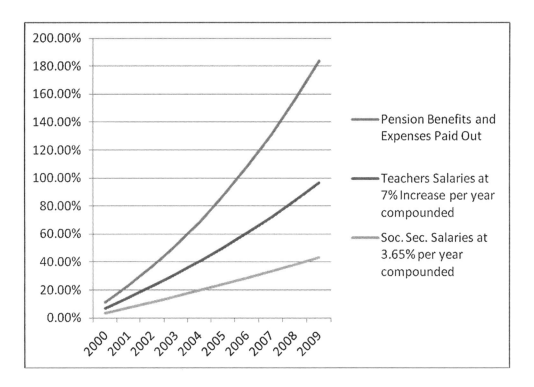

CLAIM: By offering a Defined Benefit plan, a firm is likely to attract workers who prefer to remain with an employer for their entire career.

I have seen no evidence of this; if there is a valid study I would like to see it. Most people who start working at age 21 or 22 don't even think about retirement benefits. A much more likely reason people go to work for the public sector, as studies by the Center for Retirement Research at Boston College have found, is the level of CRRA (Coefficient of Relative Risk Aversion) a person has. Those with a higher CRRA are more likely to choose a job with less employment risk (risk aversion) and are willing to pay for the stability by accepting lower compensation. In other words people go to work for government because they view the job as safer long-term not because they have a Defined Benefit plan.

What could be lower risk than a job with tenure? A job with tenure and a defined benefit plan that's what. Therefore those jobs should pay/compensate much less not more. Less risk therefore less pay.

On the other hand those with a low level of CRRA would be more likely to accept a sales position on straight commission such as real estate where both the risk and reward are much higher than say teaching.

So the stability of government jobs should lend itself to lower compensation not higher.

CLAIM: "Reducing pension benefits… has the effect as a reduction in total compensation and hinders the government's ability to recruit a skilled workforce."
If Social Security and 401K do not "hinder" private sector employers from hiring skilled people why should it hinder public employers? Assuming the Center for Retirement Research is correct we should be able to adequately staff government with lower compensation than private sector by hiring risk-averse people. By over-compensating we are diverting tax resources to compensation from higher priority areas such as services for the poor. That is exactly what is happening in Illinois where the Department of Family Services budget is cut by $180 million and $400,000/yr. retirees get $12,000/yr. COLA increases.

When public vs. private "quit rate" is the same then compensation is balanced.
There is a simple metric for determining when or if compensation is adequate: when turnover in the public sector matches that of the private sector. According to the BLS (Bureau of Labor Statistics) the average quit rate in state and local government is one-third that of the private sector. So logically it would follow that public compensation should be reduced to the point where the quit rates are equal. According to Boston College's research that point would be where public compensation is well below private sector compensation not vice-versa as in Illinois.

According to ISBE (Illinois State Board of Education) the retention rate for teachers is 96% (net of retirements) the highest rate of any white-collar profession. That same report shows at least 50,000 teachers with IL Certification are not teaching giving an unemployment rate of about 25%. So why do we have to pay 14,000 public school employees over $100,000/yr. when there are 50,000 waiting in the wings? In a free market the cost of teachers would be coming down not going up. High teacher compensation, including pensions, is a direct result of a monopolistic enterprise.

Of course this argument applies equally to university professors.

Part 2: Numerology 101 – A study in the mythology of false numbers.

Is 8.5% ROI a reasonable assumption for establishing a pension benefit?

When you set a pension up the *major* determinate of its success or failure is the assumed Interest Rate, which is also the assumed ROI. The larger you make this made-up number the lower the theoretical contribution rate required to fund your pensions thru eternity. Thus the higher the assumed interest rate the lower the assumed contribution rate. The lower the assumed contribution rate, the higher the potential taxpayer guaranteed pension payout rate. Notice "interest rate" and "contribution rate" are both "assumed" while the "payout rate" is "guaranteed". Herein is the source of the current problem. Taxpayers guarantee the "payout rate" regardless whether the "assumed rate" is correct or not.

In this way you can promise teachers and university professors 75% and 80% of their salaries as retirement income at age 55 compared to the maximum $22,000 Social Security payout at age 62 representing about 20% of your income.

The total employee lifetime contributions in dollars for $100,000 state pensions and $22,000 Social Security pensions are about the same – educators contributing a slightly higher percentage (7.5% vs. 6.2%) for fewer years. Compared to self-employed paying in 14.4% to Social Security, public employee contributions are considerable less.

This mythical math is why 54 year-old music teachers can retire with pensions of $130,000/yr. and kindergarten teachers making $75,000/yr. can retire on $155,000/yr. And, by the way, why a U of I professor with 5 years of service can retire on $130,000 at age 63 after contributing all of $155,000 to her pension. Nice deal if you can get it.

What happens if the mythical 8.5% ROI is not achieved? What if salary increases are higher than assumed? What if ever increasing benefits are legislated without corresponding employee contribution increases? What if retirees live longer than expected? Taxpayers pay every single penny of the extra cost. That's what is happening right now.

As pension assets become ever larger over time, recovery from large losses becomes impossible: the Zettler Ratio.

I am sure what follows has been discussed somewhere and has a better name than the Zettler Ratio but I was unable to find it. It is similar to Sequence of Returns Risk but different because that term involves large losses for an individual near retirement and public pension funds never retire – they go on forever.

Basically it is a compound interest problem – if you assume your ROI is going to be consistently 8.5% but your contributions are only increasing at 4.2% a large investment loss becomes more difficult (or impossible as I show below) to recover from as time goes on. So the ratio is investment loss divided by employee contributions. I use the employee contribution because it is a fixed rate not a variable rate like the employers contribution.

As most people know aiming for an 8.5% investment return over a long period of time, say the next 35 years as the state pension funds are, requires investment in more risky assets such as hedge funds, real estate, sub-prime mortgages (oops), derivatives and leverage. Obviously you cannot achieve your 8.5% ROI by purchasing Treasury Bonds paying 4%.

The problem is easily demonstrated by using numbers provided by TRS. In 2008 and 2009 TRS market value of assets fell from $42 billion to $28.5 billion a decrease of 32% or $13.5 billion in investable assets. The employee contributions for 2009 were $876 million resulting in a Zettler Ratio of 15.4 or 15.4 additional years of employee contributions to make up the losses.

If we go back to 1995 when the current 50-year pension-balancing scheme was enacted we see there were $12.6 billion worth of TRS assets. Using 32%, the same loss ratio as the 2008-2009 losses, we come up with losses of $4 billion. Since member contributions in 1995 were $421 million we come up with a ratio of 9.5 years of member contributions. Thus losing 32% early in the asset building process is much easier to recover from by upping contributions whether from employees or employers.

But what happens if we lose 32% in 2045, the last year of our 50-year plan? Well if we meet the unlikely goal of 8.5% ROI from now to 2045 we will have $488 billion in assets combined in all five state pension funds. And it follows if we have the same 32% loss as 2008-2009 we will be in the hole by an unimaginable $156 billion giving us an insurmountable 28.9 years of employee contributions to make it up. Losses of this magnitude would require even more risk-taking than the current 8.5% assumption. And no amount of increased employee contributions could offset the huge loss.

The point of this exercise is to show that by assuming an 8.5% ROI taxpayers are increasingly at risk as time goes by, a point never mentioned by the professors or the politicians and union bosses who set this up to begin with. If we had known that would we have agreed to it? No, of course not.

Just because it is legal does not mean it is not corrupt.

"Annuities are very expensive to buy." – The Professors, page 12.
It's nice to see them admit this point since annuities are exactly what taxpayers are paying for when a teacher retires. In fact in the 2011 TRS Actuarial Report the term "annuity" or "annuitant" is used 98 times. One has to wonder why college professors do not realize IL state pensions ARE annuities.

Why are annuities so expensive? Because they must guarantee they will be here in 30, 40 or 50 years to make that last payment to the annuitant. They must be careful and risk-averse. Therefore they must not assume 8.5% ROI.

Governments on the other hand will always be with us and can, theoretically at least, take financial risks prudent men would not. And that means they can always raise taxes to pay for things like annuities, Boston Tunnels and F-22 fighters that they vastly underestimate the cost of. It goes without saying: governments make mistakes and taxpayers pay for them. IL state pension systems are huge mistakes waiting to be paid for by unsuspecting taxpayers.

So what rate do insurance annuities and Social Security use to calculate pension costs? They use what is known as a "risk free" rate or about one-half of the 8.5% assumed by TRS. Why "risk free"? Because if you are guaranteeing risk free payouts (no one has ever missed a Social

Security payment) then you should be using risk-free assets to back them up. Otherwise you have a 32% loss, as illustrated in the previous section, and suddenly there is no money to make all the annuity payments.

How expensive are risk-free annuities? Well to fund upfront our 54-year old $130,000/yr. music teacher's annuity would require a $3 million plus payment to an insurance company. Compare that to a 66-year old with a max $28,000/yr. Social Security's annuity value of about $440,000 or one-seventh the value of the teacher's.

Taxpayers do not think public pension values seven times their Social Security are reasonable, fair or contractual.

Part 3: Why don't the professors do something worthwhile like examining the risk-profile of the 8.5% ROI Assumption?

Why 8.5% ROI for the next 35 years is unlikely and should not be used by any "prudent man".
In 1830 a Massachusetts court case, Harvard vs. Amory, determined investment trustees must use the "prudent man rule" when investing for others benefit. That ruling stipulates that trustees should "observe how men of prudence, discretion and intelligence manage their own affairs, not in regard to speculation, but in regard to … the probable safety of the capital to be invested."

I think by definition then, a 32% loss indicates a lack of "prudence" and/or "discretion" and/or "intelligence" and that was due directly to the risky assumption of an 8.5% ROI. Therefore it would be prudent and intelligent to consider whether it is reasonable going forward to assume 8.5% even though the SURS administrative staff indicate the last 30 years have averaged 8.2% or so ROI.

The following table shows the change in investment emphasis since 2000 for TRS. Note the big decrease in the safety of bonds and Domestic Equity (McDonalds and Microsoft for example) and the increase, from zero, in the "Real Return" and "Absolute Return" categories. The definition of "Real Return" and "Absolute Return" strategies, as shown at the bottom of the table, include such terms as "derivatives", "leveraged", and "options on futures". Do those techniques sound like something a "prudent man" would use for his own investments? Well, not according to Warren Buffet who said bluntly: "I view derivatives as time bombs".

So what Warren Buffet considers to be a 'time bomb" the professors consider to be "prudent".

Less Than Prudent TRS Asset Allocation 2011 vs. 2000
In Percentage of Assets

Asset Class	2011	2000	2011 vs. 2000
Domestic Equity	20%	26%	-6%
International Equity	20%	20%	0
Fixed Income	16%	41%	-25%
Real Estate	14%	10%	4%
Private Equity	14%	3.50%	10.50%
Real Return *	10%	???	
Absolute Return **	8%	???	

* A **"Real Return"** strategy may use to a significant degree derivative instruments such as options, futures and options on futures.
** An "**Absolute Return**" strategy that seeks return through active asset allocation by using long and short positions.
Implementation is through derivatives, and is leveraged.

NOTE: Rounding error causes total to exceed 100%

Debt and Demographics will overwhelm investment returns going forward.

1. The world has been in a 30 year-interest rate bubble

In June 1981 the Fed Funds rate was 20%. In June 2011 it will be .25%. Obviously the rate is not going to go down by 19.75% again over the next 30 years. As interest rates go up, as they surely must, equities and bonds will go down. How does ever increasing interest rates fit into your 8.5% projected outcome?

2. A world awash in 10's of trillions of dollars of debt will grow slowly if at all for an extended period. Dollars used to pay debt and interest cannot consume or invest.

3. The human population will never double again.

This has never been true before but demographers say the world's population will level off at about 11 billion in 2100 from 7+ billion now. This is important because new workers are an important part of economic growth as they work, earn, consume and invest. By contrast, the population doubled between 1960 and 2000 the era of highest economic growth in history.

4. Major economic powers have birth rates below replacement rate.

Economic powerhouses China, Japan, Russia and Europe will all have decreasing populations in the next decades, another historical first. For example Russia's population is predicted to drop to 110 million from the current 140 million by 2050. Economic growth will almost certainly slow from past decades.

5. Life expectancy is growing.

Related to number 3 and 4 above, this means more senior citizens supported by fewer workers. For example China's life expectancy has gone from 46 to 75 in just the last 50 years. This means current actuarial assumptions for life expectancy are almost certainly too low, resulting in future pension and health care obligations that will be larger than currently assumed.

6. People are retiring at an earlier age.

Earlier retirement age (Illinois teachers for example) plus longer life expectancy means slower economic growth and more taxes on fewer workers. See 3, 4 and 5 above.

7. All of the above.

All of the above means more income/wealth will need to be transferred via taxes from fewer working/productive people to more non-working/non-productive people thus greatly decreasing investment and economic growth. We only need to look at Japan where 25% of the population is now over 65 growing to 45% by 2050. A given dollar cannot go two places, investment and tax, at the same time. Barack Obama, please take note.

8. The terrorist risk premium.

A handful of terrorists with dirty bombs (let alone nuclear weapons) could simultaneously shut down Manhattan, Toronto, London, Paris, Amsterdam and Berlin causing complete financial chaos and bringing the world economy to a halt. It would make the credit crisis look like a walk in the park. Unstable political entities Iran and Pakistan have nuclear weapons and who knows what they will do. I do not know whether the risk premium is one percent, two percent or more but I do know it is greater than zero.

I certainly would not expect everyone to agree with me on the above 8 points but I think most people would agree they are worth discussing when you are projecting high rates of return 35 years into the future. If the "prudent men" running the pension trust funds have discounted the above risks (and other risks unmentioned) and still came up with an 8.5% ROI assumption then they should put that forward and not hide behind the meaningless statement " that's what we did before" "Before" is never coming around again.

Call me a cynic but my guess is the powers that be used 8.5% because that made their numbers work. Anything lower would increase the unfunded liability by more than they care to accept. I would also guess we will never see anything from TRS or our learned professors justifying the 8.5% rate going forward 35 years. And that's because it can't be justified.

Part 4: Confusing the numbers for the benefit of the self-interested.

Confusing fixed contribution rates (employee) with variable contribution rates (taxpayers).
The same old canard is repeated in this report as with every other report put forward by self-interested parties: "Illinois has simply not set aside enough funds to pay promised benefits." That is semantically true according to the corrupt rules in place that require the taxpayer (euphemistically known as the "state") to pick up 100% of additional amounts accruing for every unfunded benefit, investment loss and obscene salary increase.

Employees on the other hand always pay a fixed amount unchanged by poor investment results or benefit outcomes. This policy is not holy writ, it is purposeful design.

But what if we had designed it differently including a fairer rule whereby employees and employers split the cost 50/50? In other words both employee and employer rates would be variable based upon assumption outcomes. Well then suddenly employees would have "not set aside enough funds to pay promised benefits." That is because the state (taxpayer) has paid 256% more for pensions than employees have since 2000. With a 50/50 split employees are 75% "under-funded" and the state is 75% "Over-funded". You can make the numbers come out any way you want them based upon the system design but in IL it is always the taxpayers that pay for political self-dealing.

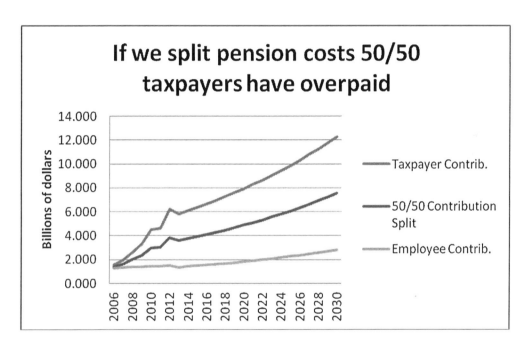

Confusing Wisconsin with Illinois.
In an attempt to conflate WI with IL our intrepid professors use pension numbers that are at best disingenuous and at worst ignorant. Perhaps they should read championnews more often: then they would know more about WI pensions than they let on in their report.

For example on page 28 they make the statement "the government cost of pensions is nearly twice that of Illinois" which is only correct if you are comparing apples to oranges and you ignore the actual WI pension statute.

First of all WI uses Social Security as part of its "retirement plan" but it is not a traditional "pension plan" as we all know. In Social Security the costs are "fixed" not variable as they are in a traditional pension plan. The WI "pension plan" which matches in concept and funding with the IL state pension plans is a separate entity all together. They also attempt to use Milwaukee Teachers Pension System as part of WI pensions but fail to use Chicago Teachers Pension System as part of the IL system they are analyzing. Could it be because the contribution rates are much higher for Milwaukee Teachers than for WI state pensions thus adding bias to their argument? Nah, not possible.

So if we compare only the traditional pension systems WI state actual contribution rate for 2011 is 6.6% compared to IL actual contribution rate of 29%. This is because the WI statutes require a 5% contribution from the employee although the employer has an option to pay the 5%, which virtually all WI employers did until this year. The IL contribution rate shown in the report (11.3%) is only true if the investment rate of return over the next 35 years is indeed 8.5% AND in addition the taxpayers pay off the $85 billion plus interest on the $17 billion in pension bonds. Alas, pension bond interest is not mentioned in the report. It is as if it does not exist. If we used the same interest rate as WI (7.2%) instead of the TRS 8.5% ROI the IL contribution rate (Employer normal cost) would be 15% of payroll not 11.3%.

So a more realistic comparison would be 15% IL to 6.6% WI.

The real reason the WI rates are lower is the better design of the system. Here's why:
1. IL teacher average salaries are 33% more than WI.
2. WI retirement age 65, IL age 55.
3. WI max. pension 70% of salary, IL TRS 75%
4. WI Cost-of-living-adjustment can increase or decrease depending upon investment returns, IL it is always 3%.
5. WI no sick leave credit for retirement, IL up to 2 years credit.
6. IL early retirement on full pension, WI none.

Part 5: Why does everyone stick with status quo answers and what is plan B?

Our professorial group has not come up with anything new. In fact it is the tired old song – IL taxpayers are stuck with paying obscene taxes to provide benefits to public workers they will never have themselves. The professors, like others before them, refuse to consider the idea that by providing no real reform options they leave IL taxpayers with only two possibilities: First, repeal the constitutional pension guarantee via referendum or secondly, leave the state for more reasonable tax climes and allow Illinois to slowly become the new Michigan with its declining tax base, joblessness and fractured public services. Chicago will join other mid-western cities like Detroit, Cleveland and Pittsburgh in a slow decline to irrelevance.

Also without even considering the terrible outcome that would be represented by the likely possibility of much lower investment returns over the next 35 years than the current assumed rate of 8.5% they ill-serve the IL citizens that pay them.

If investment returns between now and 2020 are 4% what do we do (plan B)?
According to CGFA (Committee on Government Forecasting and Accountability), Illinois' financial watchdog, under best-case scenario, the unfunded pension liability will grow from $85 billion today to $115 billion in 2020 and that is only if we achieve 8.5% ROI. If we achieve half of that then the unfunded will be $160 billion and the value of all pension assets will be lower than in 2010 and decreasing every year. In essence a ticking time-bomb.

So why do the powers that be and their lackeys in the media refuse to talk about a plan B? I would argue it is self-interest that motivates them to ignore what's looming ahead. If you are a politician you may have to answer for previous votes and support and if you are a college professor in the SURS retirement system your $100,000 plus pensions may be at risk. The salaries of the five authors vary from $120,000 to $220,000 meaning they will all be over $100,000 pensions if they work say 30 years. In fact in 2008-2009 the 63 SURS member who retired on $100,000 plus pensions averaged 29 years worked in IL.

Was this project part of their state salary or did it cost us extra?
I have to ask this question because if you look at the bios of the authors at the end of the paper they all seem to have responsibilities other than teaching, which I would have thought is what they were hired for. Also I don't think it was worth much since it did not break any new ground.

For example Robert Rich the lead author is Director of IPGA. Is that an extra paid duty or is that included in his university salary? And how about as coordinator at Partnership Illinois Program is that an extra stipend? And does he still serve as a "consultant" to a wide variety of federal and state agencies?

Prof. David Merriman is director of the Fiscal Futures Project, which is modeling the long-term trends in state budgets. In that model is he considering the effects a 4% or less ROI on the $50 billion in pension assets will have on future budgets? If not, why not?

Prof. Laurie Reynolds provided a summary legal analysis of current legal thought on pension reform options. Though not nearly as thorough as University of Minnesota's Amy Monahan's it was never the less well done. Prof. Reynolds also does consulting with municipal attorneys, public interest law firms and local government units. I assume she is paid for these consultations.

Reading this paper makes me wonder if we are hiring more consultants than teachers at IL universities. If the purpose of universities is to educate then one would assume we should be hiring teachers not consultants. So if I may be so bold, exactly how many hours a week do these five professors spend in the classroom? How much of the ever increasing cost of tuition is the result of too many highly paid non-teacher consultants? And if they are allowed to make money as consultants, i.e. outside of their duties as teachers, and they are not teaching a full load of classes then should we not get a discount on their state salaries (and subsequent pensions)? Being a college professor is a great (free) marketing tool for any consulting business. Shouldn't the provider of such marketing power get a commission? And in order to arrive at the proper commission we would need to know how much outside income they are generating. Reasonable I say.

As Exhibit A I give you former Governor Jim Edgar who is considered to be a full-time employee (FTE) and a "Distinguished Fellow" at a salary of $177,630/yr. May I ask exactly how many hours per year does Mr. Edgar spend lecturing or "Fellowing" for the taxpayers of Illinois? Would we save money by just paying him $500/hr. for the time he does work? And since Edgar also receives a state pension of $138,888 that makes his IL taxpayer-take $316,000 per year. No wonder he's against reform.

So in the final analysis **"Public Pension Policy in Illinois – An Introduction to a Crucial Issue"** does not provide any new information or new ideas: it simply plows old ground. It seems to me to be self-serving and takes the usual course of putting the burden of every back-room deal, every political payoff, every unjustified benefit increase, every risky investment loss and every corrupt (though probably legal) political decision on the backs of the unsuspecting taxpayer.

So my recommendation: save your time, read my book instead.

SOURCES:
Actuarial Reports TRS, SURS, SERS, GARS 2000-2010
TRS Comprehensive Financial Reports 2000, 2011
CGFA Five State Systems Combined
Wisconsin Department of Trust Funds Fact Sheet on State Pension Plans
Wisconsin Statutes "Public Employee Trust Fund Chapter 40"
Wisconsin Legislative Fiscal Bureau Informational Paper 84 WI Retirement System
Wisconsin Comprehensive Financial Report June 30, 2009

APPENDIX A:

PENSION DATA

Pension Numbers Matrix as of June 30, 2011.

	TRS	**SURS**	**SERS**	**Total**
Active members 2011	170,190	81,611	66,363	318,164
Full Time	137,711	75,999	unknown	213,710
Part Time	32,479	5,612	unknown	38,091
Inactive Members 2011	115,295	79,922	21,298	216,515
Retirees& Benefit 2011	101,532	51,370	60,055	212,957
TOTALS	387,017	212,903	147,716	747,636
Total Active, Inactive and Retired>>>>>				**747,636**

	TRS	**SURS**	**SERS**	**Total**
Payroll Billions 2011	9.6	3.9	4.2	17.7
Annuities Paid Out Billions 2011	4.4	1.6	1.5	7.5
Yearly Increase Number of Retirees	3,556	2,467	1,391	7,414

	TRS	**SURS**	**SERS**	**Total**

MV Assets Billions 2011	37.5	14.2	11.0	62.7
PBO Billions 2011	81.3	31.5	31.4	144.2
Unfunded Billions 2011	**43.8**	**17.3**	**20.4**	**81.5**
Per Cent Funded	**46.13%**	**45.08%**	**35.03%**	**43.48%**

	TRS	SURS	SERS	Total
Employer Contrib. Rate 2011 %	**28.43**	**22.00**	**36.10**	
Employer NC Billions	**0.85**	**0.70**	**0.57**	2.12
Interest on UAAL Billions	**3.72**	**1.34**	**1.58**	6.64
Total Employer Cost	**4.57**	**2.04**	**2.15**	8.76
Employer Normal Cost Rate 2011 %	8.81%	17.95%	13.57%	
Employee Contribution 2011 Billions	0.875	0.260	0.240	1.38
Employer minus Employee Cost	3.694	1.781	1.911	7.39
Employer Cost % of Employee Contrib.	522%	785%	896%	
Employee Rate 2011 %	9.40	8.00	4.00	
Assumed Interest Rate/ROI %	8.50	7.75	7.75	
Assumed Salary Annual Increase %	7.00	5.00	5.50	
Post-retirement Annual Increase %	3.00	3.00	3.00	

NOTE 1: Assets, PBO and Unfunded as of 06/30/2011

NOTE 2: Employee Rate Annuity Only no beneficiary

NOTE 3: SURS Employee Contribution Rate Average all contributors

TRS = Teachers Retirement System

SURS = State University retirement System

SERS= State Employees Retirement System

1. Top 100 Statewide Pensions as of April 1, 2012.

Illinois State Pensions Top 100 as of April 1, 2012				
NAME	Employer	Annual Pension	Pension Paid Out To Date	System
Das Gupta, Tapas	University of Illinois - Chicago	426,885	3,001,481	SURS
Abraham, Edward	University of Illinois - Chicago	414,709	1,979,315	SURS
Barmada, Riad	University of Illinois - Chicago	397,919	4,627,975	SURS
Mafee, Mahmood	University of Illinois - Chicago	370,141	1,949,910	SURS
Abcarian, Herand	University of Illinois - Chicago	338,731	1,096,816	SURS
Albrecht, Ronald	University of Illinois - Chicago	337,451	1,562,785	SURS
Ausman, James	University of Illinois - Chicago	309,894	1,232,874	SURS
Wilensky, Jacob	University of Illinois - Chicago	288,864	1,973,506	SURS
Forman, Phillip	University of Illinois - Chicago	281,591	2,410,085	SURS
Sugar, Joel	University of Illinois - Chicago	274,096	1,926,831	SURS
Bangser, Henry S	New Trier TWP HSD 203	269,531	1,366,454	TRS
Bazzani, Craig	University of Illinois - Urbana	265,592	2,289,503	SURS
Murray, Laura L	Homewood-Flossmoor CHSD 233	263,993	902,084	TRS
Honig, George	University of Illinois - Chicago	263,576	1,938,081	SURS
Milner, Joel	Northern Illinois University	261,396	1,210,564	SURS
Folse, John	Southern Illinois University - Carbondale	255,967	2,604,032	SURS
Schuler, James	University of Illinois - Chicago	254,138	1,583,445	SURS
Moss, Gerald	University of Illinois - Chicago	251,102	1,513,373	SURS
Weaver, Reginald L	National Education Association	249,937	843,928	TRS
Kutska Elizabeth R	Park District Risk Mgmt Agency	247,821	1,635,040	IMRF
Lopata, Melvin	University of Illinois - Chicago	247,247	1,898,335	SURS
Rugg, Stephen	University of Illinois - Urbana	243,554	1,057,915	SURS
Oldham, Greg	University of Illinois - Urbana	243,413	879,391	SURS
Pavel, Dan	University of Illinois - Chicago	242,707	1,544,785	SURS
Hintz, James S	Adlai Stevenson HSD 125	241,854	1,406,575	TRS

Blair, Norman	University of Illinois - Chicago	241,337	1,237,356	SURS
Neumann, Frederick	University of Illinois - Urbana	238,710	2,174,090	SURS
Conyers, John G	Palatine CCSD 15	237,648	1,774,861	TRS
Catalani, Gary T	Community Unit SD 200	237,195	1,127,336	TRS
Dada, M Mohsin	Schaumburg CCSD 54	236,904	177,678	TRS
McCampbell Roy F	Village of Bellwood	236,752	625,571	IMRF
Winer, Jerome	University of Illinois - Chicago	235,488	1,608,848	SURS
Jonas, Jiri	University of Illinois - Urbana	235,406	2,144,956	SURS
Gmitro, Henry A	Community CSD 93	234,803	645,708	TRS
Greenough, William	University of Illinois - Urbana	232,585	594,937	SURS
Hager, Maureen L	North Shore SD 112	231,703	637,182	TRS
Swalec, John	Waubonsee Community College	230,596	2,129,035	SURS
Kelly, Dennis G	Lyons TWP HSD 204	230,034	380,296	TRS
Applebaum, Edward	University of Illinois - Chicago	229,849	2,258,124	SURS
Steinberg, Salme	Northeastern Illinois University	229,179	1,012,067	SURS
Defanti, Thomas	University of Illinois - Chicago	227,542	1,539,409	SURS
Gislason, Eric	University of Illinois - Chicago	227,094	703,178	SURS
Curley, Mary M	Hinsdale CCSD 181	226,645	1,077,194	TRS
Flickinger Theodore B	ILL Assoc of Park Districts	226,584	481,360	IMRF
Alkire, Richard	University of Illinois - Urbana	226,550	784,775	SURS
Bultinck, Howard J	Sunset Ridge SD 29	226,246	953,960	TRS
Wetzel, Norman R	Community USD 300	225,602	1,841,999	TRS
Greene, Joseph	University of Illinois - Urbana	224,347	1,664,353	SURS
Werner, David	Southern Illinois University - Edwardsville	224,327	1,560,710	SURS
Baskin, Lawrence M	Glen Ellyn CCSD 89	223,864	1,338,482	TRS
Gibbons, Robert	University of Illinois - Chicago	221,692	360,167	SURS
Jorndt, George	Triton College	221,615	2,045,570	SURS
Levitsky, Sidney	University of Illinois - Chicago	219,650	2,000,815	SURS
Baym, Gordon	University of Illinois - Urbana	218,942	373,021	SURS
Patton, Ronald C	Bloom TWP HSD 206	218,686	1,482,911	TRS
Edwards, Marvin E	School District U46	217,973	1,825,494	TRS
Kimball, Clyde	Northern Illinois University	217,675	2,164,437	SURS

Gibori, Geula	University of Illinois - Chicago	217,046	352,620	SURS
Strange, Gary	University of Illinois - Chicago	214,889	549,663	SURS
Chapman, Gerald D	Palatine TWP HSD 211	214,825	1,945,722	TRS
Kumar, Arvind	University of Illinois - Chicago	214,302	1,113,885	SURS
Conti, Dennis R	Woodland CCSD 50	212,475	1,270,387	TRS
Gallagher, James J	Evergreen Park CHSD 231	211,607	744,077	TRS
Tondeur, Philippe	University of Illinois - Urbana	211,384	1,783,722	SURS
Harris, Zelema	Parkland College	211,128	1,126,994	SURS
Chambers, Donald	University of Illinois - Chicago	210,917	1,384,380	SURS
Snoeyink, Vernon	University of Illinois - Urbana	210,720	1,383,791	SURS
Hryhorczuk, Daniel	University of Illinois - Chicago	210,235	308,040	SURS
BERMAN, ARTHUR	Not Applicable	209,531	1,837,857	GARS
Stukel, James	University of Illinois - Urbana	209,250	1,484,513	SURS
McGee, Glenn W	Wilmette SD 39	209,014	872,219	TRS
Flaherty, Joseph	University of Illinois - Chicago	208,852	205,519	SURS
Weber, Donald E	Naperville CUSD 203	208,751	1,596,374	TRS
Bridge, Susan J	Oak Park-River Forest SD 200	208,156	914,717	TRS
Beak, Peter	University of Illinois - Urbana	208,121	825,857	SURS
Hanson, Linda M	Highland Park TWP HSD 113	207,606	1,554,833	TRS
Linke, Charles	University of Illinois - Urbana	207,194	2,342,266	SURS
Ulen, Thomas	University of Illinois - Urbana	206,961	352,608	SURS
Bhat, Rama	University of Illinois - Chicago	206,603	472,073	SURS
Hess, Karl	University of Illinois - Urbana	206,543	1,116,897	SURS
Burns, Kevin G	Community HSD 218	206,495	981,423	TRS
Delia, Jesse	University of Illinois - Urbana	206,317	525,881	SURS
McDonald, John	University of Illinois - Chicago	205,805	1,240,371	SURS
Diener, Edward	University of Illinois - Urbana	205,290	711,153	SURS
Ward, Christopher J	Lockport TWP HSD 205	205,282	1,410,121	TRS
Gardner, Chester	University of Illinois - Urbana	205,182	268,576	SURS
Johnson, Michael	University of Illinois - Chicago	204,740	267,986	SURS
White, James W	Queen Bee SD 16	204,621	719,512	TRS
McGrew, Jean B	Northfield TWP HSD 225	204,528	2,256,296	TRS
Hencken, Louis	Eastern Illinois University	204,487	827,184	SURS

Bartke, Andrzej	Southern Illinois University - Carbondale	204,331	332,196	SURS
Palermo, Joseph A	Berkeley SD 87	203,753	532,674	TRS
Easter, Robert	University of Illinois - Urbana	203,514	103,645	SURS
Buckius, Richard	University of Illinois - Urbana	203,438	689,458	SURS
Trick, Timothy	University of Illinois - Urbana	202,912	1,436,118	SURS
Guenther, Ronald	University of Illinois - Foundation	202,808	166,507	SURS
Peterson, Russell	College of Lake County	202,796	1,412,304	SURS
Franz Robert D	Village of Deerfield	202,720	929,648	IMRF
La Tourette, John	Northern Illinois University	202,544	1,881,659	SURS
Warnecke, Richard	University of Illinois - Urbana	201,758	991,245	SURS
	Average annual pension>>>>>>	234,748	1,283,839	

2. **Top 25 Politician Pensions (GARS) as of November 2011.**

Politicians (GARS) Top 25 Pensions as of Nov 2011			
Retiree Name	Annual Pension	Total Pension Paid out to date	Employee Contributions
BERMAN, ARTHUR	203,428	1,751,569	109,293
PETKA, EDWARD	161,280	291,434	171,449
ERWIN, JUDITH	141,476	171,140	238,038
FRIEDLAND, JOHN	140,649	1,993,957	66,716
EDGAR, JAMES	134,853	1,229,827	164,657
THOMPSON, JAMES	131,031	2,001,519	84,996
PHILIP, JAMES	130,414	936,318	330,125
BURRIS, ROLAND	129,162	1,721,424	134,680
JONES JR, EMIL	126,004	308,354	206,924
NETSCH, DAWN	125,372	1,644,511	87,778
HOMER, THOMAS	123,621	993,784	78,093
HANNIG, GARY	123,057	41,019	176,273
DALEY, RICHARD	117,629	53,755	88,434
HAWKINSON, CARL	116,768	629,550	136,036
DEGNAN, TIMOTHY	115,516	1,480,211	85,291
BOWMAN, H	115,447	1,399,297	73,377
KARPIEL, DORIS	114,234	797,209	95,999
MCGREW, SAMUEL	113,719	1,022,415	76,963
MOLARO, ROBERT	112,074	306,260	109,860
GRANBERG, KURT	111,716	305,557	121,757
DANIELS, LEE	110,553	482,663	181,640
RYDER, WILLIAM	110,110	748,894	138,330
HARTKE, CHARLES	109,668	380,218	112,308
KUSTRA, ROBERT	109,070	1,229,306	104,039
WATSON, FRANK	108,480	249,502	181,198

Average Top 25 GARS pension = $127,937

SOURCE: State Employees Retirement System.

3. **Top 25 State Employee Pensions (SERS) as of April 1, 2012.**

SERS State Employee Retirement System Top 25 Pensions as of April 1, 2012			
Retiree Name	Final Employer	Annual Pension	Total Pension Paid out to date
PARWATIKAR, SADASHIV	HUMAN SERVICES	184,470.00	1,464,787.02
MODIR, KAMAL	HUMAN SERVICES	166,732.44	1,981,427.87
VALLABHANENI, NAGESWARARAO	HUMAN SERVICES	142,229.52	1,526,129.07
BAIG, MIRZA	HUMAN SERVICES	139,529.16	1,084,048.77
KADKHODAIAN, HOOSHMAND	HUMAN SERVICES	136,378.08	1,391,602.68
HARTMAN, EDITH	HUMAN SERVICES	135,853.80	1,243,368.75
LOFTON, JOHN	STATE POLICE	134,026.08	1,077,048.24
HODGE, CAROLYN	GOVERNORS OFFICE	130,055.64	85,125.41
MARLIN, GENE	STATE POLICE	129,268.20	1,402,163.19
DARLINGTON, LARRY	MISCELLANEOUS BOARD AND COMMISSIONS	128,982.36	1,036,516.47
KARNETT, LARRY	STATE POLICE	125,984.28	653,748.41
WELBORN, GEORGE	CORRECTIONS	124,866.48	1,027,364.97
BANGHART, ROSA	HUMAN SERVICES	124,698.60	1,439,778.69
NOWACZYK, ROBERT	STATE POLICE	124,446.96	383,123.58
KENT, DANIEL	STATE POLICE	122,991.24	988,370.61
DAROSA, TIMOTHY	STATE POLICE	122,991.24	986,265.57
MURPHY, GEORGE	STATE POLICE	122,991.24	988,370.61
COOPER, KEITH	CORRECTIONS	122,661.60	985,114.32
BAKER, EDWARD	STATE POLICE	121,800.36	148,702.89
HAYDEN, ROGER	STATE POLICE	121,416.84	148,234.65
DANIEL, JOHN	STATE POLICE	121,295.04	687,401.64
ESPER, LARRY	STATE POLICE	121,188.36	968,696.31
THUNDIYIL, GRACE	HUMAN SERVICES	120,996.60	584,378.19
BECKER, TIMOTHY	STATE POLICE	120,672.00	10,056.00

Average Top 25 SERS pension = $130,687

SOURCE: State Employees Retirement System.

4. **Top 25 Judges Pensions (JRS) as of April 1, 2012.**

JRS - Judges Retirement System Top 25 Pensions		
Retiree Name	**Annual Pension**	**Total Pension Paid out to date**
BARRY, TOBIAS	186,764.40	1,749,400.08
HARRISON II, MOSES	182,008.56	1,507,588.64
FITZGERALD, THOMAS	181,286.40	253,500.93
RARICK III, PHILIP	181,125.72	1,184,038.90
HEIPLE, JAMES	180,080.88	1,721,032.17
MILLER, BENJAMIN	180,080.88	1,701,098.39
MCMORROW, MARY	180,067.92	945,251.42
SCOTT, RICHARD	178,453.08	1,191,513.23
LUCAS, RICHARD	176,316.48	626,257.44
NICKELS, JOHN	172,320.00	1,875,696.24
BYRNE, ROBERT	171,622.44	604,354.82
CALLUM, THOMAS	171,622.44	604,354.82
CAMPBELL, CALVIN	171,622.44	541,446.88
GREIMAN, ALAN	171,622.44	541,446.88
GROMETER, ROBERT	171,622.44	525,403.24
MCNULTY, JILL	171,622.44	605,621.43
BUCKLEY, ROBERT	171,302.76	1,387,195.78
COHEN, JUDITH	171,302.76	1,387,195.78
COUSINS JR, WILLIAM	171,302.76	1,387,195.78
SOUTH, LESLIE	171,289.32	444,797.26
TULLY, JOHN	171,289.32	370,579.29
WOLFSON, WARREN	171,289.32	431,776.56
OBRIEN, SHEILA	170,624.52	206,529.74
OMARA FROSSARD, MARGARET	170,624.52	219,889.00

Average Top 25 JRS pension = $174,679

SOURCE: State Employees Retirement System

5. Top 25 University Pensions as of April 1, 2012.

SURS – State University Retirement System Top 100 as of April 1, 2012			
	Retirement Employer	Annual Pension	Retiree's Total Pension paid since 1/1/98
Das Gupta, Tapas	University of Illinois - Chicago	426,885	3,001,480.83
Abraham, Edward	University of Illinois - Chicago	414,709	1,979,314.50
Barmada, Riad	University of Illinois - Chicago	397,919	4,627,975.28
Mafee, Mahmood	University of Illinois - Chicago	370,141	1,949,910.14
Abcarian, Herand	University of Illinois - Chicago	338,731	1,096,816.33
Albrecht, Ronald	University of Illinois - Chicago	337,451	1,562,784.76
Ausman, James	University of Illinois - Chicago	309,894	1,232,873.92
Wilensky, Jacob	University of Illinois - Chicago	288,864	1,973,506.40
Forman, Phillip	University of Illinois - Chicago	281,591	2,410,084.89
Sugar, Joel	University of Illinois - Chicago	274,096	1,926,830.91
Bazzani, Craig	University of Illinois - Urbana	265,592	2,289,503.40
Honig, George	University of Illinois - Chicago	263,576	1,938,080.68
Milner, Joel	Northern Illinois University	261,396	1,210,563.92
Folse, John	Southern Illinois University - Carbondale	255,967	2,604,031.86
Schuler, James	University of Illinois - Chicago	254,138	1,583,445.04
Moss, Gerald	University of Illinois - Chicago	251,102	1,513,372.96
Lopata, Melvin	University of Illinois - Chicago	247,247	1,898,335.25
Rugg, Stephen	University of Illinois - Urbana	243,554	1,057,914.68
Oldham, Greg	University of Illinois - Urbana	243,413	879,390.84
Pavel, Dan	University of Illinois - Chicago	242,707	1,544,784.71
Blair, Norman	University of Illinois - Chicago	241,337	1,237,356.17
Neumann, Frederick	University of Illinois - Urbana	238,710	2,174,089.70
Winer, Jerome	University of Illinois - Chicago	235,488	1,608,848.12
Jonas, Jiri	University of Illinois - Urbana	235,406	2,144,956.44
Greenough, William	University of Illinois - Urbana	232,585	594,936.76
	Average Top 25 University Pensions	286,100	

6. Top 25 Teacher Retirement System pensions as of April 1, 2012.

TRS - Top 100 Teacher Pensions as of April 1, 2012			
Name	**School District**	**Annual Pension**	**Pension Paid Out To Date**
Bangser, Henry S	New Trier TWP HSD 203	269,531	1,366,454
Murray, Laura L	Homewood-Flossmoor CHSD 233	263,993	902,084
Weaver, Reginald L	National Education Association	249,937	843,928
Hintz, James S	Adlai Stevenson HSD 125	241,854	1,406,575
Conyers, John G	Palatine CCSD 15	237,648	1,774,861
Catalani, Gary T	Community Unit SD 200	237,195	1,127,336
Dada, M Mohsin	Schaumburg CCSD 54	236,904	177,678
Gmitro, Henry A	Community CSD 93	234,803	645,708
Hager, Maureen L	North Shore SD 112	231,703	637,182
Kelly, Dennis G	Lyons TWP HSD 204	230,034	380,296
Curley, Mary M	Hinsdale CCSD 181	226,645	1,077,194
Bultinck, Howard J	Sunset Ridge SD 29	226,246	953,960
Wetzel, Norman R	Community USD 300	225,602	1,841,999
Baskin, Lawrence M	Glen Ellyn CCSD 89	223,864	1,338,482
Patton, Ronald C	Bloom TWP HSD 206	218,686	1,482,911
Edwards, Marvin E	School District U46	217,973	1,825,494
Chapman, Gerald D	Palatine TWP HSD 211	214,825	1,945,722
Conti, Dennis R	Woodland CCSD 50	212,475	1,270,387
Gallagher, James J	Evergreen Park CHSD 231	211,607	744,077
McGee, Glenn W	Wilmette SD 39	209,014	872,219
Weber, Donald E	Naperville CUSD 203	208,751	1,596,374
Bridge, Susan J	Oak Park-River Forest SD 200	208,156	914,717
Hanson, Linda M	Highland Park TWP HSD 113	207,606	1,554,833
Burns, Kevin G	Community HSD 218	206,495	981,423
Ward, Christopher J	Lockport TWP HSD 205	205,282	1,410,121
	Average Top 25 TRS Pensions>>	226,273	

APPENDIX B.

1. <u>TRS Benefit Cost Increases vs. Teachers Contributions. (1.1)</u>

What this chart shows is how the benefits kept increasing while the contributions barely moved over 40 years.

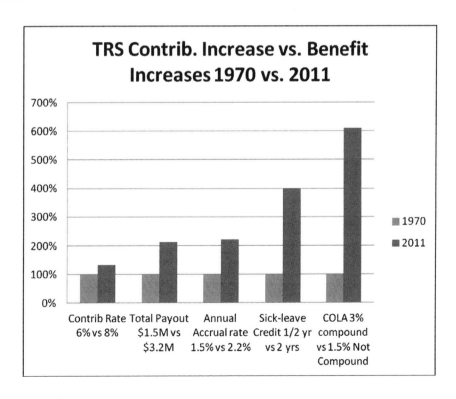

2. ERO (Early Retirement Option) Payments over $200,000. (1.2)

ERO Allows teachers to retire early without a pension discount of 6%/yr. if the school district coughs up big dollars. This table only shows people who received pension contributions from their local school district (and thus local taxpayer) in excess of $200,000. This is paid during the retirement year.

NAME	SCHOOL	ERO Payment by School	Annual Pension	Years Work In IL
Codell, Neil C	Niles TWP CHSD 219	361,097	163,344	20
Herrmann, Mary B	Winnetka SD 36	287,875	131,560	14
Petersen, Jerry D	Community HSD 218	285,686	140,080	16
Steyskal, James L	Reavis TWP HSD 220	253,383	139,471	30
Vogler-Corboy, Dale A	Niles TWP CHSD 219	251,630	96,991	19
Wardzala, Edward J	Lake Park CHSD 108	251,338	129,917	31
Gonzalez, Janet E	Adlai Stevenson HSD 125	226,579	122,748	23
Peterson, David W	SEJA 804 NSSED	223,631	141,598	31
Surber, Rebecca L	Woodridge SD 68	217,165	119,299	31
McGee, Glenn W	Wilmette SD 39	209,903	184,119	32
Brown, Timothy F	Consolidated HSD 230	209,652	131,020	21
Sostak, Susan P	Norridge SD 80	207,423	85,431	22
Heuerman, Steven L	Niles TWP CHSD 219	206,672	115,108	31
Sorensen, Larry W	Park Ridge CCSD 64	205,472	97,150	26
Broughton, Cynthia A	ISBE - Assistant Supt	205,114	126,455	32
Stramaglia, Michael F	Schiller Park SD 81	203,275	107,228	22
Nielsen-Hall, Denise M	Deerfield School District 109	201,541	110,895	32

3. "Service Credit" years Vs. Actual Years Worked in IL. (1.4)

Note how in every case the "Service Credit" years used to calculate pensions is less, oftentimes substantially less, than years worked in IL. Why should IL taxpayers have to pay for years not worked in IL?

TABLE : Service Credit Years versus Actual Years Worked					
Name	Age At Retire	Total Years Pension With Service Credit	Years Worked in IL	Current Pension	School District
Codell, Neil C	56	26	20	163,344	Niles TWP CHSD 219
Herrmann, Mary B	55	26	14	131,560	Winnetka SD 36
Petersen, Jerry D	55	26	16	140,080	Community HSD 218
Steyskal, James L	55	32	30	139,471	Reavis TWP HSD 220
Conyers, John A	57	30	18	230,724	Palatine CCSD 15
Wardzala, Edward J	55	34	31	129,917	Lake Park CHSD 108
Gonzalez, Janet E	55	28	23	122,748	Adlai Stevenson HSD 125
Peterson, David W	55	33	31	141,598	SEJA 804 NSSED
McGee, Glenn W	56	34	32	184,119	Wilmette SD 39
Brown, Timothy F	55	27	21	131,020	Consolidated HSD 230
Heuerman, Steven L	55	33	31	115,108	Niles TWP CHSD 219
Sorensen, Larry W	55	28	26	97,150	Park Ridge CCSD 64
Broughton, Cynthia A	55	34	32	126,455	ISBE - Assistant Supt
Stramaglia, Michael F	55	23	22	107,228	Schiller Park SD 81
Nielsen-Hall, Denise M	55	33	32	110,895	Deerfield School District 109
Markavitch, Vickie L	55	21	12	91,613	Niles TWP CHSD 219
Schau, Pamela S	55	24	16	92,993	Maine TWP HSD 207
Mitz, William M	55	34	31	113,622	Adlai Stevenson HSD 125
Breunlin, Richard J	54	35	33	112,099	Palatine TWP HSD 211
Young, Jennifer	54	34	29	101,075	Adlai Stevenson HSD 125

4. $100,000 Pensions, work 15 years or less in Illinois. (1.11)

Pension Greater than $100,000 Work Less Than 15 Years in Illinois

Last Name	Annual Pension	Years work in IL	Pension System
Hartz	134,353	5.0	SURS
Debrun	105,888	7.8	SURS
Polley	113,154	9.3	SURS
Spigos	115,944	9.3	SURS
Scommegna	119,325	10.3	SURS
Hamilton	104,338	11.5	SURS
Hoffman	104,435	11.5	SURS
Rauch, Lynne E	145,809	12.0	TRS
Rice	107,633	12.0	SURS
Carnes, Duwayne D	108,991	12.0	TRS
Gross	136,694	12.3	SURS
Cipfl	102,130	12.3	SURS
Geil	124,708	12.7	SURS
Frohman	155,940	12.8	SURS
Mucci	101,341	12.8	SURS
Kimmelman, Paul L	103,552	12.8	TRS
Shomay	112,289	12.8	SURS
Van Der Bogert, Mary R	169,050	13.0	TRS
Mozes	109,267	13.0	SURS
Schowalter	100,467	13.0	SURS
Ripps	167,251	13.0	SURS
Erdoes	139,249	13.1	SURS
Rich	103,682	13.3	SURS
Morrissey, W Michael	110,954	13.3	TRS
Herrmann, Mary B	131,560	14.0	TRS
Jordan, William H	128,132	14.0	TRS
Kosobud	113,386	14.2	SURS

Hentges, Joseph T	105,438	14.3	TRS
Anderson	148,502	14.5	SURS
Pappas	183,993	14.7	SURS
Wu	104,515	14.8	SURS
Zahed	130,982	14.9	SURS
Graupe	119,853	15.0	SURS
Lumber	111,588	15.0	SURS
McDonald	127,036	15.0	SURS
Ennis, Elizabeth A	159,647	15.0	TRS
Arndt, Kenneth M	136,433	15.0	TRS
Roberts, Leonard E	101,422	15.0	TRS

SOURCES: Teachers Retirement System and University Retirement System

5. Employee Contributions versus ERO School Contributions. (1.3)

This chart shows how the local taxpayer under ERO pays huge amounts to allow teachers and administrators to retire early without penalty.

Note how in every case except one the local district (local taxpayer) paid more for Early Retirement than the employee contributed to his pension over his entire career.

Employee Contributions versus ERO School Contributions

Name	Current Pension	School District	Employee Contrib.	School Dist. ERO Contrib.
Codell, Neil C	163,344	Niles TWP CHSD 219	234,371	361,097
Herrmann, Mary B	131,560	Winnetka SD 36	201,755	287,875
Petersen, Jerry D	140,080	Community HSD 218	-	285,686
Steyskal, James L	139,471	Reavis TWP HSD 220	199,755	253,383
Vogler-Corboy, Dale A	96,991	Niles TWP CHSD 219	151,247	251,630
Wardzala, Edward J	129,917	Lake Park CHSD 108	188,596	251,338
Gonzalez, Janet E	122,748	Adlai Stevenson HSD 125	162,397	226,579
Peterson, David W	141,598	SEJA 804 NSSED	189,567	223,631
McGee, Glenn W	184,119	Wilmette SD 39	260,525	209,903
Brown, Timothy F	131,020	Consolidated HSD 230	-	209,652
Heuerman, Steven L	115,108	Niles TWP CHSD 219	170,001	206,672
Sorensen, Larry W	97,150	Park Ridge CCSD 64	169,737	205,472
Broughton, Cynthia A	126,455	ISBE - Assistant Supt	163,408	205,114
Stramaglia, Michael F	107,228	Schiller Park SD 81	-	203,275
Nielsen-Hall, Denise M	110,895	Deerfield School District 109	174,362	201,541
Markavitch, Vickie L	91,613	Niles TWP CHSD 219	-	196,061
Schau, Pamela S	92,993	Maine TWP HSD 207	162,715	195,858
Mitz, William M	113,622	Adlai Stevenson HSD 125	182,810	195,781
Breunlin, Richard J	112,099	Palatine TWP HSD 211	179,938	191,502
Young, Jennifer	101,075	Adlai Stevenson HSD 125	125,457	187,999
Soc Security Age 62 Same salary (approx)	22,000	Social Security age 62 same salary	130,000	-

Note: "-" Indicates Records without available data

6. Total School District Employee Cost Final Year of Employment (1.3)

Combining the ERO payment from the school district plus the salary for the final year adds up to a "Golden Parachute" for some K-12 employees.

Name	Annual Pension	School District	School Dist. ERO Contrib.	+	Last Annual Salary	=	Total School Cost Final Year
Codell, Neil C	163,344	Niles TWP CHSD 219	361,097	+	411,511	=	772,608
Herrmann, Mary B	131,560	Winnetka SD 36	287,875	+	245,000	=	532,875
Petersen, Jerry D	140,080	Community HSD 218	285,686	+	236,071	=	521,757
Steyskal, James L	139,471	Reavis TWP HSD 220	253,383	+	223,466	=	476,849
Vogler-Corboy, Dale	96,991	Niles TWP CHSD 219	251,630	+	242,914	=	494,544
Wardzala, Edward J	129,917	Lake Park CHSD 108	251,338	+	225,169	=	476,507
Gonzalez, Janet E	122,748	Adlai Stevenson HSD 125	226,579	+	222,056	=	448,635
Peterson, David W	141,598	SEJA 804 NSSED	223,631	+	240,341	=	463,972
McGee, Glenn W	184,119	Wilmette SD 39	209,903	+	273,235	=	483,138
Brown, Timothy F	131,020	Consolidated HSD 230	209,652	+	216,986	=	426,638
Heuerman, Steven L	115,108	Niles TWP CHSD 219	206,672	+	187,278	=	393,949
Sorensen, Larry W	97,150	Park Ridge CCSD 64	205,472	+	174,870	=	380,342
Broughton, Cynthia	126,455	ISBE - Assistant Supt	205,114	+	161,213	=	366,327
Stramaglia, Michael	107,228	Schiller Park SD 81	203,275	+	223,709	=	426,984
Nielsen-Hall, Denise	110,895	Deerfield School District	201,541	+	163,070	=	364,611
Markavitch, Vickie	91,613	Niles TWP CHSD 219	196,061	+	163,384	=	359,445
Schau, Pamela S	92,993	Maine TWP HSD 207	195,858	+	178,137	=	373,995
Mitz, William M	113,622	Adlai Stevenson HSD 125	195,781	+	191,124	=	386,905
Breunlin, Richard J	112,099	Palatine TWP HSD 211	191,502	+	162,981	=	354,483
Young, Jennifer	101,075	Adlai Stevenson HSD 125	187,999	+	159,999	=	347,998

7. <u>Service Credit Years versus Actual Years Worked. (1.4)</u>

This chart shows how retirees work fewer years than they use for pension calculations. Every time this happens taxpayers costs increase.

Name	Age At Retire	Total Years Pension With Service Credit	Actual Years Worked in IL	Current Pension	School District
Codell, Neil C	56	26	20	163,344	Niles TWP CHSD 219
Herrmann, Mary B	55	26	14	131,560	Winnetka SD 36
Petersen, Jerry D	55	26	16	140,080	Community HSD 218
Steyskal, James L	55	32	30	139,471	Reavis TWP HSD 220
Conyers, John A	57	30	18	230,724	Palatine CCSD 15
Wardzala, Edward J	55	34	31	129,917	Lake Park CHSD 108
Gonzalez, Janet E	55	28	23	122,748	Adlai Stevenson HSD 125
Peterson, David W	55	33	31	141,598	SEJA 804 NSSED
McGee, Glenn W	56	34	32	184,119	Wilmette SD 39
Brown, Timothy F	55	27	21	131,020	Consolidated HSD 230
Heuerman, Steven L	55	33	31	115,108	Niles TWP CHSD 219
Sorensen, Larry W	55	28	26	97,150	Park Ridge CCSD 64
Broughton, Cynthia A	55	34	32	126,455	ISBE - Assistant Supt
Stramaglia, Michael F	55	23	22	107,228	Schiller Park SD 81
Nielsen-Hall, Denise M	55	33	32	110,895	Deerfield School District 109
Markavitch, Vickie L	55	21	12	91,613	Niles TWP CHSD 219
Schau, Pamela S	55	24	16	92,993	Maine TWP HSD 207
Mitz, William M	55	34	31	113,622	Adlai Stevenson HSD 125
Breunlin, Richard J	54	35	33	112,099	Palatine TWP HSD 211
Young, Jennifer	54	34	29	101,075	Adlai Stevenson HSD 125

8 TRS Pensions Greater than Final Salary. (1.6)

An unbelievable list showing some of the retirees whose pension is more than 100% of their final salary.

Name	School	Annual pension	Ending Avg. Salary	Pension Greater $	
Smith, Annette T	Peoria SD 150	155,352.96	75,860.66	79,492.30	Elementary Teacher
Zender, Frances T	Community HSD 155	146,430.00	98,904.96	47,525.04	High School English
Watson, Arcelia R	Paxton-Buckley-Loda 10	100,498.20	63,570.00	36,928.20	Middle School Teacher
Emmons, Joyce R	Bradley School District	100,602.12	66,639.75	33,962.37	Special Ed
Ellman, Jean	SEJA 804 NSSED	115,986.96	92,846.20	23,140.76	Social Worker
Wassell, Fred J	New Berlin CUSD 16	76,308.48	53,648.13	22,660.35	Biology Teacher
Roth, Ruth C	Morton CUSD 709	91,056.48	77,674.32	13,382.16	High School English
Burtzos, Ioanna	Downers Grove GSD 58	87,352.44	78,525.82	8,826.62	Social Science Teacher
Ford, Gordon H	Springfield SD 186	75,575.16	67,754.91	7,820.25	Psychologist
Gordon, Melva E	Peoria SD 150	79,020.12	71,771.72	7,248.40	Elementary Teacher
Vondrak, Edward	Thornton TWP HSD 205	108,729.72	101,513.50	7,216.22	Phys ED
Ferguson, Ronald	Winnebago CUSD 323	74,911.68	68,724.04	6,187.64	Administrator
Lovett, Marna D	Rockford School District	85,494.72	79,421.85	6,072.87	Elementary Teacher
Hauptman, Gail C	Olympia CUSD 16	74,043.36	68,196.65	5,846.71	Special Ed
Full, James C	Freeport School District	75,487.08	71,112.97	4,374.11	Drivers Ed
Parker, John E	Granite City CUSD 9	76,996.56	73,051.31	3,945.25	Administrator
Hwastecki, Ralph P	Northbrook-Glenview SD 30	85,473.36	83,067.28	2,406.08	Elementary Teacher
Giannamore, Frank T	Mundelein CHSD 120	128,830.08	127,352.12	1,477.96	Guidance Counselor
Kinnan, Anna P	Oak Park ESD 97	106,994.52	106,427.35	567.17	Elementary Teacher

9. 7% per year Increases at Avoca District 37 Teachers Contract September 10, 2010 (2.5)

How is it possible any school board can approve a contract that increases public employees pay by 35% thru 2014?

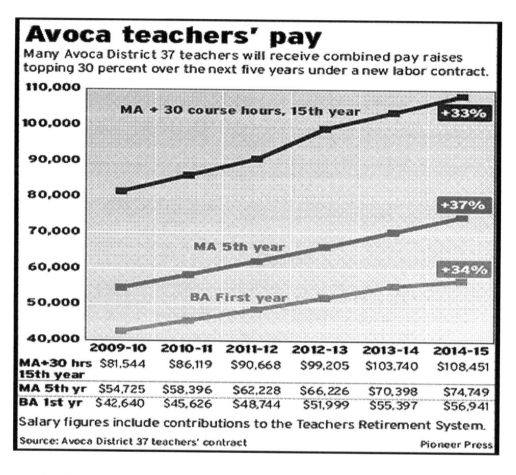

Graphic from Pioneer Press

10. State Retirees With Pensions Greater than Contributions. (1.8)

Top 10 GARS (Politicians) with Annual Pensions Greater than career contributions

Name	Annual Pension	Total Contrib.	Pension in Excess of Contrib.	Pension as Pct. Of Con-trib.
Social Sec. Age 86	37,000	140,000	(103,000)	26%
BERMAN, ARTHUR	203,428	109,293	94,135	186%
FRIEDLAND, JOHN	140,649	66,716	73,933	211%
THOMPSON, JAMES	127,215	84,996	42,219	150%
NETSCH, DAWN	121,720	87,778	33,943	139%
HOMER, THOMAS	120,021	78,093	41,927	154%
BOWMAN, H	115,447	73,377	42,071	157%
KARPIEL, DORIS	114,234	95,999	18,234	119%
DEGNAN, TIMOTHY	112,152	85,291	26,861	131%
MOLARO, ROBERT	112,074	109,860	2,214	102%
MCGREW, SAMUEL	110,407	76,963	33,444	143%

Top 10 SERS (State) with Annual Pensions Greater than career contributions

Name	Final Employer	Annual Pension	Total Contrib.	Pension in Excess of Contrib.	Pension as Pct. Of Con-trib.
Social Sec. Age 86		37,000	140,000	(103,000)	26%
PARWATIKAR, SADA	HUMAN SERVICES	179,097	121,041	58,056	148%
MODIR, KAMAL	HUMAN SERVICES	161,876	101,605	60,271	159%
BAIG, MIRZA	HUMAN SERVICES	135,465	124,340	11,126	109%
COOPER, KEITH	CORRECTIONS	119,089	94,287	24,802	126%
BAKER, MICHAEL	CORRECTIONS	116,050	77,520	38,530	150%
AHITOW, RODNEY	CORRECTIONS	113,754	101,847	11,906	112%
CASTRO, JOHN	CORRECTIONS	113,754	87,583	26,171	130%
OLEARY, MICHAEL	CORRECTIONS	113,754	108,897	4,857	104%

| HARDY, STEPHEN | HUMAN SERVICES | 113,650 | 86,948 | 26,702 | 131% |
| DOBUCKI, KENNETH | CORRECTIONS | 112,830 | 90,804 | 22,025 | 124% |

Top 10 TRS (Teachers) with Annual Pensions Greater than career contributions

Name	Employer	Annual Pension	Total Contrib.	Pension in Excess of Contrib.	Pension as Pct of Contrib.
Social Sec. Age 86		37,000	140,000	(103,000)	26%
Conyers, John G	Palatine CCSD 15	230,726	217,805	12,921	106%
Baskin, Lawrence	Glen Ellyn CCSD 89	217,344	216,134	1,209	101%
Patton, Ronald C	Bloom TWP HSD 206	212,316	203,340	8,977	104%
Howard, Robert T	Community CSD 59	195,503	168,445	27,058	116%
Pekoe, Lawrence C	Deerfield School Dist109	189,853	139,232	50,621	136%
Schildt, Nicholas N	Quincy SD 172	188,994	163,010	25,983	116%
Geppert, Edward J	IL Federation Of Teachers	185,851	170,210	15,641	109%
McKanna, Robert A	Palatine CCSD 15	180,396	147,826	32,570	122%
Van Winkle, David	Valley View CUSD 365	179,929	170,188	9,741	106%
Anderson, John C	Lake County Special Ed	178,987	140,192	38,795	128%

Top 10 SURS (University) with Annual Pensions Greater than career contributions

Last	First	Employer	Annual Pension	Total Contrib.	Pension in Excess of Contrib.	Pension as Pct. Of Contrib.
Social Sec. Age 86			37,000	140,000	-103,000	26%
Riad	Barmada	University of Illinois - Chicago	386,334	361,950	24,384	107%
Dan	Pavel	University of Illinois - Chicago	235,638	215,327	20,311	109%
Frederick	Neumann	University of Illinois - Urbana	231,767	227,101	4,666	102%
John	Swalec	Waubonsee Community College	223,891	146,673	77,218	153%

George	Jorndt	Triton College	215,161	180,700	34,461	119%
Sidney	Levitsky	University of Illinois - Chicago	213,252	184,505	28,748	116%
Philippe	Tondeur	University of Illinois - Urbana	205,243	198,691	6,552	103%
Peter	Beak	University of Illinois - Urbana	201,831	155,810	46,021	130%
Charles	Linke	University of Illinois - Urbana	201,162	190,775	10,387	105%
Louis	Hencken	Eastern Illinois University	198,420	182,195	16,225	109%

JRS – Judges Retirement System.

Judges tend to be in the system fewer years than other members but still pull down substantial pensions. These top10 averaged about 25 years to get their large 6-figure pensions and two of them actually contributed less than our SS recipient.

Top 10 JRS (Judges) with Annual Pensions Greater than career contributions

Name	Annual Pension	Total Contrib.	Pension in Excess of Contrib.	Pension as Pct. Of Contrib.
Social Sec. Age 86	37,000	140,000	(103,000)	26%
BARRY, TOBIAS	181,325	171,583	9,742	106%
MILLER, BENJAMIN	174,836	172,652	2,183	101%
LUCAS, RICHARD	171,181	154,218	16,963	111%
GREIMAN, ALAN	166,624	124,138	42,485	134%
MCNULTY, JILL	166,624	163,800	2,824	102%
COHEN, JUDITH	166,313	132,310	34,003	126%
COUSINS JR, WILLIAM	166,313	159,250	7,064	104%
TULLY, JOHN	166,300	148,775	17,525	112%
BARTH, FRANCIS	165,031	153,775	11,256	107%
INGLIS, LAWRENCE	164,551	157,394	7,157	105%

11. IL Pensions More Than $100,000 Work 20 Years or Less (1.11)

How is it possible that Illinois taxpayers have to pay $100,000 plus pensions to employees who only worked in Illinois for part of their career?

Top 50 of 133 Total

	NAME	Mo. Pension	Year Pension	Work Years
1	Abcarian	$ 26,607	$ 319,286	20
2	Ausman	$ 24,342	$ 292,105	17
3	Moss	$ 19,724	$ 236,688	24
4	Pavel	$ 19,065	$ 228,774	20
5	Sandlow	$ 14,931	$ 179,173	20
6	Pappas	$ 14,886	$ 178,634	17
7	Ross	$ 14,707	$ 176,479	17
8	NICKELS, JOHN	$ 13,536	$ 162,428	20
9	Ripps	$ 13,532	$ 162,380	15
10	Brody	$ 13,015	$ 156,185	20
11	Ehrlich	$ 12,907	$ 154,886	20
12	Van Der Bogert, Mary R	$ 12,704	$ 152,453	20
13	Frohman	$ 12,601	$ 151,213	13
14	Goldberg	$ 12,516	$ 150,192	20
15	Bailie	$ 12,361	$ 148,328	18
16	DOUGLAS, LORETTA	$ 12,323	$ 147,882	20
17	JAFFE, AARON	$ 12,288	$ 147,451	20
18	MADDEN, JOHN	$ 12,288	$ 147,451	20
19	GILL, TIMOTHY	$ 12,249	$ 146,990	20
20	DOZIER, RONALD	$ 12,216	$ 146,590	20
21	HEISER, LARRY	$ 12,216	$ 146,590	20
22	Anderson	$ 12,181	$ 146,173	17
23	THOMPSON, PERRY	$ 12,130	$ 145,562	19
24	MILLER, GEORGE	$ 12,088	$ 145,050	20
25	Hughes	$ 12,030	$ 144,365	18

26	WILLIAMSON DARRELL G	$ 11,957	$ 143,479	20
27	ANDREWS, H	$ 11,857	$ 142,278	20
28	Moriarty	$ 11,840	$ 142,079	20
29	BRODHAY, STEPHEN	$ 11,739	$ 140,869	20
30	RIZZI, DOM	$ 11,724	$ 140,689	19
31	KENNEDY, JAMES	$ 11,681	$ 140,168	19
32	KUHAR, LUDWIG	$ 11,605	$ 139,260	20
33	Valli	$ 11,548	$ 138,581	20
34	KLITZ, CARSON	$ 11,461	$ 137,531	20
35	GAUSSELIN, EDWIN	$ 11,451	$ 137,408	20
36	TESCHNER, JOHN	$ 11,372	$ 136,461	20
37	MANNING JR, ROBERT	$ 11,361	$ 136,327	20
38	ROBINSON, RONALD	$ 11,357	$ 136,283	20
39	HETT, THOMAS	$ 11,275	$ 135,303	19
40	Erdoes	$ 11,266	$ 135,193	13
41	Wollstadt	$ 11,245	$ 134,943	17
42	DONNERSBERGER, DAVID	$ 11,111	$ 133,337	17
43	BERMAN, EDWIN	$ 11,093	$ 133,116	20
44	Cook	$ 11,061	$ 132,731	20
45	Gross	$ 11,059	$ 132,713	12
46	SEYMOUR, STEVEN	$ 10,904	$ 130,853	19
47	HOLT, LEO	$ 10,902	$ 130,826	18
48	SCHERMERHORN, THOMAS	$ 10,895	$ 130,737	18
49	Hartz	$ 10,870	$ 130,439	5
50	MC COOEY, BRENDAN	$ 10,833	$ 129,998	19

SOURCES: Teachers Retirement System (TRS)
State University Retirement System (SURS)
State Employee Retirement System (SERS)

12. Projected $10 million pensions using 30 year life expectancy. (1.12)

What follow is just the Top 10 estimated pension payouts. The Top 100 totals $702 million.

Several items to note:
1. Compared to early retirement on Social Security none of these millionaires worked a full career.
2. The state pension payout ratio "Payout to Contrib. Ratio" runs to over 40 times compared to Soc. Sec. max. 6 times. By limiting pension payouts to 20 times contributions we would save 50% on these public pensions. Who except the politically entitled would think 20 times is unfair?
3. Every one of these Top 10 Payouts is a K-12 employee.
4. Assumes 30 year life expectancy.
5. Original pension is used to calculate "Total Pension Payout".

Name	Employer	Current Pension	In-state Years Service	Estimated Total Pension Payout	Employee Pension Contrib.	Payout to Contrib. Ratio
Social Security Max	Retire age 62	22,000	40	780,000	130,000	6
Curley, Mary M	Hinsdale CCSD 181	226,645	31	10,765,641	248,707	43
Catalani, Gary T	Community SD 200	237,195	35	10,721,225	289,150	37
Gmitro, Henry A	Community CSD 93	234,803	34	10,613,087	282,749	38
Murray, Laura L	HomewoodFlossmoor	238,882	36	10,248,021	298,590	34
Bangser, Henry S	New Trier HSD 203	261,681	32	9,889,792	275,365	36
Burns, Kevin G	Community HSD 218	206,495	34	9,808,492	223,196	44
Hintz, James S	Adlai Stevenson125	234,810	29	9,568,607	235,017	41
Many, Thomas W	Kildeer Countryside	201,405	33	9,566,755	288,263	33
Hager, Maureen L	North Shore SD 112	231,703	33	9,430,296	277,773	34
Johnson, Michael	IL AssocSchoolBoards	193,273	33	9,180,483	229,060	40

13. Annual Pension Contributions Assuming an 8% ROI. (2.1)

Over time the taxpayers pension contribution (top line) increase at a much fatser rate than employees' contributions. Why isn't it at least 50-50?

Top line "Taxpayer Pays".
Bottom line "Employee Pays".

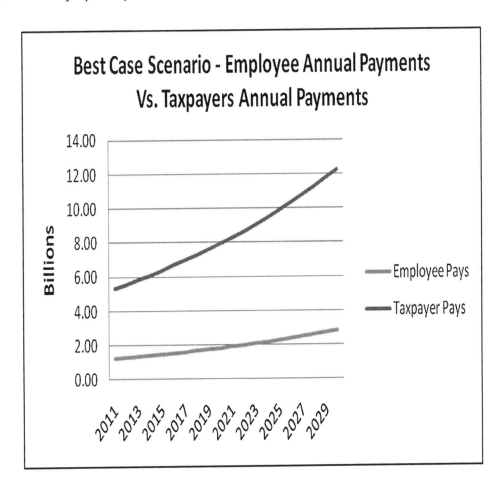

14. Taxpayer Pension Contribution vs. Teacher Contribution 2001 – 2011.

The common misperception that taxpayers are not paying their fair share is put to rest by this table taken from TRS actuarial report data.

Since when is more than 200% not a fair share?

Teachers vs. Taxpayers			
State Pension Contributions to TRS 2001 - 2010			
In millions of dollars			
YEAR	Taxpayer Contrib. (Employer)	Teacher Contrib. (Employee)	Taxpayer to Teacher %
2001	821	643	128%
2002	907	681	133%
2003	1,021	732	139%
2004	5,489	769	714%
2005	1,055	762	138%
2006	658	799	82%
2007	854	826	103%
2008	1,172	865	135%
2009	1,604	876	183%
2010	2,200	899	245%
2011	2,300	910	253%
TOTAL>>	18,081	8,762	206%
Pension Bond Interest	2,072	-	
Total Paid In	20,153	8,762	230%
SOURCE: Teachers' Retirement System of the State of Illinois			
June 30, 2010 - 2011			
Actuarial Valuation of Pension Benefits.			

15. Top Teacher Union Political Contributions as of 12/31/2010. (2.5)

Democrats $12,332,815
Republicans $2,236,400

Blagojevic Total	1,866,697	D	Saviano A Total	147,997	R
Hynes D	1,379,580	D	Moffitt D Total	145,325	R
Madigan L Total	929,996	D	Bond M Total	144,014	D
Jones E Total	641,900	D	Harmon D Total	140,655	D
Quinn Total	640,199	D	Franks J Total	137,940	D
Kilbride T Total	588,834	D	Murphy H Total	137,394	D
Demuzio D	533,882	D	Mitchell J Total	132,777	R
Madigan M Total	495,900	D	Turner A Total	126,794	D
Cross T Total	487,438	R	del Valle Total	126,200	D
Miller D Total	305,667	D	Elman S Total	126,055	D
Ryan G Total	289,506	R	Halvorson Total	124,274	D
Forby G Total	285,861	D	Eddy R Total	124,182	R
Smith M Total	261,171	D	Ronen C Total	122,300	D
White J Total	243,450	D	Dillard K Total	122,050	R
Link T Total	232,907	D	Garrett S Total	121,137	D
Netsch D Total	228,742	D	Kosel R Total	117,171	R
Hassert B	213,486	R	Giles C Total	116,770	D
Kotowski D	199,202	D	Cronin D Total	115,000	R
Hoffman J	193,606	D	May K Total	111,171	D
Schoenberg	188,523	D	Scully G Total	107,407	D
Hannig G Total	184,401	D	Myerscough	104,779	D
Clayborne Total	182,631	D	Kelly R Total	103,175	D
Crotty M Total	176,457	D	Flider B Total	102,620	D
Bomke L Total	171,225	R	Delgado W	102,250	D
Welch P Total	162,468	D	Schock A Total	101,874	R
Luechtefeld	158,369	R	Lang L Total	101,000	D
Granberg K	154,806	D	Preckwinkle	100,000	D

16. Top Individual Donations by Teacher Unions. (2.5)

Top Individual Contributions

350,000	Quinn
300,000	Blagojevic
300,000	Blagojevic
250,000	Blagojevic
225,000	Blagojevic
200,000	Blagojevic
150,000	Kilbride T
150,000	Quinn
125,000	Hynes D
100,000	Blagojevic
100,000	Blagojevic
100,000	Hynes D
100,000	Hynes D
100,000	Miller D
100,000	Preckwinkle
100,000	Hynes D
100,000	Madigan M
100,000	Hynes D
100,000	Hynes D
100,000	Kilbride T
100,000	Kilbride T
100,000	Kilbride T

17. Donations by Teacher Union Affiliate. (2.5)

Contributions by Organization

14,220,141	IPACE Springfield IL
9,525,563	Chicago TU
6,245,530	IFT Westmont IL
4,664,347	AFT Washington
3,226,655	IFT Springfield IL
2,686,161	IFT Oakbrook IL
1,564,552	Lake Cty Fed. Of Teachers
1,538,190	AFT, Joliet IL
1,058,598	College Teachers
983,502	West Suburban Teachers Union
600,004	SW Suburban TU
369,012	Peoria IFT
292,269	North Suburban Teachers Union
152,514	McHenry County

18. $100,000 Teacher Union Pensions Paid for by Taxpayers. (2.6)

Why do taxpayers have to pay huge pension for people who are not public employees?

TRS Teacher Union Officials Pensions in Excess of $100,000	Column1	Column2	Column3	Column4	Column5
Name	Employer	Annual Pension	Pension Paid out to date	In-state Years Service	Highest Salary
AVERAGE FOR GROUP>>>>>>>>>>		119,023	834,753	28	164,325
Geppert, Edward J Jr.	IFT	185,851	1,081,079	25	260,038
Smith, Glenn P	IFT	160,348	898,826	31	226,069
Drum, Kenneth J	IFT	159,348	2,056,286	31	165,058
Davis, Anne P	IEA	148,295	760,178	41	197,037
Abrahamson, Barbara J	IFT	142,466	721,949	29	203,700
McKenzie, Karen S	IFT	142,466	721,949	27	203,700
Baird, Andrea	IFT	140,742	805,127	16	197,173
Amato, Thomas J	IFT	136,354	1,214,090	31	189,204
Koster, Lanita	IFT	132,739	567,058	31	193,341
Betterman, Lieselotte N	IEA	130,899	1,780,120	31	118,654
Turley, Terry W	IFT	129,905	658,023	34	184,051
Peickert, Robert	IFT	127,461	1,036,936	32	163,281
Bron, James L	IFT	126,483	182,347	29	211,053
Zinn, Dennis	IFT	126,048	1,093,398	33	155,865
Haisman, Robert W	IEA	125,985	1,051,766	32	116,589
Wright, Tavey L	IFT	125,145	534,614	34	182,280
Bell, Michelle R	IFT	123,129	82,086	33	203,911
Miller, Gerald	IFT	121,504	688,860	31	203,700
Arterburn, Laura L	IFT	116,377	543,092	28	193,341
Penca, James F	IFT	114,967	1,412,541	32	119,082
Deboer, Virgil W	IFT	112,668	1,386,984	34	117,193
Ewing, Bertram	IFT	109,263	1,423,247	26	126,393
Blackshere, Margaret R	IFT	107,868	1,407,423	30	110,607
Bowman, Martha V	IEA	100,090	513,074	37	143,556

19. Taxpayers Contribute 227% More Than Teachers 2000-2010 (3.1)

Teachers vs. Taxpayers			
State Pension Contributions to TRS 2001 - 2010			
In millions of dollars			
YEAR	Taxpayer Contrib. (Employer)	Teacher Contrib. (Employee)	Taxpayer to Teacher %
2001	821	643	128%
2002	907	681	133%
2003	1,021	732	139%
2004	5,489	769	714%
2005	1,055	762	138%
2006	658	799	82%
2007	854	826	103%
2008	1,172	865	135%
2009	1,604	876	183%
2010	2,200	899	245%
TOTAL>>	15,781	7,852	201%
Pension Bond Interest	2,072	-	
Total Paid In	17,853	7,852	227%
SOURCE: Teachers' Retirement System of the State of Illinois			
June 30, 2010			
Actuarial Valuation of Pension Benefits.			

20. Teacher Salary Increases vs. Social Security Salary Increases. (4.7)

If teachers' salaries increased at the same rate as the private sector workers enrolled in Social Security there would be no pension problem.

Top line = Pension Cost
Middle line = Teacher Salaries
Bottom line = Social Security Salaries.

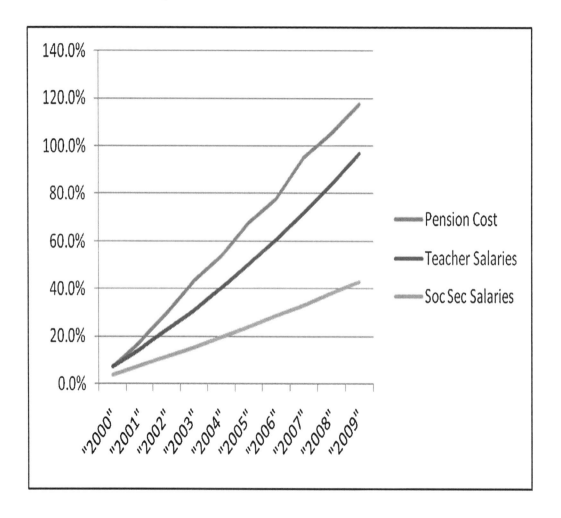

21. Decreased Pension Cost if Salary Increased by 3.65% per year. (4.7)

Top line shows historical raises for K-12 employees, bottom line if salaries had increased by 3.65%/yr. the average Social Security wage increase instaed of 7%/yr. Unfunded TRS would be zero under this scenario showing the problem is salaries being too high not taxpayers not contributing enough.

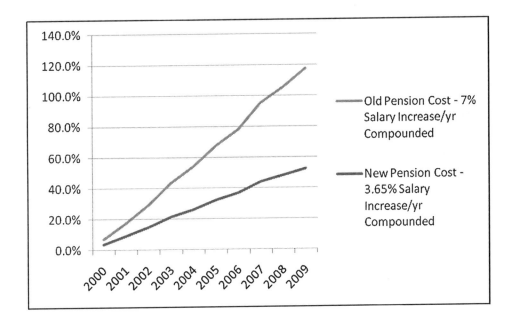

22. Teacher Salaries by Subject 2011 (4.8)

Why are 903 Drivers Ed and Phys. Ed teachers making more than $100,000/yr.?

Subject	2011 High Salary	Greater $100K 2011
Art	179,660	213
Automotive Repair	175,122	24
Cabinet maker	146,295	21
Clothing/Apparel	131,620	8
Drama	179,660	30
Drive Ed	166,658	143
Elementary Education	161,104	1006
English	174,300	545
Foodservice	135,997	17
French	176,600	55
Latin	135,912	10
Librarians	155,546	53
Music	182,686	284
Nurse	136,166	35
Phys Ed	203,154	760
Radio and TV Broadcasting	154,413	15

$100,000 Teacher Salaries By Subject — Fiscal Year Ending June 30, 2011

23. Bremen District 228 Superintendent and Pension Costs.

The cost of education is not limited to the current staff.

Top table shows cost of all Bremen superintendents retired and working.

Early retirements and short terms as superintendent mean higher taxpayer costs.

If public employees had to work to 65 there would be many fewer retirees and much lower pension costs because their life expectancy would be lower.

Bremen Dist. 228	Annual Pension	Pension-able Salary	Employee Contribution	Pension Paid To Date	In-state Years Service
Wheat, Robert M	110,268	69,400	-	1,991,404	35
Riordan, James E	178,490	193,275	-	1,458,735	31
Evans, Frank H Jr.	123,252	136,939	142,865	703,446	32
Reiplinger, Raymond	168,339	185,971	175,988	1,007,413	39
Kendall (Salary)	220,188				
TOTALS>>>>>>>>>	800,538			5,160,998	

Bremen District 228 Top 10 Pensions as of 03/01/2011					
	Mo. Pension	Annual Pension	Employee Contribution	Pension Paid To Date	Years Worked
Riordan, James E	14,874	178,490	-	1,458,735	31
Reiplinger, Raymond M	14,028	168,339	175,988	1,007,413	39
Coleman, Geraldine	11,663	139,959	166,642	598,215	36
Beishuizen, Robert A Sr.	11,161	133,931	133,263	859,558	33
Welch, Patricia J	10,984	131,811	174,908	482,784	33
Glenn, Marianne	10,843	130,110	164,759	477,793	32
Evans, Frank H Jr.	10,271	123,252	142,865	703,446	32.2
Meyer, Vita J	10,249	122,990	-	1,095,316	33.7
Moy, Edward S	10,040	120,479	135,209	728,388	31.2
Carter, Richard R	9,973	119,674	138,543	511,514	37
Social Security at 66	2,350	28,200	161,000		45
		1,369,037	1,232,178	7,923,161	33.8

24. Top Grade School Teacher Salaries 2009 (4.10)

Why are any 3rd grade teachers making over $150,000/yr?

K-5th Grade Teacher Salaries 2009					
NAME	SCHOOL	2009 Salary	2008 Salary	1 Year Increase	Per cent Increase
O'Hara	Lake Forest D 67	158,699	134,224	24,475	18%
Hiler	North Shore D 112	158,515	120,420	38,095	32%
Ehnert	Des Plaines D 62	153,466	127,691	25,775	20%
Jannusch	Des Plaines D 62	151,932	126,857	25,075	20%

25. Public Vs. Private Sector Compensation BLS. (4.11)

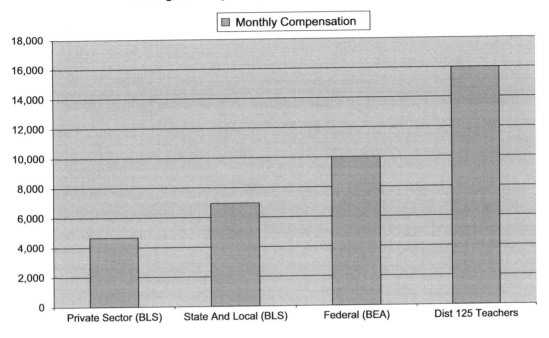

Average Monthly Compensation-Public Vs. Private Sector

26. Pension Costs "Best Case Scenario" 2011-2045. (5.1)

If, in the "Best Case", we are going to pay $230 billion in pension taxes by 2031 and the unfunded will grow from $85 billion to $142 billion what does a "Worst Case" scenario look like?

$ 85 billion	- **2010 Unfunded Pension Liability**
$ 230 billion	- **2009-2034 Pension taxes paid in**
$ 160 billion	- **2034 Unfunded Pension Liability up $64 billion from 2009.**
$ 4.5 billion	- **2010 Pension Tax Payment**
$ 15 billion	- **2034 Pension Tax Payment**
$ 24 billion	- **2044 Pension Tax Payment**

When does the current $85 billion unfunded decrease? Not until 2044. Best case.

27. Top Pensions Stevenson Dist. 225 vs. St. Libory Dist. 30. (5.2)

Why do taxpayers in St. Libory have to pay state taxes to fund outrageous pensions for overpaid employees from Stevenson District 125?

Why doesn't Stevenson pay their pensions and St. Libory pay theirs?

Stevenson HS Dist. 125 High Pensions			St Libory Dist 30 High Pensions		
NAME	Mo. Pension	Annual Pension	NAME	Mo. Pension	Annual Pension
Hintz, James S	16,787	201,444	Brickey, Carol S	2,864	34,366
Kanold, Timothy D	15,973	191,674	McCormack, Carol	2,578	30,936
Dufour, Richard P	15,751	189,015	Diecker, Charlotte	2,423	29,082
Martin, John D	12,199	146,386	May, Ruth	2,172	26,068
Galloway, Dan A	11,636	139,634	Mueth, Marian L	1,893	22,715
Giglio, Beth	10,778	129,340	Kellerman, Rebecca L	1,349	16,193
Green, Richard P	10,578	126,934	Compas, Celeste	740	8,881
Karhanek, Gayle A	10,512	126,141			
Gallenberger, Catarina V	10,497	125,968			
Raffaelli, Philip N	9,918	119,021			

28. Compensation Defined and Possible Compensation Cuts. (5.3)

"Total compensation" defined for every job description as consisting of the following elements for budget purposes:
1. Salary
2. Plus overtime cost
3. Plus pension contribution cost (local, state, federal)
4. Plus health insurance cost
5. Plus other insurance (life, disability) cost
6. Plus sick days accrual cost
7. Plus personal days cost
8. Plus vacation days cost
9. Plus holiday's cost
10. Plus education reimbursement cost.

Possible Compensation Cuts to Fund Pensions:
1. Salary cuts, furloughs and layoffs.
2. Health insurance contribution increased substantially including retirees.
2. Vacations cut.
3. Sick days retirement accruals eliminated completely.
4. Holidays cut from 12 to 8.
5. Life insurance eliminated.
6. Outsourcing begins including Drivers Ed back to private sector.
7. 100% of pension costs transferred to local school districts.
8. Tenure law opened for revision including elimination or severe limits.
9. Collective bargaining law reopened for revision.
10. Open Meetings Act expanded to include public participation in all labor contracts.
11. New law requiring voter approval of all contracts increasing costs more then the Cost-of-Living.
12. End of career (last 5 years) raises limited to cost-of-living.
13. Option to pay all pension amounts over $75,000/yr with state IOU's.
14. Education funding frozen or cut.
15. Allow Community Colleges to offer 4-year degrees thus lowering state costs by cutting enrollment at high cost state universities.
16. Initiate change arbitrarily and let the courts decide if it's legal.
17. Begin Constitutional Amendment process (300,000 signatures or 60% vote in House and Senate).

29. $100,000 Salaries K-12 Employees 2001 thru 2011
And $100,000 Pensions Statewide 2004 Thru 2011

$100,000 Salaries K-12 Employees 2001 Thru 2011		
YEAR	$100K Salaries K-12	% INCREASE
2001	3,026	
2002	4,026	33%
2003	4,976	24%
2004	6,469	30%
2005	7,778	20%
2006	8,477	9%
2007	9,593	13%
2008	11,244	17%
2009	12,418	10%
2010	14,049	13%
2011	14,866	6%

$100,000 State Pensions 2004 Thru 2011		
YEAR	$100,000 Pensions	% INCREASE
2004	1,129	
2005	1,578	40%
2006	1,847	17%
2007	2,535	37%
2008	3,195	26%
2009	3,597	13%
2010	4,200	17%
2011	5,467	30%
2020 Estimate	25,000	357%

Made in the USA
Charleston, SC
17 May 2012